I0120580

Everyday Life in the Spectacular City

The publisher and the University of California Press Foundation gratefully acknowledge the generous support of the Fletcher Jones Foundation Imprint in Humanities.

Everyday Life in the Spectacular City

MAKING HOME IN DUBAI

Rana AlMutawa

UNIVERSITY OF CALIFORNIA PRESS

University of California Press
Oakland, California

© 2024 by Rana AlMutawa

All photographs were taken by the author.

Library of Congress Cataloging-in-Publication Data

Names: AlMutawa, Rana, 1989– author.
Title: Everyday life in the spectacular city : making home in Dubai /
   Rana AlMutawa.
Other titles: Making home in Dubai
Description: Oakland, California : University of California Press, [2024] |
   Includes bibliographical references and index.
Identifiers: LCCN 2023020731 (print) | LCCN 2023020732 (ebook) |
   ISBN 9780520395053 (hardback) | ISBN 9780520395060 (paperback) |
   ISBN 9780520395077 (ebook)
Subjects: LCSH: Middle class—United Arab Emirates—Dubayy (Emirate) |
   Belonging (Social psychology)—United Arab Emirates—Dubayy
   (Emirate) | City and town life—United Arab Emirates—Dubayy
   (Emirate) | Urban anthropology—United Arab Emirates—Dubayy
   (Emirate) | Dubayy (United Arab Emirates : Emirate)—Social life and
   customs.
Classification: LCC DS247.D74 A46 2024 (print) | LCC DS247.D74 (ebook) |
   DDC 307.76095357—dc23/eng/20230520
LC record available at https://lccn.loc.gov/2023020731
LC ebook record available at https://lccn.loc.gov/2023020732

33 32 31 30 29 28 27 26 25 24
10 9 8 7 6 5 4 3 2 1

Contents

Acknowledgments

Writing this book would not have been possible without the help of so many people. First, I want to thank those who shared with me their stories and, through that, allowed me to write this book. I hope you enjoy it and your reflections therein.

Thanks also goes to Ian, who read and provided feedback on my many drafts, even though he was not familiar with the topics of this research, and to my family for being my sounding board as I reflected on my research. This includes not only my parents and sisters but also my cousins, aunts, uncles, and other members of my extended family.

A big thank you also goes to Sneha Krishnan, my PhD supervisor at the University of Oxford, who helped me conceptualize my theoretical frameworks, offered me challenging and motivating comments, and provided all-around helpful advice and a sympathetic ear when I needed it. To Natalie Koch, Shaundel Nicole Sanchez, and May Al-Dabbagh—your feedback, conversations, and sympathy throughout the years gave me the strength to soldier on.

Likewise, I want to thank my editor, Niels Hooper, for believing in this book from the beginning and making it happen, as well as Naja Collins, the associate editor. Thanks also go to my developmental editor, Shanon Fitzpatrick, for her help throughout the many drafts and iterations.

My gratitude also goes to the peers, colleagues, and mentors who read drafts of this book and offered invaluable feedback, as well as those who I had many conversations with, helping me to reflect on and sharpen my research: Laure Assaf, Onoso Imoagene, Todd Reisz, Idil Akinci, Nadeen Dakkak, Abdulkhaleq Abdulla, Melanie Sindelar, Laavanya Kathiravelu, Hasnaa Mokhtar, Manishankar Prasad, Deepak Unnikrishnan, Wafa Al Sayed, Maryam Al Kuwari, John O'Brien, Noora Lori, Ryan Centner, Rashed AlMulla, Sultan AlQassemi, Rend Beiruti, Budoor Alrahmah, Lubnah Ansari, and many others. Thank you to Abu Bakr, who drove me to so many different locations in the city. A special thank you goes to Mustafa Al Zarooni, who gave me access to newspaper archives that otherwise would have remained unavailable to me and thus deprive my work of this valuable source material.

Finally, I would like to sincerely thank New York University in Abu Dhabi for their support and funding; I am blessed to have found my academic home at this institution.

To all of you and many others, thank you—truly, you have my deepest gratitude. None of this would have been possible without you.

Introduction

In a shopping center in an affluent part of Dubai, a group of old, retired Emirati men congregate daily in Starbucks. When I asked these men about places in Dubai where they felt a sense of community, they argued there was no real community anymore: it only existed in the old days, when everyone knew one another and everyone was Emirati—and these days were long gone. Likewise, popular and scholarly accounts depict similar narratives about the sense of alienation inhabitants of Gulf cities endure in cities dominated by neoliberal spectacles.[1] Yet, a more complex picture emerges when one follows the everyday lives of these very individuals and learns the ways that they adapt and make meanings *within* (and *not* just behind or against) the glitzy and rapidly changing urban landscape they inhabit, which has created Dubai's reputation as "the spectacular city." It also highlights the need to understand people's everyday lives holistically, beyond just interview data, as people's experiences of the city do not always mirror how they speak about them.

These men, for instance, had appropriated the chain coffee shop (located in what would normally be considered a sanitized shopping center) in a "traditional" manner, almost like they would a *majlis*.[2] They consumed little from it, as evidenced by the lone bottle of water sitting at the table, and brought their own food from home, such as a stainless-steel bowl of dates. One of them—who was the most vocal about his dislike of the city's "superficiality" and its catering to tourists—often frequented the city's fancy restaurants and five-star hotel lobbies, potent symbols of top-down and commerce-oriented spectacular development for which Dubai has become known.[3] While this does not negate the sense of loss he and others experience, it draws attention to the reality that many inhabitants' everyday lives—and the social meanings they make—do not only take place beyond the spectacular city but also *within* it. Even as these men considered the new Dubai to be less "authentic" than the city of their childhood, they were still making it their home. The example of their coffee shop outing ritual draws attention to ongoing processes of *inhabiting spectacle* pursued by *adaptive agents* to create meaningful everyday lives amid rapid development in the new Dubai, and not only beyond it.

Everyday Life in the Spectacular City is an urban ethnography that reveals how middle-class citizens and long-time residents of Dubai adaptively interact with the city's spectacular spaces—such as its big shopping centers, gleaming new developments, and upscale coffee shops—to create meaningful social lives. I use the phrase "spectacular places" to refer not only to big developments but also to more mundane spaces, such as small coffee shops and malls. I do this because the latter still represent the spectacular and rapid scale of development in the city, which is often considered to be inauthentic, alienating, sanitized, too modern, and too foreign in popular and mainstream accounts. This book argues that these citizens and residents inhabit spectacle as adaptive agents: they adapt themselves to imposed structures while at times also making these same structures serve their own social needs, which evolve in tandem with the changing urban landscape of a now iconic metropolis defined by neoliberal patterns of modernization and globalization. Belying popular and scholarly portrayals of Dubai as inherently "inauthentic," and therefore objectively alienating and disempowering, it presents *adaptivity* as a new framework for understanding how agency operates beyond the conceptual binary of resistance and capitulation within the increasingly twinned developments of illiberal society and neoliberal spectacle.

In response to Dubai's dramatic development trajectory, it has become a common scholarly and popular pursuit to seek, implicitly or explicitly, to uncover the "real" city that lies beneath the veneer of the high-profile architecture and newly renovated, often privatized indoor and outdoor spaces of Dubai. This pursuit contrasts supposedly "authentic," "local" spaces with "inauthentic," "tourist" ones, which are often depicted as objectively alienating to local populations. While this vein of critique can voice sincere concerns about neoliberalism, exclusionary urbanism, and the losses that can accompany rapid changes, it is often mired in unexamined Orientalist attitudes and has little regard for the everyday realities of the many inhabitants of these layered landscapes. Indeed, while the new Dubai of today has been built by the state and globalized finance capital largely outside the oversight or control of Dubai's citizens and residents, the significance of the city's transformations is never fully determined by the intentions of its developers. This book, therefore, centers the ongoing adaptive work inhabitants do to transform Dubai's spectacular places into personally important cultural sites, sites that house memories; provide places to gather, connect with one another, and "see and be seen"; and serve as public spaces where residents observe and negotiate social norms and various regimes of inclusion and exclusion. For adaptive agents, the spectacular city becomes a site of not only loss and marginalization but also belonging and community.

Inhabitants' activity in forming meaningful connections with and within spectacular spaces grounds the book's conceptual contribution to understanding how contemporary subjects living in illiberal societies actively respond to their societies' neoliberal developments. Dominant discourses conceptualize a limiting triptych of ways residents might relate to spectacular developments such as those in Dubai by (at least subtly) resisting the neoliberal agenda the developments represent; helplessly watching as the spectacle unfolds; or maybe enthusiastically accepting the new status quo.[4] In this schema, agentic engagement with urban spaces is conflated with acts of defiance toward the spectacular city, which is not depicted as a "real" place. For instance, Yasser Elsheshtawy, considered one of the foremost urbanism scholars writing on the Gulf, asserts that "in the midst of the spectacular city, *between its cracks*, another city emerges."[5] "The city's 'placelessness' and temporariness is defied in many ways through small acts of resistance."[6] Such narratives privilege overt or subtle resistance to spectacle as meaningful, while positioning other experiences within the spectacular city as superficial, lacking in a deep engagement with urban space, or even the manifestation of false consciousness. This resistance-centered discourse prioritizes liberal conceptions of agency, overlooking the experiences of individuals deemed politically passive while simultaneously investing spectacular urban space with a level of power that can seem completely totalizing.[7] Alternatively, my ethnography shows that middle-class citizens' and residents' attitudes toward the top-down developmental model do not fit into a triptych of supporters, oppressed, resistors. Instead, many are adaptive agents who inhabit and make meanings in a spectacular and illiberal city that shapes, but can also be shaped by, their desire to live a meaningful life and the practices they enact to achieve this goal.[8]

Through its focus on contemporary Dubai and those who inhabit its spectacular spaces, this book offers a deeper look at an understudied middle- and upper-class population of people living everyday lives within an urban landscape that has recently undergone dramatic transformations. Because of the scale and rapidity of its developmental trajectory, and the spectular spaces that have resulted, Dubai has frequently been portrayed as an exceptional place by both critics of the city and its boosters. Yet while some aspects of Dubai are unique to the city, its trajectory of spectacular development has echoes in other times and places within the Gulf region and across other parts of the world. Therefore, this research offers broader insights into how people create everyday life within top-down and commerce-oriented development through negotiating ongoing processes of loss and marginalization while also forging dynamic forms of belonging and community. Ultimately, adaptive agency offers a tool for understanding not only the actions of middle-class inhabitants in Dubai but also a more globalized phenomenon, for some of Dubai's spectacles, this book argues, can be seen as *un*exceptional in today's changing world.

HOW DUBAI BECAME THE SPECTACULAR CITY

A brief history of Dubai's development trajectory can help us contextualize the city's spectacular development, which is a function not only of its modern urban aesthetic but also of the quick pace and large scale of the changes that have unfolded across the city over the last few decades.

Pre-oil Dubai was a business hub, due in part to its rulers' efforts to encourage merchants and traders to settle there. In 1900, Arab and Persian merchants and traders who had been living in Persian port cities moved to Dubai after the Persian government began levying taxes on its ports and the ruler of Dubai instituted a variety of business-friendly economic and political incentives designed to attract them.[9] The city remained small, however; for the next several decades, urban Dubai was less than 320 hectares (3.2 km²), and the entire population lived in three enclaves at the mouth of Dubai Creek.[10]

In 1960, Dubai began to develop under the direction of Sheikh Rashed bin Saeed Al Maktoum, who hired British architect John Harris to develop the city's first master plan. An electrical grid and a road system were built; the area of the creek near the port was dredged; a new town center was constructed; and land was zoned for industrial, commercial, and residential uses.[11] In 1966, oil was discovered in commercial quantities, and by 1968, migrant laborers constituted 50 percent of Dubai's population. These developments spurred significant expansion and development of infrastructure, including schools, hospitals, roads, and telecommunications networks.[12] A new port and terminal building were constructed at Dubai International Airport, and the largest manmade harbor in the world was built at Jebel Ali, where a free-trade zone was created.

The making of Dubai as a spectacular city has often been associated with the city's recent developments, beginning particularly with the building of the iconic luxury hotel Burj Al Arab at the end of the 1990s. However, similar endeavors began as early as 1959 with the construction of Dubai's hospitals and its first national bank, which may be considered mundane today but were once themselves spectacles.[13] Dubai's airport, now considered an essential service, was often described while it was being built as "a vanity project 'to enhance Dubai's name.'"[14] Developments like these were used to fashion Dubai's image as a modern, safe, and regulated place—and to ensure citizens' loyalty. For example, Sheikh Rashid found hospitals in neighboring emirates to be a political threat, as he was concerned that other ruling families offered better health care for Dubai's citizens.[15] The building of Al Maktoum Hospital in the 1960s "signaled Dubai as a legitimate place of welfare and safety"[16] and presented the city "as a place where one could live comfortably. Medical care—with its dual needs of refrigeration and heating . . . antiseptic surfaces, and its aura of serenity delivered by assured technology—also exhibited Dubai's capacity for technological advancement."[17] Vaccination campaigns demonstrated to people coming to Dubai through the ports that Dubai was regulated and safe.[18] During this time as well, Dubai's confined passageways were exchanged for wider roadways. Construction standards, and the enforcement of those standards, were associated with health, so various new inspectors emerged. In 1961, there was a "Sanitary Inspector." By this time, Spinney's supermarket had already opened in Deira and offered the optical assurance of hygienic packaging, though the store still could not offer fresh milk."[19] All these developments advanced Dubai's desire to present itself as a modern, safe, and orderly place, an effort that continues today.

In discussing Sheikh Rashid's visits to London, Reisz says that while London was not a template for Dubai, "it was presented to the ruler as a sales catalogue of discrete parts and experiences," ranging from escalators, theme parks, high streets, metros, and hotel suites.[20] A hospital, airport, and bank were built not only for the services they provided but also for their aesthetics: they presented Dubai as a modern place, a safe place, a regulated place. Dubai's desire to present itself as a modern, safe, and orderly place continues today through various initiatives.

In 1971, Dubai became one of the emirates that constitute the United Arab Emirates (UAE). After the union, a new master plan replaced the older one (with the same architect). A tunnel beneath the creek, now called the Shindagha Tunnel, was constructed to connect Bur Dubai and Deira. The Maktoum and Garhoud bridges were constructed and Port Rashid was opened in 1972.[21] After Sheikh Rashid's death in 1990, his son, Sheikh Mohammed bin Rashid, became the de facto ruler of Dubai (his brother, Sheikh Maktoum, was the official ruler until 2006, when he passed away). Sheikh Mohammed bin Rashid is credited for creating the Dubai that is known today. He envisioned a Dubai that could sustain itself without oil as an international tourist hub where big multinational corporations would establish their Middle Eastern headquarters and investors would want to spend money. He wanted Dubai to be a well-functioning, modern city that offered services such as a metro and efficient electronic information and communication technologies in both the government and the private sectors.

The city grew, particularly along Sheikh Zayed Road toward Jebel Ali, an area that has come to be known as the "new Dubai."[22] Sheikh Zayed Road, and "new Dubai" in general, house the city's skyscrapers and new commercial and financial centers. New Dubai instantiates the "glitzy" and "sanitized" side of the city, where the most spectacular developments take place.[23] To forward Sheikh Mohammed bin Rashid's goal of transforming Dubai into a major tourist destination, in the 1990s the city began constructing megaprojects such as the artificial islands known as Palm Islands; Burj Al-Arab Hotel; Dubai Marina, which features luxury hotels, high-rise apartment buildings, and cafés; Jumeirah Beach Residence, a beachfront apartment and hotel community featuring restaurants, a boardwalk, a park, and chair and cabana rentals; Internet City, an IT business park that houses 1,400 companies; Media City, a regional hub that houses 1,300 media companies; and many others. By 2005, Dubai's urban area was 190 times bigger than it had been in 1900.[24]

Although many new developments have been erected on empty land, some megaprojects are now being built on the old sides of the city and are gentrifying these areas. While the new Dubai may be seen as the sanitized and wealthy side and the old Dubai as the "gritty" side, one can find working-class neighborhoods and lower-income residents sharing big villas in parts of new Dubai. Nevertheless, many parts of the city are clearly segregated by class. This segregation facilitates a common distinction observers make between "new Dubai" and "real Dubai": realness is associated with the older neighborhoods where Emiratis used to live and that now house the foreign working class, and realness is dissociated from the new developments and their emphasis on capitalist development and attracting foreign capital.

But everyday life is not as clear cut as this common dichotomy suggests. Middle-class inhabitants engage with new Dubai as a "real" space in ways that they find meaningful. While some of them describe experiences of loss and alienation in relation to new Dubai, many also describe social gains made through enacting rituals of belonging there. By illuminating the complexities of their relationships to new Dubai, and the agential work they do to inhabit the city, this book fills in some of the shades of gray that are missing from prevailing black-and-white images of life in old and new Dubai.

LOOKING BEYOND BINARY PARADIGMS
TO THEORIZE ADAPTIVE AGENCY

In my first weeks as a PhD student at the University of Oxford, I attended an Arab student group dinner. As we were socializing in a Syrian restaurant in town, an Arab student sitting next to me informed me that she had been to Dubai but didn't like it—she found it superficial. I had heard these comments before. A few weeks ago, on a plane ride from Dubai to London, a British woman told me she preferred Abu Dhabi to Dubai because the former was slower paced, and you could see more Emiratis there—she described Abu Dhabi as more authentic. I constantly hear comments about Dubai's perceived superficiality from various people: Arabs, South Asians, Westerners, and others; people from different backgrounds and occupations; and people with different relationships to the city, including tourists, new residents, and, occasionally, the city's inhabitants, both Emiratis and long-term resident non-Emiratis. While this narrative persists in academia and mainstream accounts—and there has been very insightful research highlighting the Orientalist nature of such stereotypes—there is still a need for a large-scale intervention to thoroughly investigate this omnipresent authenticity discourse and the consequences its narratives play in our understanding of certain geographies and the people who inhabit them.

Therefore, a central contribution of this book is its critique of binary paradigms that have dominated popular and scholarly portrayals of Dubai and how the city is inhabited by its long-term residents. Foremost among these is the pervasive discourse that the city is inauthentic, and therefore totally alienating, to its residents. This "discourse of inauthenticity" shapes, and is shaped by, portrayals that characterize the city as an exceptionally illiberal and neoliberal urban landscape, in which the authoritarian state and global capital work together to exert overwhelming power. While attentive to the dramatic scale of Dubai's development and the political economy in which such changes have taken shape, my ethnography foregrounds alternative conceptualizations of Dubai's urban environs and the ways they achieve meaning through ongoing practices of interaction between middle-class residents and the city they inhabit. This book eschews binary notions of authenticity/inauthenticity and liberalism/illiberalism to focus on the meaning-making practices of adaptive agents who negotiate complex and layered political, economic, social, and cultural geographies to create everyday lives within the spectacular city.

Binary conceptualizations of fake versus authentic environments lead people to fetishize so-called authentic places, while at the same time dismissing so-called fake places (whether whole cities like Dubai or specific spaces such as shopping malls) as nonplaces unworthy of studying and learning about—except to critique. When we use binaries of fake/authentic to understand certain spaces and geographies, we fail to recognize the multiplicity of roles spectacular places assume. They are home for some people, places of memories, places where people negotiate social norms, and important cultural sites in various ways—not just inherently alienating spaces of neoliberal spectacle. Overlooking these realities results in narratives that depict inhabitants of Gulf cities as constantly isolated, helpless as they are forced to live in soulless cities changing beyond their consent. It also reproduces ideas about these cities being exceptionally exclusionary and unsustainable, without linking the exclusionary and unsustainable nature of neoliberal urban development in Dubai to global processes happening simultaneously elsewhere. For instance, in *The Independent*, the public intellectual Ziauddin Sardar writes:

> The place looks and feels unreal. That's the conclusion I reach every time I visit a Gulf state. It is not just the Disney World architecture, the obscene display of wealth, the ubiquitous presence of poor migrant laborers, the insidious racism of the natives, and the segregation and seclusion of the women. What really strikes you is the fact that the region is totally out of sync: the contradictions between imported hypermodernity and the reactionary and anachronistic local traditions are just too stark. I always leave thinking: this isn't going to last long.[25]

Valuations of modernity are political, as are judgments of modernity: "when observers accept or reject an individual's or a group's effort to be seen as modern, their evaluations are political pronouncements."[26] Sardar's depiction of the supposed clash between "imported hypermodernity" and "anachronistic local traditions" categorizes the Gulf's modernity as a facade covering up a lack of modernity underneath.[27] Sardar's assessment exemplifies the Orientalist lens that often implicitly or explicitly pits Gulf states against the rest of the (typically Western) world. In this quote, for example, the exploitation of workers and exclusion of women are depicted as primary characteristics of Gulf states, not as social ills that plague many states. Koch demonstrates that there is an abundance of these narratives in Western newspapers and academic work.[28] Yet, these narratives do not only emerge from the West. For instance, Centner shows that people from Istanbul and Beirut contrast Dubai to their own cities, portraying Dubai as a cultureless place in comparison to their cities of "civilization" and "history."[29]

One of the aspects often associated with Dubai's "inauthenticity" is its illiberalism, wherein inhabitants do not play a role in how their cities develop, which coexists with *neo*liberalism to create the spectacular city. Authoritarianism and neoliberalism are linked: Debord says that the modern spectacle is "the autocratic reign of the market economy which had acceded to an irresponsible sovereignty, and the totality of new techniques of government which accompanied this reign."[30] A society of spectacle therefore appears to uphold neoliberalism's basic principles, where state and capital come together and further empower one another, which can magnify authoritarian political arrangements. However, it is important to foreground that state spectacles exist both in liberal and illiberal settings, even if they are more dominant in the latter because creating spectacles requires resources (financial or political) that are easier to arrange in settings with minimal organized opposition.[31] While illiberal settings may produce more overt forms of spectacle, spectacular cities share the same characteristics and problems of other neoliberal cities, and neoliberal forms of governance exist both in liberal and illiberal states.

States build spectacular cities—signified by megaprojects and "starchitecture"—for a variety of reasons, such as to facilitate capital accumulation, project themselves as tourist destinations, and portray themselves as modern to both the world and their own residents.[32] Spectacles promote a city's modernity and a state's global visibility, showing it as a "vital and dynamic place" while legitimizing development projects without a high level of scrutiny.[33] When spectacular developments or events are tied to national pride and patriotism, they are less prone to being criticized, as doing so might risk someone being seen as unpatriotic.[34]

Because they aim to attract foreign capital, tourists, and wealth, spectacular cities are often neoliberal cities (although cities not deemed spectacular also share similar characteristics). Neoliberal development privileges elites with economic capital while disadvantaging those without it, as it allows for the redistribution of wealth in a manner that benefits the economic elite—for example, by lower taxation of economic elites, by giving the private sector control over the public sector, or by lower welfare distributions.[35] The general lack of regulation safeguarding rights of low-wage laborers or the lack of social benefits for noncitizens corroborates the idea of Dubai as a neoliberal city. However, it is not sufficient by itself to explain the extensive social benefits offered to citizens, such as free land or housing, free higher education and health care, high job security, and the availability of public sector jobs with short hours and relatively high pay. Nevertheless, we do see forms of neoliberal governance dominating the landscape in many ways, even for citizens. For instance, the fact that most Emiratis in Dubai attend private rather than public schools reinforces the reality that private services are fulfilling the roles that the public sector otherwise could, as these public services are seen as deficient compared with private ones.

The depiction of cities such as Dubai as *exceptionally* illiberal and neoliberal, however, may lead us to miss out on mundane realities of people's everyday lives and critique their political subjectivities (or supposed lack thereof) to higher degrees than when similar research is conducted elsewhere. While there are states with a higher saturation of illiberal practices than others, pockets of liberalism and illiberalism exist everywhere, and authoritarian and democratic states use many of the same tools to engage with their subjects.[36] More importantly, there are people and places in so-called liberal states, such as Indigenous communities or Black Americans in the US, who experience illiberalism more than others in the same state.[37] Rather than locating liberalism/illiberalism geographically or spatially, liberalism/illiberalism should be located by practice.[38] This allows us to begin de-exceptionalizing Dubai's forms of illiberalism and neoliberalism to gain a better understanding of the forms of subjectivity and agency that take place there.

In this book, critiquing the pervasive "discourse of authenticity" built on binaries of authentic/fake and liberal/illiberal allows a more nuanced portrait of Dubai's middle-class residents to emerge, one that highlights their adaptive practices of inhabiting spectacle. This is important because it allows us to theorize a mode of agency operating beyond the binary of passivity/resistance that has often framed popular and scholarly portrayals of Dubai's residents despite the well-known limitations of this framing.

Take, for instance, this scholarly account:

> Dubai, Abu Dhabi, Doha and others. Their soaring towers, spotless shopping malls, immaculate transport systems and ultramodern airports are suggestive of an urbanity that does not tolerate any kind of informal intervention. A *detached populace* moves through these sites, consuming a visual landscape that is predicated on the spectacular. It must remain clean, sanitized, free from any traces of human interaction. *People are behaving as if they are on a stage set, playing a predetermined role and following a carefully written script.*[39]

Here, inhabitants of spectacular cities are described as entranced subjects who are incapable of feeling "real" belonging or having meaningful lived experiences; their actions have been predetermined for them. Some scholars of the Gulf at times engage in similar narratives: the Bahraini scholar Omar AlShehabi depicts inhabitants of Gulf cities as without agency in relation to their cities' development: "They are generally marginalized and without any active role in defining its physical and social features. Here they see buildings and towers rising around them, and they cannot do anything except watch."[40]

It is perhaps not unexpected, then, that a lot of the academic discourse on the Gulf is focused on locating resistance, whether explicitly or implicitly. Abu-Lughod says that scholars who find "something admirable about resistance have tended to look to it for hopeful confirmations of the failure—or partial failure—of systems of oppression."[41] Elsheshtawy, for example, highlights the "toiling populace" who are "bravely defying prevailing norms" as the exception to an otherwise detached population.[42] Yet if we allow resistance to spectacle to appear to be the only legitimate (or even possible) form of agency, we simplify some of the more complex dynamics of subjectivity through which people in Dubai relate to their city, to themselves, and to one another.

Everyday Life in the Spectacular City charts an alternative path to the common academic quest to locate a certain type of (resistive) agency among inhabitants in Gulf states. In this way, it advances a perspective informed by critical scholarship that decenters resistance in conceptualizing agential human subjectivities. Mahmood, for example, argues that academics still emphasize women's acts of "resistance," even "when an explicit *feminist* agency is difficult to locate."[43] The trend among feminists of different leanings to assume that Muslim women's participation in socially conservative (Islamic) movements is either based on some sort of false consciousness (which has been abandoned since the 1970s) or indicative of subversive resistance—a trend scholars like Mahmood and others have critiqued. Yet a similar pattern in scholarship emerges in the context of the Gulf, with the discourse of "false consciousness" still being used at times, not only in Western narratives but sometimes also among Gulf intellectuals, to describe urban denizens. Indeed, most people living in Gulf cities cannot participate in the official making of their cities, which is also true for residents of many non-Gulf cities. As a result, many of them experience alienation and loss, something that I explore later, as have many other scholars writing about the Gulf.[44] Yet many also feel belonging and create community in the city's spectacular spaces through adapting to the city's spectacular developments; and in some cases, they also adapt aspects of the city to their own needs.

In conceptualizing middle-class Dubai inhabitants as adaptive agents, I build on Alexei Yurchak's work on "normal subjects."[45] While Yurchak's normal subjects lived in a very different context than my interlocutors—the late communist-era USSR—the similarity between his ethnographic context and mine lies in the centrality given to groups of people who have been dismissed as indifferent and passive in the face of illiberal state spectacle. Yurchak argues that academic and media representations of Soviet life are built on the idea that most people living under (late) socialism in the USSR experienced it as simply "bad" or viewed it as "imposed" on them (although it is important to emphasize here that his reference is to people living in the USSR and not in Eastern Europe). He notes the presence of various dichotomies in the academic literature on Soviet life, such as repression/freedom, oppression/resistance, and official culture/counterculture, as well as hidden/official selves. He criticizes works that attempt to uncover a "hidden resistance," arguing that common narratives ignore that there were many people living under late socialism in the

Soviet Union who genuinely supported the values associated with it, even though their actions sometimes transgressed many of the system's norms. In his analysis, transgressing some of these norms was not typically resistance (hidden or not) but rather part of the articulation of normal subjectivity.[46]

Yurchak's useful definition of a normal subject is one who knew they could live a "normal" life—defined as safe, self-manageable, and enjoyable—"away from the official sphere, provided he/she took no active interest in it."[47] These normal subjects varied from those who attended Komsomol meetings but mostly napped during them; to those who refused to attend any of these meetings, not because they were anti-Soviet but because they differentiated themselves from both anti- and pro-Soviet groups; to those who fully believed in the goals of communism but enjoyed playing banned rock music, not seeing it as a transgressive act. Many of Yurchak's interlocutors self-consciously labeled themselves as normal subjects, particularly as their everyday lives included interactions with political contexts that they then navigated in "apolitical" ways.

The central figures in my study do not self-consciously refer to themselves in this way nor are they in similar political contexts, living as they do in a neoliberal and globalized city. My questions to them about their everyday socializing practices and the urban spaces of the city are also markedly different from what Yurchak may have asked his own interlocutors, as I attempted to understand their attitudes toward Dubai's late-twentieth and twenty-first-century developments. Many of my interlocutors, though not all, are generally supportive of Dubai's top-down developmental model while also possessing some reservations about certain issues, which vary from one person to another and take forms from ambivalence to forthright critique. Still, what is common among most of them is that they are generally adaptive, rather than resistant, to the city's changes, even if they do not feel favorably toward all of them. This is what makes them normal subjects—their strategies of adaptation fashioned away from the official sphere and geared toward the construction of safe, self-manageable, enjoyable lives, ones amenable to pursuits of belonging and community formation. Framing these residents of Dubai as normal subjects throws into relief their actions and identities as adaptive agents.

Adaptive agents, as I conceptualize them, often negotiate an ambivalent sense of belonging to Dubai, adapting to its spectacles in some ways—and not in others. Like Yurchak's use of "normal subjects," my point here is to contest binaries of antagonists/supporters as well as to challenge the depiction of certain criticism as a form of resistance. It is also to call attention to the myriad quotidian negotiations of everyday desires through which residents—including not only citizens but also noncitizens—respond to the norm of spectacular development as an iterative and ongoing process.

Like Mahmood, I also criticize "normative liberal assumptions about human nature" that assume that "all human beings have an innate desire for freedom, that we all somehow seek to assert our autonomy when allowed to do so, that human agency primarily consists of acts that challenge social norms and not those that uphold them, and so on."[48] By saying that freedom is not everyone's priority I do not mean to draw essentialist arguments that imply freedom is only sought or able to be experienced in the West. Many in the Gulf seek for their voices to be heard or advocate with varying degrees of directness for specific changes. But not everyone seeks freedom for the same purposes, nor do they seek it all the time, my research shows. An overemphasis on freedom can elide other desires, including desires for social ties, material objects, new experiences, comfort and safety, and so on.

Seeing Dubai's residents as adaptive agents opens space to explore modes of inhabitation that might otherwise be hard to understand as agential, including states like acceptance and indifference. Discussing the illiberal and spectacular city of Astana in Kazakhstan, Koch says that Western media and academic discourse about Kazakhstan erases the agency of Kazakhstanis, many of whom support the nondemocratic regime.[49] Their support does not imply unawareness of structural inequalities and violence, nor that there are no critics and forms of discontent.[50] Rather, there are many more ambivalent and complex attitudes toward their state that cannot be easily understood through narratives about supporters/antagonists. Furthermore, Koch argues that common depictions of Astana as "false" and "strange" exclude "from sight the realities of the ordinary people, including their complex attitudes towards their state—whether it is their admiration and support for it; their fear of persecution; or more commonly, their mere political indifference."[51]

Indifference is a political subjectivity that maintains the status quo and its power relations. It is inhabitants' indifference that sustains the system and its structural inequalities, marking their actions (or inaction) as significant and political.[52] Importantly, there are a variety of reasons that Koch's interlocutors are indifferent: some are living relatively well and would rather not rock the boat; they want themselves and their families to be safe; they believe the government is doing what it can to make their country better; they think things will not change anyway, even if one is politically active; or sometimes it is "truly painful for many people to think about this injustice actively and constantly."[53] Thus, apparent passivity can often be quite conscious (as opposed to an indication of "false consciousness"), and while safety is one concern in such contexts, there are a variety of other reasons that people remain accepting or indifferent. These modes, of course, also exist in various ways in "liberal" contexts, starting from the way that millions of Americans do not vote in US elections, for a variety of reasons, to the indifference shown by populations around the world to everyday forms of inequality.[54]

While some argue that indifference can allow human atrocities to take place, such as in the case of Nazi Germany, indifference does not lead to the same power structures and inequalities in every setting.[55] Yurchak shows this in the late Soviet context, where he argues that people's indifference contributed to a crisis in the system that eventually led to the USSR's dissolution.[56] More mundane examples point to the ways that indifference can sometimes undermine rather than maintain a system. In the UAE, for instance, begging is criminalized, and police campaigns instruct people *not* to give mendicants money and to report them; yet, during Ramadan, people notice an increase in begging and the giving of money. People who donate when police campaigns instruct them not to are not always convinced by their own actions. Some of them do not feel they have done a "good deed," as they are suspicious of the legitimacy of these requests, but they also do not want to dismiss someone who might be in genuine need and feel embarrassed for not helping them during Ramadan. Complicating matters, they often otherwise support punitive laws against begging, not only because they are concerned with it being a form of organized crime but also because they share the state's vision that begging "defames the image of the state and its cultural appearance."[57]

Their range of reactions, in other words, can blur the lines between indifference and support/antagonism to state policies that aim to project a certain (sanitized) image of the UAE.

Academic (and popular) discourse often assumes that politically active populations—rather than indifferent ones—produce more equitable societies. Yet politically active individuals can also be racist, sexist, classist, etcetera. In the example above, an active citizen may be more likely to report illegal behavior to the authorities, placing precarious individuals at higher risk of deportation or imprisonment, than an indifferent person might. This is not to claim that marginalized groups are treated the same in all political systems but rather to highlight the need for a more nuanced understanding of these different systems, which my ethnography provides in regard to Dubai—which shares qualities with many other places, including cities in so-called liberal contexts. For instance, in Western universities, some faculty members may criticize neoliberalism and its practices in their teaching and writing, and perhaps through protests and petitions. However, some engage in the very practices that support a neoliberal and exclusionary system so that they can lead a "normal" life: they prioritize publishing and neglect teaching and service work, publish in journals that are not open access, engage in citational practices that further bolster the works of established (often white) scholars and marginalize underrepresented ones, write in inaccessible languages, and so on. These academics, like other people in illiberal systems, want to live "normal" lives. They may engage in forms of protest against the neoliberal system that do not rock the boat rather than acts that can radically change the system, and which can harm their chances of living a normal life. In that sense, they also share some similarities with normal subjects in different political systems, including the UAE.

Aside from the fake/authentic, liberal/illiberal, and supportive/resistant binaries, my book also challenges binaries of belonging/exclusion—which are often also discussed through citizen/noncitizen binaries in the case of the Gulf. As I conducted my research, one of the questions that was often asked of me was how we can talk about urban belonging in Dubai when there is the glaring matter of limited citizenship and no permanent residency. This is an important question. In Dubai, 90 percent of the population—including many of the people interviewed for this book—have no path to being naturalized and therefore lack permanency in the place they consider home. Joining other scholars who have examined the impacts of this citizenship regime on residents' experiences of belonging, my work argues that while the citizen/noncitizen binary in the UAE certainly structures aspects of everyday life in many important ways for residents, it does not neatly predict dichotomous experiences of belonging/exclusion.[58] *Noncitizens* in the Gulf often experience a sense of belonging by virtue of their familiarity with and memories of a place, proximity to family members, social and personal connections, familiarity with the language and cultural traditions, and access to material advantages and social benefits, among other factors.[59] Meanwhile, *citizens* in Gulf cities may not experience full belonging in their states or cities, such as when Emiratis navigate being minorities in their country of citizenship (which I discuss more in chapter 3). Contributing to a wider argument, my research affirms the limitation of lenses that primarily emphasize binary citizenship status as the determinant of inclusion or exclusion.[60] Instead, I consider citizenship status to be one variable among many affecting how middle-class residents of Dubai encounter the city and craft meaningful lives within its spectacular developments.

Belonging and the politics of belonging inform the way middle-class residents on whom my work focuses—as well as other segments of society—experience inclusion and exclusion in the city.[61] Belonging is about feeling safe and "at home," although "home" should not be understood in a physical sense but rather as a psychological attachment, imagined and felt.[62] The politics of belonging, meanwhile, "refers to a set of potentially exclusionary political discourses that seek to shape notions of who does belong—and crucially, who does not."[63] My research is attentive to both these aspects of belonging. Furthermore, my research shows that the ways people create belonging in the spectacular city can reinforce or alter the politics of belonging, especially in regard to influencing how classed and gendered exclusions are exacerbated or mitigated. As people pursue belonging, they shape the politics of belonging, and my research traces this unfolding dynamic.

Where top-down developments seek to maximize profits, individuals can have power to access certain spectacular spaces. In doing so, they might feel degrees of belonging while a politics of belonging is being enacted. Practices of belonging influence what politics of belonging operate in the space of urban Dubai, and vice versa. Some exclusions are being rearranged, while others are being reinforced. There are new arrangements of gender power, class power, and globalization that are being produced in spectacular spaces. For example, for some Emirati women, Dubai's new developments allow them to seek out places where they have more social freedoms than they do in "local" spaces. Yet this is based on a model of consumption that includes only people of a certain social and economic class, excluding others.

Similar themes emerge in regard to globalization. While many spaces in new Dubai are inclusive of people from different national backgrounds, this is a classed cosmopolitanism. There is an increasing number of people accessing glitzy developments full of consumer places and items, and also often full of people from many parts of the world; yet at the same time, the difference between working-class and middle-class Dubai inhabitants is getting starker, which can lead to less comingling between social groups. In this sense, the politics of belonging being orchestrated through the new spectacle and people's engagement with it has rearranged gender, national, race, and ethnic dynamics along different lines than those that existed a few decades earlier. My research offers insights into such changes.

AN INHABITANT'S RESEARCH ON INHABITING SPECTACLE

This urban ethnography was conducted with middle-class and upper-middle-class Emirati citizens and long-term residents of Dubai (as well as, in chapter 4, inhabitants from the neighboring emirates and Gulf Cooperation Council [GCC] states).

I interviewed over one hundred citizens and noncitizens, including men and women of different age groups. My Emirati interlocutors ranged from 18 to 65 years old; most were under 40, and only a few were over 50. All my non-Emirati interlocutors were between 20 and 50 years old. About 60 percent of my interviewees were women, due to my larger number of friendships with women, who then introduced me to other women.

I found most of my interlocutors through my social circles and snow-balling word-of-mouth referrals. Although I have friendships with both Emiratis and non-Emiratis, having Emirati family immediately meant more access to UAE citizens; as a result, about 60 percent of my interlocutors are Emiratis. Except for one British interviewee, all my noncitizen interlocutors were Arab or South Asian, which is tied not only to my sampling methods but also to UAE demographics. In addition to drawing on my social circles to find interviewees, I posted information about my project on my public Instagram and Twitter accounts and received many messages from people I did not know who wanted to be interviewed. Most of the interviewees I did not know were those who had reached out to me through friends or social media.

Interviews averaged about two and a half hours; the shortest was about an hour, and the longest was five hours. The majority were audio recorded and then transcribed. When interviewees did not want to be recorded, I handwrote notes during the interview and typed them at home. When I discuss these interviews in the following chapters, I use pseudonyms to protect anonymity. Because of the political connotations behind terms such as "expats," which is often used to refer to middle-class and wealthy residents, and "migrants" or "workers," which is used to refer to low-income residents such as laborers, I refer to any non-Emirati in Dubai as a resident. I refer to Emiratis as citizens and also use the term *khaleeji* to refer to citizens from the GCC states. I use the term "inhabitants" for both Emiratis and non-Emiratis, to emphasize that they live in Dubai.

Along with these interviews, I conducted participant observation in new Dubai, including its shopping malls (especially Dubai Mall, the city's largest mall); the beach and public parks; and developments such as the Canal, City Walk, Jumeirah Beach Residence, and La Mer. The latter developments are mixed-use residential and commercial spaces often used by the middle and upper-classes; some are used more by Emiratis, and others by residents and tourists. These settings constitute spectacular parts of the city and are popular places to visit among those I interviewed. I spent many hours walking in shopping malls and new developments, going to coffee shops, Ramadan pop-up shops, and social gatherings in new Dubai. I also went to old Dubai to compare my experiences of it to those of new Dubai and to deepen my understanding of the experiences described by those who had grown up in old Dubai. During my observations, I occasionally interacted with people I came across, but these interactions were minimal.

I often used my mobile phone to note my observations and to photograph behavior in the settings I was observing. It was a challenge to take photos in Dubai, as the UAE prohibits taking photos of people without their permission. The photos I took were often not focused on any one person or group, although I later cropped these photos to zoom in on the activities or behaviors I originally intended to capture. I blurred the faces of anyone who appeared in these. The photos I took represent moments of people inhabiting spectacle that caught my attention and were chosen subjectively by me to document. In that sense, the way I understand these photos or what they represent may very well be different from how the people in these photos understand their own experiences. With that caveat in mind, the photos appearing in this book are nevertheless illustrative of everyday realities that are difficult to capture only in words.

Finally, I also used social media, particularly Instagram and Twitter, not only to find interviewees but to understand how people spoke about Dubai's urban spaces. I looked at posted photographs and videos that showed the places those in my research groups go to, their social activities, and their attitudes toward different urban spaces. I used Instagram and Twitter because they are popular among Gulf citizens and middle-class residents, including both men and women and multiple generations, from teenagers to people in their sixties (although not necessarily by the same audiences, as Twitter is considered more "serious").[64]

In conceptualizing this project, I used class and duration of residency in Dubai to decide who to include in this ethnography for various reasons. Interviewing interlocutors who lived in the UAE for at least two decades was important to understand how individuals who had a strong attachment to Dubai—and who witnessed its rapid changes—felt about the city's transformations. In that sense, both citizens and noncitizens here share at least one similarity in regard to their relationship to the city in that they witnessed and lived through its major changes (and the implications of that). My interest in studying long-term residents and middle-class citizens together arose initially from the relative absence of work on this demographic intersection.[65] Understanding the urban experiences of both citizens and residents together allows us to move beyond binaries of citizen/noncitizen inherent in the earlier literature, especially because class, regardless of citizenship, is an important determinant of how people subjectively experience many aspects life in Dubai.

While residency length is in many cases easy to determine, class is admittedly a more complicated category. My interlocutors varied in terms of their class positions within the broad category of middle class, with many of them being what I would term upper-middle class. The social location of the "middle class" in Gulf societies is complex, particularly because this term is not necessarily used among Emiratis (or many *khaleejis*, for that matter).[66] In fact, Gulf citizens, especially in the wealthier states of the UAE, and in Kuwait and Qatar, are often considered to constitute the privileged class at the top of the social hierarchy. However, many Gulf citizens, although wealthy by international standards, are not the elite among other citizens—they are not part of the ruling family or the big merchant families that wield influence on a policy level. While I did not ask explicit questions about socioeconomic status in my interviews, in some of my everyday conversations and interactions I did come across Emiratis who were quite well-off (and might be seen by other non-Emiratis as upper-middle class or even elites) but who saw themselves as middle class. This was particularly because they were comparing themselves to other Emiratis (rather than the UAE population as a whole). In some ways, this group may be seen as elites, such as a family with parents in their fifties who could afford certain luxuries (dining out often, traveling often) with only one parent working. They, however, considered themselves middle class in the sense that they felt they were more or less like most other Emiratis, and different from elites who had larger networks and influence (and of course, more economic capital).

Their conception of middle class works if elites are those who control the distribution of social and economic goods, the middle classes those to whom the social and economic goods are distributed, and the lower socio-economic classes those who benefit least from this distribution (the latter group among Emiratis is not large but does exist).[67] Categories can be blurred, however. For my purposes, it is important to note that spaces popular among many Emiratis, such as shopping malls, coffee shops, and other new developments in the city (Dubai Mall, City Walk, Galleria Mall, e.g.), are used by elites and middle classes more often than they are used by others.

When it comes to class among residents (noncitizens), I found it easier to distinguish class by factors such as the type of jobs individuals work in, the neighborhood they live in, the schools they (or their children) attend, and perhaps their material possessions. Basically, it is not only economic capital that distinguishes one's class. For instance, while the degree of education and type of schools attended can signify who is upper-middle class among young UAE residents, it applies differently for older individuals, particularly middle-aged or older Emiratis. Emiratis in their forties (and older) who have not had a university education (or who may not have completed high school) *can* still find high-paying careers (including owning their own businesses) that guarantee them a middle- or upper-middle-class lifestyle. This is changing today, but it is quite different from conceptions of the middle class in other places. Education, including the types of school and university one attended, is one important factor in understanding socioeconomic class among younger people in the UAE, and was one helpful indication of socioeconomic class among (younger) noncitizens that I used to loosely categorize my interviewees. As opposed to those in the upper classes, many in the upper-middle classes need their jobs so as not to experience a degradation in lifestyle (they do not live off inheritance, e.g.). Through their jobs, they tend to earn enough to be able to bring their families to live with them, to afford Dubai's pricey private schools (noncitizens have no access to free public education, but job benefits packages allow middle-class residents to afford some form of private schooling), and to enjoy varying degrees of disposable income. Most of my interlocutors could afford some (or many) aspects of the "glitzy" lifestyle of the city, such as living in new Dubai (and being comfortable in such settings) or socializing in its pricey restaurants and bars. In sum, the noncitizens whose experiences I discuss therefore have economic, social, and cultural capital that generally allows them to live in and enjoy new Dubai regularly, although the extent to which this is possible, or desirable, varies among them.

Similarly to my interlocutors, the spectacular places of new Dubai that I focus on may be considered middle-class (or in some cases, upper-middle-class and upper-class) spaces of consumption. While they are also used by elites and reproduce classed exclusions, they are not necessarily elite spaces per se. Rather, they vary greatly in their level of accessibility. Restaurants in five-star hotels are highly exclusive, for instance, but shopping malls are not neatly segregated in terms of class and race. Thus, the spaces of Dubai where my research took place were often traversed, albeit in sometimes unparallel ways, by members of different classes. It is also the case that places like shopping malls in Dubai cater to different groups and socioeconomic classes over time. For example, Deira City Center, once popular among the middle classes, is now frequented by lower- to middle-income residents, as is the case with other older malls such as Al-Ghurair Center and Burjuman. There are other smaller malls that are purposely built for low-income inhabitants as well and are placed in labor camps. Although the fanciest central spaces are used more by those with higher disposable incomes, they can also be spaces where different classes and groups congregate at and across different times.

Although important, class by itself is limited as a marker to describe the nuances of belonging and exclusion in the spectacular city, highlighting the need to focus on intersectionality. It is thus important to look beyond just economic capital and toward cultural capital to understand who is included and who is excluded. One of my interlocutors commented, for example, that she often encountered her working-class, South Asian male employee walking around the Mall of the Emirates. While he is a lower-income resident, her employee still had a much better command of English, access to the metro, and a higher salary than a construction worker or janitor. The "glitzy" Mall of the Emirates, therefore, is more accessible to people like him than it is to the working poor, while more upscale parts of the city (such as the fancy hotels) are largely inaccessible to both groups. Thus, while my ethnography focuses on middle-class citizens and residents of Dubai, it also emphasizes the diversity among groups and places assumed to be homogeneous. Recognizing that those who may be considered working class or middle class vary in their economic and social capital also helps move us beyond binaries that depict some spaces simply as exclusionary or alienating and others as simply inclusive.

At times, exclusions appear clear cut. An official working for Emaar, Dubai Mall's developer, said that laborers are allowed in the mall so long as they do not enter wearing overalls, their work clothes. His reasoning was that working on a construction site leaves laborers' clothes dirty and unfit for the mall. This reinforces the idea that these spaces are sanitized in order to project a certain image and illuminates the working of the politics of belonging.[68] The politics of belonging "refers to a set of potentially exclusionary political discourses that seek to shape notions of who does belong— and crucially who does not." In this case, the working poor (and particularly laboring men, who are often South Asian) are seen as disruptive of the sanitized environment of the spectacular city. Race (or ethnicity), class, and gender intersect here, and this perception goes hand in hand with middle-class views of low-income South Asian men as a threat to women's safety.

At other times, exclusions may be very much present but more indirect. For instance, not having enough days off from work to go out, the fact that malls and other spectacular developments are too expensive for the working poor to enjoy, or not being able to afford public transportation—are all examples of indirect exclusions. But again, intersectionality matters here. Working-class women with certain forms of cultural capital needed to enjoy the spectacular city, for instance, have better (yet not complete) access to it. For instance, Alawadi found that Filipinas living in Satwa (a working-class, central location) both socialized in their neighborhood as well as enjoyed going to American chains (such as Applebee's, Pizza Hut, or Tim Horton's) on Sheikh Zayed Road.[69] The latter is a more middle-class area lined with Dubai's skyscrapers and businesses (restaurants there range from Pizza Hut to expensive restaurants in hotels).

Some people advised me to look at people's clothes to get a better idea of who might be included or excluded from places like shopping malls. For instance, they said that *shalwar kameez* was often a sign that an individual was from a working-class background, while middle-class South Asian men usually wore Western-style trousers and shirts. Yet not everyone who wore *shalwar kameez* was working-class, and there were many individuals dressed in that way walking in the mall, as can be seen in figure 1. This does not mean that others like them were not excluded from these places, but it makes it difficult for me to conclude who *is* and who is *not* included and based on which factors.

Middle classes often view shopping malls and new developments as safe and comfortable places because they are, to a large extent, excluding those deemed a "threat" to their safety.[70] A large number of workers,

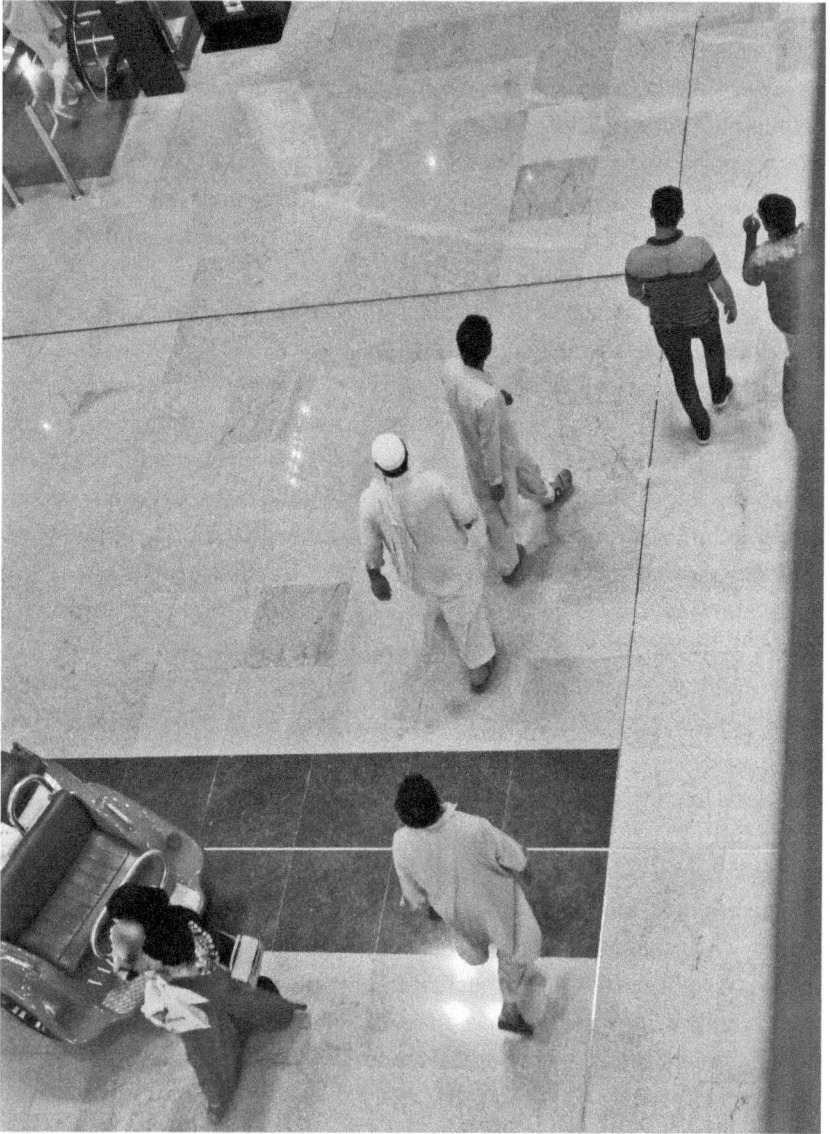

Figure 1. Men in *salwar kameez* in Dubai Mall.

primarily from South Asia, came to the UAE without their families because of requirements that restricted individuals working in some professions, such as drivers, from sponsoring them. These laws were changed and relaxed in 2019 (although not everyone can afford to bring their families, even if legally permitted).[71] Therefore, the people one sees at a place like a mall or new developments do not accurately depict the demographics of Dubai's population, which is predominantly male.

On one hand, male-dominated spaces can be understandably uncomfortable for women, who may fear for their safety among men or have cultural or religious values that influence with whom they want to socialize. On the other hand, there is no doubt that the city is still built in a manner that privileges elites and middle classes, including women in these groups. The challenge is to be able to recognize these exclusions and challenge them without reproducing dichotomies of belonging and exclusion (e.g., by recognizing that belonging is built on exclusions almost everywhere, and that even idealized public spaces have excluded certain groups, we may move beyond binaries of inclusive/exclusive spaces).[72]

For some, the mall is an aspirational space, a place to negotiate the politics of belonging, where people attempt to stake claims to a part of the city where their class status does not allow them to fully belong. These aspirational places can therefore be intimidating. A friend said that her ex-boyfriend, a working-class Sri Lankan who had just arrived in Dubai, felt uncomfortable in its malls because of how he was dressed compared with people around him. He felt that while he wore trousers and shirts with different colors and patterns, other people matched their clothes in different ways. My own interlocutors did not express these types of sentiments, however, both because they came from higher socioeconomic backgrounds and because they were long-term residents of Dubai and more familiar with its urban landscape. For some of them, the shopping mall is a familiar place, one where they may have childhood memories, where people socialize and interact: in short, a space of belonging. Taqiya, an Arab woman who was born and raised in the UAE, left for college abroad. Whenever she came back over the holidays, she told her family: "Take me to Deira City Center. I won't feel I'm home until I go there."

The city harbors various exclusions, yet at times it appears a challenge to study them without engaging in exceptionalist narratives. Indeed, some have overemphasized the city's segregation, criticizing even the projects that have been most used by non-elites. Acuto, for instance, used the example of the Dubai metro, where the majority of riders are working- and middle-class residents, to claim that it is a tool for those with economic capital to segregate themselves: "Thanks to the Dubai Metro [...] tourists and businessmen are able to [...] reach ... the Burj or Dubai Mall from the airport in a matter of minutes ... [without ever] exiting anywhere else than in their comfort-proof enclave."[73] I move beyond these exceptionalist narratives while at the same time highlighting the specific ways that belonging is often built on exclusion in the spectacular city. Many of the city's new developments are ideal for the middle classes precisely because the "lowest segments" of the population, such as its laboring male population, are not the majority of people they will encounter there (as opposed to some areas of old Dubai). Recognizing these nuances of class adds complexity to our understanding of belonging and exclusion in Dubai.

POSITIONALITY

As an Emirati woman who grew up in Dubai, my position with respect to the city and the people I research is often very personal, particularly as I study parts of the city that I grew up in and which are, still today, part of my life. My positionality provides me with both opportunities and limitations, something I refer to throughout my research. One of the opportunities is that I am able to reflect on how my interlocutors experience the city and its changes in ways that are not commonly conveyed in academia. For instance, interviews with middle-aged *khaleeji* men and women, as well as the discourse in Arabic newspapers in the Gulf, provide some academics with the perception that these individuals feel marginalized amid the large presence of noncitizens in the country.[74] This is very true. Yet in daily life, we can see contradictions. Some of the very people who criticize the loss of "cultures and traditions" due to the influx of foreigners boast about Dubai's multinationalism and how it has made them more "open-minded" in other circumstances. These nuances are lost when interview responses or discourses in newspapers are used to report on people's stated experiences without deeper research into people's daily realities.

As a privileged Emirati woman doing an ethnography about middle- and upper-middle-class citizens and residents, I recognize that what I present in this book is not representative of how many of Dubai's inhabitants encounter the spectacular city. Both my citizen and noncitizen interlocutors generally lead relatively privileged lives, meaning that not only my voice, but the voices I am reporting on, represent a specific segment of society. To augment limitations of my approach, I supplemented my work with existing literature focused on other populations and the structural inequalities they face, which helped me to demonstrate that with inclusion there is often also exclusion taking place.

While ethnographies are normally focused on a small group of people, I often wondered what realities I was missing since I was not directly engaging with low-income inhabitants and therefore did not have access to their experiences of the city. Logistical constraints in terms of doing fieldwork but also in terms of my positionality guided my decisions about how I focused my research. Not only did I not speak Urdu, Hindi, or Malayalam (the main languages spoken by low-income inhabitants in Dubai), but power dynamics meant that I would not be able to establish trust or truly understand the experiences of low-income inhabitants in my time frame. Although there were a few times when I engaged in conversation with low-income individuals in public spaces, I often wondered if my questions were uncomfortable for them. What if they thought I was someone from the security services? Even if not, why would they tell me, a stranger, their accounts of the city truthfully? For this reason, I relied on the works of other scholars to inform my research.

As I show in chapter 3, I often did wonder about my responsibility to gain a better personal understanding of lower-income neighborhoods in the city. My discomfort in male-dominated, working-class neighborhoods raised other uncomfortable questions: Was I uncomfortable because these spaces were male dominated, because they were unfamiliar, or because of racist and classist stereotypes? This question of what the "moral" role of a privileged researcher is in an illiberal context constantly came to my mind as I was conducting this research, and even after completing it. I continue to ask questions about it throughout this book. I ask these questions when I am thinking of Dubai's low-income inhabitants whom I did not interview, but I also ask them when I analyze my discussions with the more privileged individuals I did engage.

While I share many similarities with some of my interlocutors, I do not claim to understand all their experiences. After speaking about my research with students at New York University Abu Dhabi, one of them asked me about how I (as a citizen) went about writing about belonging among noncitizens. Indeed, I do not feel the precarity of noncitizens who worry about not having their visas renewed every few years. In these cases, I have supplemented my findings with the existing literature and at times asked some of those I interviewed to read different parts of my work. This does not mean I have managed to represent every person's experiences accurately, but I hope that I have come close to representing the views of many of them.

One might assume that, as an Emirati, I can write more easily about Emirati experiences compared with those of non-Emiratis. This is not entirely true. While there are many legal and social aspects of noncitizen belonging that I have never experienced, I realized I have a better understanding of my upper-middle-class interlocutors' relationships to urban spaces than I do those of Emiratis from lower-income backgrounds, such as people I discuss in chapter 5. I have more familiarity with some noncitizens' relationships to the city because all my schooling in the UAE took place at institutions that had a mix of Emiratis and non-Emiratis, and my friendships followed a similar pattern. This meant not only going to schools with non-Emiratis but also socializing in the city—in malls, restaurants, cafés, etcetera—together. I felt more concerned about my positionality when I spoke to Emiratis who grew up in low-income or lower-middle-class neighborhoods. Because I did not grow up with the community life of the *freej* (neighborhood) that they described, I realized that my childhood memories were different and that I did not know enough about their everyday lives and forms of socializing—and that I could therefore be at risk of easily misunderstanding them. Meanwhile, although I have privileges that my noncitizen interviewees did not have, I sometimes felt like I had a closer understanding of their everyday lives in the city in terms of their daily interactions with others. Particularly as I am not seen as visibly Emirati (since not wearing the "national dress" marks someone almost immediately as a non-Emirati), I assume that the interactions and silent negotiations I had with people I did not know in public spaces were based on them interacting with me as they would a noncitizen.[75] I note this because those who wear the national dress are often said to be treated with more "respect."[76] I bring up these example to illustrate different ways my experiences do and do not intersect with different subgroups of Emiratis and noncitizens.

Writing about my own society, my subjectivity and many of my biases may be clear to my readers (as opposed to non-Emirati academics writing about the UAE, who may be viewed as more neutral). My positionality as I write this book reflects this location, as I am privileged in the UAE, albeit also part of a minority as an Emirati, but not necessarily in the Western academic world where there is a serious underrepresentation of Emirati scholars writing about their own societies. The question from the student who asked me about my positionality concerning researching noncitizens made me wonder whether the same questions are asked of noncitizens (including those in the Western academy) writing about Emiratis. I suspect that oftentimes, they are not.[77]

In a Twitter post with a high level of interactions, Kuwaiti academic Talal Al-Rashoud wrote: "As Gulf academics we often find ourselves in a delicate position. We must criticize the gross injustices plaguing our region, yet we must also debunk the potent orientalist discourse that all too often pervades such criticism. We thus end up attacking & defending simultaneously."[78] This accurately reflects how I often felt about my academic experience, with one major caveat—that I had to also negotiate how to do this in a more constrained political context, for while Kuwaiti academics also engage in some self-censorship, they have a much larger space for academic freedom. Given this positionality, my place in the academy affords me both opportunities and limitations that shaped this book. The former includes the reality that I have better access to and familiarity with certain parts of UAE society. The limitations include working with assumptions that my research is necessarily more biased than that of noncitizens, dealing with a sense of alienation of writing from that position, and navigating specific concerns (self-censorship) that other academics writing about the region may not have to consider in the same way.

CHAPTERS

There are certain main characteristics associated with Dubai's spectacular development that are also related to its so-called inauthenticity. For some people, Dubai is not as traditional as they expect a Middle Eastern city to be. It's hypermodern or *too modern*. Its urban landscape is dotted with globalized, commercialized "nonplaces" such as shopping malls and franchise chain coffee shops. They see it as a *neoliberal city* built to generate profit through wealthy investors and visitors rather than a city built for inhabitants. In a similar vein, some people find that it is *too foreign*, that there is not enough Emirati culture in Dubai, nor even Emiratis. For others who do not mind the diversity, Dubai is still not "authentically" cosmopolitan, for it is more segregated than cosmopolitan. They point out that Dubai privileges the experiences and lifestyles of the elites, particularly Western elites, to whom much of the city's "modernity" supposedly caters. Furthermore, it is a politically *illiberal city* where inhabitants do not have a say over the way their environs develop, and where informality is shunned in place of *tightly controlled* and *surveilled* spaces. All these characteristics together constitute an idea of Dubai, and particularly its spectacular spaces, that make it hard to conceptualize people living everyday lives there. This book, divided into five chapters, follows my interlocutors as they interact with these widely lambasted axes of Dubai's spectacle: (1) its so-called inauthenticity, (2) its neoliberalism, (3) its noncosmopolitan foreignness, (4) its pandering to Western ideals of modernity, and (5) its sanitized overregulatedness.

Chapter 1, "(In)Authenticity in Brand Dubai," explores discourses of authenticity that circulate not only in Western media and academia but also among some of Dubai's inhabitants. In particular, it demonstrates how these inhabitants negotiate the impermanence of their city's built environment as well as its top-down developmental ethos that hails tourists, expats, and international finance capital. These changes have spurred widespread cultural and intellectual debates over the authenticity of Dubai, leading to common stereotypes of this city as unreal, shallow, foreign, and totalizing in its power over residents. My research argues that certain citizens and residents, particularly those I label as the creative class, participate in mobilizing discourses of authenticity to interpret the city's changes and what they mean. Social contestations over authenticity can function to animate old memories, serve as an idiom for social critique, and help articulate visions of hoped-for future change. They can also enable some to differentiate themselves from the so-called masses who are enthralled by the city's glitz. The creative class simultaneously demonstrates how quests for authenticity can be intertwined with Orientalist attitudes and practices of social distinction while also raising important critiques about the city's developmental trajectory.

Chapter 2 is "Negotiating Belonging in Dubai's Glitzy, Neoliberal Spaces." In the middle of Dubai's fanciest shopping mall, we see South Asian teenagers practice their dance moves and old Emirati men have their daily chat at a coffee shop. These scenes are at odds with descriptions of Dubai's neoliberal developments as sterile, alienating, and hostile to personal expression and community bonds. While common discourses depict inhabitants of politically "illiberal" cities either as helplessly watching as elite-driven spectacles unfold around them or engaging in (at the very least, subtle) acts of resistance toward the spectacle, this chapter instead centers the work residents do to adapt themselves to the neoliberal city, and at times even adapt the city to themselves. Through this work, Dubai's spectacular places are transformed into personally important cultural sites. Shopping centers, we see, house memories; provide a place to gather, connect with one another, and "see and be seen"; and serve as public spaces where residents observe and negotiate social norms. The spectacular city becomes a site of not only loss and marginalization but new class-based ways to assert belonging, and thereby participate in the enactment of a broader politics of belonging, in new Dubai's commercial spaces.

Chapter 3, "Globalization and Diversity at a Cosmopolitan Crossroads," begins by showing the various forms of cosmopolitanism that exist in new Dubai and how people not only interact with them but also posit their own preferred forms of cosmopolitanism. Participants in my research experience an ambivalent sense of belonging in relation to many of these forms of cosmopolitanism and respond to them with various adaptations. They speak of their experiences when a setting is dominated by what they see as "Western" behavioral norms—or "Westerners" themselves—in other words, when a so-called cosmopolitan space actually feels insufficiently cosmopolitan to them. Sometimes, this leaves inhabitants, including

Emiratis, marginalized in their own country, while at other times, it can be useful for those seeking out spaces to get away from their own community. As a result, they experience an ambivalent, layered, and intersectional belonging within the city's cosmopolitanisms that leaves them feeling included in some contexts and excluded in others. The classed nature of Dubai's cosmopolitanism renders it not superficial but, rather, limited in its abilities to mediate difference without reinforcing social and cultural hierarchies.

The focus of chapter 4, "An Appropriately Modern City," is Dubai. The academic discourse on new Dubai understandably examines the city's aims in attracting Western visitors, tourists, and residents. Yet there has rarely been any academic attention to Dubai's closest neighbors who use and experience the city, be they Emiratis or residents from other emirates or GCC states. Through focusing on these groups who come to live or vacation in Dubai, this chapter investigates the ways non-Western inhabitants pursue mobility and modernity via locating themselves within the spectacular city. I show that for these upper-middle-class individuals who are privileged segments of society in Dubai, the city is a place to live a "normal" life because it indicates for them a way of being in the world that is accommodating of what they deem to be modern lifestyles while allowing them to inhabit a certain set of historically and contextually specific ethical practices that bind them to family and place. Being in Dubai does not mark them as minorities as they fear might happen in the West, thus allowing them to maintain their privileged status. As opposed to immigrating to the West, moving to Dubai does not indicate that they are breaking with their cultural norms or rebelling against them. Rather, it allows them to claim access to more modern ways of living (which they associate with order, regulations, and diversity) in an Arab/Muslim/non-Western milieu.

The making of the ordered and safe city that many Dubai inhabitants admire is made possible through a high degree of state control and regulation, as well as modes of sanitization that stamp down on informality. In chapter 5, "The Costs and Benefits of Safety in Sanitized Spaces," I show that a high degree of urban state control and sanitization affect my interlocutors in various ways but most evidently impact upwardly mobile Emiratis who grew up in low-income neighborhoods in Dubai and who were moved by the state to middle-class neighborhoods. Not only have they "become more VIP," as one of them put it, but their peers, who they described as having been "gang leaders" and troublemakers, "grew up," are working in government jobs and living in villas, and have families and children for whom they are responsible today. As adaptive agents who have ambivalent attitudes toward the city's developments, many of these inhabitants miss the old days when life was informal and less ordered, when they had a sense of community and ownership over their neighborhood. At the same time, many tend to depict the increased order, policing, and surveillance positively as an example of Dubai's "modernity" as the city continues to grow in the twenty-first century. I examine how forms of ambivalence toward the spectacular city rooted in memory and nostalgia are being actively mediated by residents' desires for safety and sanitization. This elucidates what types of safety the spectacular city provides, as well as the forms of security it simultaneously withholds.

The conclusion returns to the main thesis of the book—inhabiting spectacle—reengaging with its three main themes: authenticity, belonging, and agency. It draws together the analysis of each chapter to show that many inhabitants of Dubai relate to the city's spectacular development neither as oppressed subjects nor as active resistors but rather as adaptive agents. Their pursuit of a meaningful everyday life amid the city's changes has been characterized by adaptation and a sense of belonging that is often ambivalent but no less real than other experiences of belonging. I argue that adaptation constitutes an important form of agency among members of illiberal societies—which may be becoming more, rather than less, of the norm in the twenty-first century.

My emphasis on the forms of belonging that inhabitants make in spectacular spaces, including in neoliberal developments such as shopping malls, is not an advocacy of them. Neoliberal developments become places of belonging for some people because of the prevalent circumstances. This does not make them ideal public places, and the harms of neoliberal urban development are very real, particularly for marginalized groups. There are also other issues such as sustainability, both of the urban environment and for the city as a whole, that need to be considered. Yet this is not a book proposing how Dubai's urban development should proceed and should not be read as such. Instead, the book helps us to challenge our understanding of places such as Dubai and shed our Orientalist attitudes about illiberal and spectacular cities, while recognizing that the very ills we critique in them exist also elsewhere in the world and are indeed connected. In reading this book, we should be able to hold these two thoughts at once: neoliberal developments are not good examples of urban development, and we should be addressing their harms, including their exclusions, and constantly seeking practical alternatives that are more sustainable and inclusive. Yet we should also be able to see how inhabitants make meanings in such places without engaging in sensationalist narratives that depict these people as brainwashed by capitalism, while also recognizing the harms that come with Orientalist expectations about what non-Western cities should look like, or what "authenticity" should be.

1 (In)Authenticity in Brand Dubai

I really enjoy JBR [Jumeirah Beach Residence]. I think
that's a really good space, because everybody blends. You
know that's kind of rare in Dubai, where you see all types of
society blend . . . You have tourists, yes, but you also have
low-income workers . . . and you see a lot of Emiratis
there. . . . The Marina also kind of got it right, they did a
good job. . . . The City Walk, it's kind of a hellish place . . .
it's just more shopping.

Steven, British man in his twenties, raised in Dubai

From the new developments[,] I like City Walk. It's low-
rise and feels more humble. It returned to the city its local
flavor and soul. You can even see more Emiratis there. You
don't see many Westerners. It's not their type of place. . . .
Places like JBR and Marina, these were the ones that were
built for investors and tourists and outsiders. Westerners
like to go there, it's their type of environment. You don't see
many Emiratis there.

Salman, an Emirati man in his fifties

These two quotes express contradictory subjective experiences of Dubai's
inhabitants toward the city's newer developments. JBR, the Marina, and
City Walk are all examples of master-planned, large-scale, mixed-use developments containing a mix of mostly upscale residential apartment blocks,
restaurants, and shops. As symbols of Dubai's momentous changes, observers use them to assess and interpret the city's spectacular developmental

trajectory and its impact on society and culture. As the above opinions of Steven and Salman show, some of Dubai's inhabitants who navigate these spaces in their everyday lives can have strong opinions about them, which can vary considerably from site to site and between different people and groups. These different opinions are part of broader local public conversations about what kinds of developments are right for Dubai, reflecting residents' quotidian experiences of inhabiting spectacle while providing a window onto their hopes for the future trajectory of Dubai's built environment, culture, and society.

While people's experiences of the city are diverse, as we see above, it is common for observers to paint new Dubai's developments as somehow unreal and thus uniformly alienating for locals. In some commentary, these spaces are depicted as "uncanny," "spooky," with an "unbearable absence of life."[1] The "seemingly evident metropolitan nature of the Emirati conurbation becomes questionable if one scrapes deeper beneath the glittery surface," and the city becomes a mirage, "a global city of 'non-places.'"[2] As opposed to London or New York, Dubai does not communicate "any sense of urban cohesion and vitality . . . which is usually fundamental in creating attachment to places," and is a place where "neither community spirit nor social bond have much meaning."[3] Or so the common stereotypes go.

To various degrees, similar opinions can be expressed by Dubai's inhabitants themselves. Citizens and long-term residents of Dubai I interviewed sometimes (implicitly or explicitly) referred to Dubai as superficial, contrasting the city to more "authentic" places (such as Western cities or more "traditional" parts of the Gulf). Indeed, the academic literature and my interlocutors' "folk" concepts of authenticity share some similarities. Yet my goal in this chapter is not to deconstruct "folk" concepts of authenticity, which is a social construct, nor to locate authenticity in certain parts of the city. Instead, this chapter explores who is most concerned about the "authenticity" of Dubai's glitzy spaces, what authenticity means to them, and what consequences discourses of authenticity have on our understanding of cities like Dubai and the kinds of lives that are possible to lead in them. It argues that some of Dubai's citizens and middle-class inhabitants respond to the city's developmental trajectory through participating in and selectively mobilizing discourses of authenticity with overlapping purposes.

We can see that social contestations over authenticity serve as an idiom for social critique and in some cases even help articulate visions of hoped-for future change. But they also serve other purposes: they enable some to differentiate themselves from the so-called masses who are enthralled by the city's "glitz," thereby serving as a means of creating social distinction. There are also implications to engaging in these discourses of authenticity. Whether intentionally or not, these discourses at times promote exceptionalist (and Orientalist) narratives about Dubai similar to the ones that circulate in mainstream international academic and popular culture.

Although different individuals refer to authenticity in various ways, one stratum of my research demographic appeared much more concerned with it: those I loosely refer to as the "creative class," often middle- and upper-middle-class individuals who associate themselves with arts, culture, academia, and other creative or intellectual fields. Most of Dubai's inhabitants I engaged are ambivalent about the city's developmental trajectory and find ways to adapt to it. Yet, the creative classes display some differences from others in my sample in the ways they speak about the city's developmental trajectory in that they make bold and conscious critiques of neoliberalism, exclusion, and/or classism (to varying degrees), sometimes through their art and writing, and sometimes simply through direct expression. While some of them ambivalently adapt to Dubai's urban spectacle, as do many of those we will meet in other chapters, they frequently also expressed the extent to which they explicitly rejected belonging to the spectacular elements of the city. In that sense, this chapter also demonstrates the limits of adaptivity among certain segments of society. Indeed, not all of Dubai's inhabitants adapt to (all) the spectacles, and this chapter highlights the experiences of those who do not fully adapt to the spectacle.

I begin this chapter by describing who the creative class is. After that, I focus on common threads of authenticity discourse presented by some of its members in regard to their experiences of their changing city. The first section focuses on authenticity discourse as a response to a sense of loss and alienation. I explore how some in the creative class mobilize the value of authenticity to express frustrations with Dubai's policymakers' preoccupation with "glitz and glamour," as one interlocutor termed it, which leads the emirate to ignore (or make invisible) certain spaces and people who do not fit the image of brand Dubai. This includes working-class spaces—although there were differences in the levels of concern expressed by different people about such class-based exclusions. In the next section, I explore authenticity as a paradigm through which Dubai's inhabitants can express their gripes with the city's reliance on "outsiders," such as its reliance on foreign institutions, consultants, or architects, which can be a critique of its neglect of local interests and talents. In that sense, discourses of authenticity are idioms of social critique that raise concerns about the city's developmental trajectory.

Throughout, I suggest that these discourses of authenticity, as voiced by residents who distance themselves from the city's spectacles, can sometimes intentionally or unintentionally promote a fake/authentic binary of the city. This binary leads to fetishizing and exoticizing "authentic" places, while dismissing "fake" ones as nonplaces, erasing the many meanings inhabitants make in the "superficial" parts of the city. Indeed, many Gulf "residents produce the idea that Gulf states are unique and illiberal, even though most of their daily life patterns are not much different from how they would look in another country."[4] Discourses of authenticity voiced by middle-class and elite Dubai inhabitants, I demonstrate, can also constitute practices of social distinction. They can be attempts by seekers of authenticity to distance themselves from the so-called masses, those whom they view as being mindlessly captivated by the city's spectacles. By seeking authenticity and shunning Dubai's fakeness, these individuals present themselves as more socially and politically conscious than mainstream society.

THE CREATIVE CLASS AND CONCERNS ABOUT DUBAI'S (IN)AUTHENTICITY

Various actors engage in discourses of authenticity for different reasons and in diverse ways. For instance, some older Emiratis who feel nostalgic for an older way of life when there were fewer foreigners consider the "authentic" Dubai to be one where most inhabitants are Emirati citizens and where their (narrow) definitions of what Emirati culture means is dominant.[5] These narratives align with some of the state's depictions, which portray Emirati cultures and history to be homogenous and purely

Arab, and which emphasize Bedouin culture as the "authentic" Emirati culture, eliding the Gulf's historical connections to the Indian Ocean.[6] State constructions of authenticity are important to interrogate, and there has been a fair amount of literature exploring them, including the exclusions they perpetrate.[7] Yet, with few exceptions, there has been insufficient interrogation of what discourses of authenticity look like among the Gulf's creative classes, whose views are the focus on in this chapter.[8] Of course, not everyone who works in the arts or creative fields shares the same views; some I interviewed expressed similar relationship to the city as my interlocutors in other chapters who describe adapting to, rather than rejecting, the city's spectacles (and vice versa). However, common patterns of positioning oneself in opposition to spectacle nevertheless emerged among the creative class, warranting deeper analysis of this trend.

The "creative class" are middle-class and upper-class artists, photographers, journalists, researchers, academics, and others working in the knowledge-based economy, as well as those who dabble in these areas enough to make this an important part of their self-identity.[9] There has been considerable literature that describes similar groups in different settings seeking authenticity, an alternative lifestyle, and differentiation from the "masses."[10]

In this chapter, I focus on a group similar to Ley's "cultural middle class" who distinguish themselves from others through their attitudes toward Dubai's urban spaces. While the creative classes are not gentrifiers like Ley's cultural middle class, they share similar backgrounds: many of them work in creative fields; they are artists, intellectuals, academics, journalists, and architects. Some may work in corporate jobs as lawyers and consultants but still maintain proximity to the arts and cultural world, seeking alternatives to spaces of mass consumption. For example, members of the creative class can be found attending art events, galleries, alternative music venues, independent cinemas, museums, grassroots intellectual events, and meetups. Some also choose to live in or frequent older neighborhoods they deem to be more "authentic." Often, conscious critiques of neoliberalism, exclusion, and classism shape their choices to reject the city's spectacles (which they exhibit in varying degrees). Some of them do this as part of their careers and everyday lives through their art, photography, or writing. Nevertheless, while I contrast those featured in this chapter to adaptive agents, they both share similarities at times. In fact, while they were critical of the city's spectacles and generally found them alienating, the creative class's critiques of the city varied (for instance, there were those who criticized the exclusion of low-income inhabitants from the city's new developments, and others who were less critical and more ambivalent about these exclusions).

Labeling the city as superficial was at times an idiom of social critique, a way for my interlocutors to show their dissatisfaction with the city's development trajectory. Major threads of dissatisfaction I encountered include their sense of loss and alienation; their frustrations with Dubai's policymakers' preoccupation with "glitz and glamour"; and their gripes with the city's reliance on "outsiders," such as its reliance on foreign institutions, consultants, and architects.

A CHANGING CITY: A SENSE OF LOSS, A SENSE OF BELONGING

> We used to go camping on the beach a lot. And by camping, I
> mean just go sleep on the beach. . . . It felt like it was the
> beach of the people. We came in the middle of the night and
> we painted some Japanese wave stuff on the walls. Really
> good stuff, not some graffiti. . . . One day it was all painted
> over. The municipality just painted over it and just made it
> white. . . . And eventually police will start coming up and
> telling you, "You can't sleep here." . . . As the country evolves,
> as the city evolves, stuff starts to go away. Like, I can't think
> of any beach here anymore [where] I could camp at or drive
> my car up close to the water. . . . I'm a nostalgic person.
> When I was a teenager, I felt like, okay, I'm not rich, like my
> Westerner friends. . . . But my memories and my
> experiences—that's how I got by a lot of those personal issues
> of feeling poor . . . so nostalgia was important to me. . . . And
> then as you get older you feel like your memories and your
> identity, everything is being wiped away. And a lot of the
> times it was for something that was a lot more meaningless,
> or a lot more consumer[ist]. . . . It lacked substance or

charm. . . . Things that I kind of resent would be like La
Mer. . . . I haven't gone yet. I don't care to, because I don't
want to accept that that one particular strip where so much
stuff happened [is gone] . . . people [used to] play chess;
dudes will be doing aerobics . . . kids are rollerblading;
people are riding bikes; people are *learning* how to ride
bicycles. . . . It was not about consumerism.

Sameer, an Arab man in his thirties.

Although we were about the same age, Sameer passionately told me about
his memories in areas of the city that I never had the same connections to.
Some of them were farther away, places I went to only if I was running
specific errands. Others were closer. When Sameer was a teenager, he and
his friends regularly went skateboarding at a place that was barely a five-
minute drive from my house. I occasionally went to the supermarket in
that area with my family when I was a child and teenager, and often saw a
group of (mostly British) boys skateboarding there. But until I met Sameer
for this interview, I did not see our lives intersecting.

On one hand, as Sameer spoke in detail about his memories and adventures, I felt a sense of loss for something I never experienced—or could
never experience. The city had changed so dramatically that I felt I could
never have the adventures he had, even if I wanted to. In comparison to
him, my childhood and teenage years appeared very dull. But I also knew
that until adulthood, I could in no way have had the social freedoms that
allowed me to engage in the same (gendered) activities he did. My unex-
plained sense of loss toward something I never experienced, however, was
interspersed with twinges of irritation at Sameer's references to shopping
malls (and the people who socialized in such places) as superficial. Malls
were part of *my* childhood and teenage years and were the only "public"
places that I and many other women of a similar class background were
permitted to go to without adult supervision. While they were unexciting
compared to Sameer's adventures (and while I would still advocate for the
creation of more public spaces as alternatives to the mall), I was growing
tired of finding that the simplistic tropes in academia and journalism were
being repeated by some of my interlocutors who "should know better" as
inhabitants of these cities.

Figure 2. La Mer.

Yet, referring to the city's new developments, such as La Mer (a new, mixed-use development by the beach)—which as an upwardly mobile individual, Sameer could make more use of today—as superficial was his way of expressing his sense of loss (figure 2 is of La Mer, a place often referred to in this chapter). As I show later, when the creative class implicitly or explicitly refers to certain parts of the city as superficial, they are doing so as idioms of social critique—and one of the recurring themes is the sense of loss they have regarding the rapidly changing city.

The streets, the beach, and the outdoors were places where Sameer spent his youth and created his memories. As a skateboarder, he scouted the city with his friends for new spots and formed a deep connection with various urban spaces. As the city changed, Sameer felt that his memories and identity were being erased and replaced with developments that lacked meaning—and which he seemed to believe might be less capable of becoming meaningful to others. Scholars have shown how inhabitants in different parts of the world experience alienation when there is a disruption to their place of attachment or when they are forcibly removed from such places.[11] Particularly for those who are evicted from their homes, the sense of loss is so intense that it can be sufficiently described as grief.[12] Sameer similarly expresses a sense of grief at his lost memories and connection to the city, ones that were constantly being disrupted as the city changed.

It is not only the creative classes who express such experiences and emotions of loss. The older Emirati men I referred to in the Introduction of this book, for instance, recounted similar narratives about how the city has changed and become alienating. Many of my middle-aged and older Emirati interlocutors did not necessarily use the language of "superficial" and "authentic" to describe their sense of loss. They often made the contrast between today and the "good old days" by describing how people used to be better, how they were kinder, more generous, and more "pure." They describe people today as greedy and not as "clean-hearted." Like Sameer, however, they describe their everyday lives as having been more fulfilling and enjoyable before the trajectory of spectacular development. Halima, an Emirati woman in her fifties, contrasted her childhood to that of her adult children in the following manner:

> We used to all play together in the *freej* [neighborhood], not like you now. All of us, the kids in the *freej*, would play, boys and girls. It wasn't like now, you wouldn't worry about boys and girls mixing together. People were pure inside. Boys saw the girls as their sisters. It was the best time in my life. People didn't own cars like they do now, so we all used to ride in [a neighbor's] car and go wherever he was going. All of us would sit in the open trunk and go to wherever he would take us. There was a cinema, it was called Cinema Galadari, and we had a specific line in front just for us. We loved going to the cinema. All the girls used to walk to school together. There was a pole, we would meet there every morning, and walk for maybe fifteen minutes. In the heat. We didn't mind, you didn't feel it was hot. We were naughty, when we would go in the car and on the bridge, the only bridge there at that time, we used to open our doors and let our legs fly out. We went to each other's houses all the time, kids nowadays are always bored, we were never bored. These [pointing at her children] always say they're bored, but at our age, we had so much fun. It was not like now. People used to visit each other without even calling, not like now, when you call. If you came in and your neighbor was sleeping, it was okay, you just wait for them until they wake up . . . . I wish I could go back to these days.

Both younger and older citizens and noncitizens, therefore, spoke of a sense of loss toward the changing city. But there were also some differences. For example, those of the creative class were quite critical of new megaprojects, particularly ones like Al Seef, a new mixed-use development on the creek (the "old Dubai"), whereupon modern-style buildings as well as new "traditional" ones replaced a previously open space. Some of them criticized Al Seef's exclusivity (which I discuss in the next section), and some also criticized its "inauthenticity." They were dissatisfied with Al Seef being built to replicate the old town, describing it as fake and Orientalist. Many middle-aged Emiratis I spoke to, on the other hand, were particularly excited about this development, which they said reminded them of their childhood and teenage years. To them, this place was not inauthentic.

Therefore, a sense of loss is evident among certain younger *and* older interlocutors, as well as a dissatisfaction with aspects of the city's development in recent years. Discourses of (in)authenticity make their way into various discussions and topics, such as when people in the past were described as "pure" in comparison to people today. However, the example of Al Seef shows that there are also distinct differences between the way the creative classes speak about and perceive inauthenticity.

There was also a different set of considerations between citizens and noncitizens at times, resting on the fact that noncitizens are aware of their transience in a city that is itself also rapidly changing. Tala, an Arab woman in her twenties, said that La Mer was the final stretch for her, "stomping on her entire childhood." She felt that Dubai lost focus on the fact "that not everyone in the city is transient or wants to be transient." Unlike Sameer, Tala immigrated to Europe where she could get citizenship and experience a sense of permanence. "By the end of it," she said, "nothing of what I remember Dubai to be still existed as it is."

Rapid and constant changes highlighted Dubai's transience, and my interlocutors' transience within it.[13] While citizens also experience a sense of loss at the changing landscape of the city, the issue of transience often came up in discussions among noncitizens living in the Gulf. Since Gulf countries do not offer permanent residency or citizenship except in highly exceptional cases, individuals who were born and raised in the region—and whose families have been in the same country for generations—still worried about losing their jobs and therefore their visas. Scholars assert that these cities highlight and reinforce transience through their urban policies and urban spaces, which cater to tourists and outsiders.[14] Sameer's and Tala's feelings highlight not only a sense of alienation but a double sense of estrangement as the city reinforces their impermanence as noncitizens as well.

When the people I spoke to refer to the city as superficial, it is at times a way to represent their dissatisfaction with the city's development trajectory—one that they feel erases a rich history and community patterns to make way for something superficial. These experiences of loss are often recounted in academic accounts about Gulf cities like Dubai. At times, however, they are centered as the de facto experience of Gulf inhabitants, even though my research shows they are much more common among certain demographics, namely members of the creative classes and among older generations than among other groups. When these narratives of alienation are used by other academics as representative of the Gulf citizen experience as a whole, distortion occurs.[15] For instance, Elsheshtawy discusses the work of the exiled Saudi author of *Cities of Salt*, AbdelRahman Munif, saying that

> Munif's interpretation of the fictional city of Harran is quite typical of the sense of loss accompanying massive urban transformation within cities in the Arabian Peninsula. It is not just loss however, but the resulting urban environment is a hostile one, *repelling its citizens*. He describes it as "a harsh, repulsive city." ... *The narrative of transformation offers a rare look into the mindset of Arabia's citizens* (even though they are fictional).[16]

As much as it is essential to shed light on the loss and alienation inhabitants of Gulf cities go through, these experiences have often been centered and depicted as *the* legitimate experiences of Gulf inhabitants who are expected to feel estranged from their environment as they live in illiberal cities that change without their consent. Relying on these narratives alone risks the erasure of other voices and experiences.

One of the realities being elided in these discourses of loss is the sense of belonging that can be experienced in "inauthentic" spaces, as well as the ways "authenticity" discourse can itself produce feelings of alienation. During my fieldwork I attended an event on Gulf urbanity with Sahar, a young Arab social science researcher and long-term resident in Dubai. After the event, I asked Sahar about her thoughts on what was being discussed. Among other things, she said she was slightly annoyed about the event's narrative of loss regarding the part of the beach that had been turned into La Mer; she said this narrative "puts a meaning that's not there for everyone." Sahar did not have the same connections with the beach that Sameer and Tala had. Perhaps this was one reason why, as an adult, she viewed La Mer as a social space rather than a consumerist one as Sameer did. "La Mer, when you go especially [to] the beach area, you'll see people who look like they literally have all kinds of different occupations and backgrounds. You'll see the *shalwar kameez*, and you'll see the Filipino lady groups," she said.[17] She argued that "you can have an imaginary of these spaces being purely commercial, but that overdetermines what the space is."

Similarly, Randa, a Lebanese woman in her late thirties who was also born and raised in the UAE, described La Mer as a space for family socializing. She went to La Mer in the morning with her father and sister: "We walk a bit in the sand, get my dad to exercise a bit. . . . Then my dad naps on the beach, we go have lunch, we do some shopping, walk around, eat some ice cream," she said. Huda, an Arab woman in her twenties, was also born and raised in the UAE. Although Huda and Tala were of a similar age, ethnic group, and socioeconomic background, their perceptions of the city's changes varied widely. Like all the noncitizens I spoke with, Huda shared her concern over her (lack of) permanence in the UAE as a noncitizen. However, she did not associate the city's rapid changes with transience. When I asked her how she viewed the city's constant changes, she described them as exciting, even familiar. The changes were a hallmark of Dubai, a facet of the city she had gotten accustomed to and enjoyed—it was what differentiated Dubai from other places. When I asked her how she felt about places of her childhood that had changed, she explained that she might feel nostalgic if a place she often went to had changed, but not necessarily sad. She particularly liked La Mer, "even though it [used to be] Jumeirah Beach One where I used to go with my family as a kid all the time." Adaptive agents may feel nostalgic about the "old times," but their aspirations (e.g., aspirations to be part of a more global, cosmopolitan city) and their choice of adaptability make them more in tune with the changes. For others, this sense of loss is more intense, including among many in the creative class.

Rather than reifying binaries of authenticity and superficiality, of resistance and oppression, or of belonging and exclusion, I find the work of scholars such as Brubaker who understand all nations as both inclusive and exclusive applicable also to understanding cities.[18] All places include and exclude inhabitants in varying ways and degrees.[19] The narratives of loss and alienation represent various citizens' and residents' experiences and have been well-documented by various scholars.[20] However, centering the narrative on alienation presents it as the only experience worthy of noting. Many of my interlocutors, both citizens and noncitizens, experience the city through varying shades of ambivalence.

Narratives of loss can also be interrogated more critically. While many parts of the city have been entirely transformed, other sites remain relatively unchanged and are quite vibrant places—open public spaces like Al Diyafa Street and its restaurants, different areas along the creek, the public parks—but their demographics have changed, and the majority of people present in these spaces are working-class or lower-middle-class inhabitants. Many who express a sense of loss toward the changing city have themselves "outgrown" the very spaces they are nostalgic about, highlighting that their experiences of loss are not only forced but at times also chosen based on classed (or racial) preferences of socializing.

Similarly, the depictions of informality that Sameer describes, and which other scholars argue are being lost, can often be gendered.[21] Many women who grew up in similar environments as Sameer never had the same relationship with the city that Sameer did—they did not sleep at the beach or skateboard in the streets. Many women (including myself) had memories in other places that no longer form part of our everyday lives: we might have walked on the creek with our families or had *shawarma* on AlDiyafa Road. But for some of us, these places do not stand out as sites of memories of our childhoods or teenage years any more than hanging out at the mall did. For some women, as well as children, who may have grown up in more sheltered environments, the sense of loss to the more informal city is not necessarily experienced in the same way.

When my discussants from the creative class implicitly or explicitly refer to certain parts of the city as superficial, they are doing so as idioms of social critique—one of the recurring themes is the sense of loss they have regarding the rapidly changing city. Yet focusing on these experiences of loss alone may unintentionally elide the forms of belonging that other inhabitants make in spaces often dismissed as superficial, consumerist, or alienating, some of which will be discussed in subsequent chapters.

BRAND DUBAI: THE PROBLEM WITH "GLITZ AND GLAMOUR"

Kareema, an artist who lives in old Dubai, took me on a walk in the old parts of the city which she grew up in and had a strong connection to. When we sat down on a bench, she opened the "Brand Dubai" Instagram page and showed me the photos there, contrasting the scenes in front of us with Brand Dubai's curated images.[22] There were various pictures of the Burj Khalifah and the new Dubai. But where were the sites and people of old Dubai? Pointing at a man in his *shalwar kameez* who sat at the edge of the creek throwing seeds to the birds, she said that for people like this man, feeding the seagulls was one of the few sources of entertainment he could afford, both financially and in terms of time. Why wasn't he being seen and acknowledged in Dubai's representations of the city?

Kareema compared the Brand Dubai Instagram account to the page of a Dubai-based photographer who took photos of South Asian men congregating in the streets of the old town or African women laughing and hanging out in parks, for which he used the hashtag #myrealdubai. This demographic represented a large and significant part of the city—so where were they in "Brand Dubai's" Instagram page? Why were decision-makers in the official arts and culture establishment preoccupied with the big, the sanitized, and the upscale in Dubai?

When some of my interviewees labeled parts of the city as real or fake, authentic or superficial, at times this was a way for them to show their dissatisfaction with various forms of exclusions, ranging from development projects that marginalize non-elites to official representations that privilege a sanitized Dubai. What they were arguing was that Dubai caters predominantly to certain types of audiences: often white and Western, or at least upper-middle class, while marginalizing spaces and people that do not fit into that category. Dubai's policymakers want Dubai to be seen as a place of "glitz and glamor," as Adam, a young Indian man who grew up in old Dubai, termed it. To achieve this, they seek to associate it more and more with certain groups (such as Westerners and elites). At the beginning of the COVID-19 pandemic, many noncitizen residents of the UAE were abroad and unable to enter the UAE after airports had closed. Throughout this time, they were able to apply through an online service to be repatriated. In most newspaper articles, the residents who were shown to be reuniting with their families in the UAE were Western and, most often, white. Stories and images of a blonde British woman hugging her mother at the airport or a German child reuniting with her mother were the overwhelming ones in the media landscape, despite the UAE's majority population being South Asian.[23] It is unclear whether this indeed represents the actual demographics of people being repatriated. In any case, these images represent whose stories and experiences dominate the social representational landscape among noncitizens.

Many scholars have interrogated the ways in which Dubai aims to attract and cater to white and Western residents, investors, and tourists through leisure, entertainment, and consumption patterns.[24] There is more to these discussions that will be explored in chapters 3 and 4. Nevertheless, it remains true that white and Western residents and tourists hold a privileged place in the UAE and the Gulf Cooperation Council (GCC) in general, ranging from the fact that they are paid more for the same jobs that Arabs and South Asians work in, to being the faces represented in advertisements and the media.[25] Therefore, certain parts of Dubai and certain demographics of the population are made more visible, while others (such as the places and people Kareema referred to) are made invisible. For example, middle-class Indians who live in old Dubai felt that their part of the city and their histories were becoming marginalized as new Dubai and the people within it become the focal points of the city.[26]

Those of the creative class who felt frustrated with policymakers' preoccupation with "glitz" often contended that everything is about Dubai's image—a PR campaign. During the pandemic, Dabya, an Emirati, complained that journalists were not allowed to enter the low-wage resident area of Naif, which was being quarantined. Yet, a social media influencer—who has no connection to the communities in Naif—was invited to volunteer and appeared on the news as he handed food to the area's residents. Dabya argued that they could have at least chosen another social media influencer who was well acquainted with the area and knew the communities who lived there. This emphasized to Dabya that the initiative was mostly a PR campaign that was of little substance, and which concealed multiple realities in favor of a sanitized version of the city. For officials whose vision is to attract more tourists, capital, and elites to Dubai, anything that distorts this image can be seen as damaging. This follows a neoliberal logic that prioritizes increasing capital.[27]

The frustration that people have with Dubai's policymakers' preoccupation with glitz and glamour over substance manifests not only in media representations but in everyday realities of inclusion and exclusion. One example is Al Seef. While anyone can still walk in Al Seef (the buildings are in open space rather than within an indoor mall), its critics argue that the area is now empty compared with the public space that existed before it. Kareema talked about how the once vibrant open space allowed lower-income residents (the majority in that area) to picnic on the floors, play football, or just stroll around. This is no longer the case, and these buildings now house coffee chains and relatively pricey restaurants catering to a limited clientele. Because Al Seef is more controlled and regulated, inhabitants of the area may feel uncomfortable engaging in the more informal activities that used to take place here and still take place on other parts of the creek. In the case of Al Seef, the presence of an upper-middle-class development in a lower-income area effectively takes usable space away from the very people who live there.

Policymakers' concern with sanitizing Dubai means that some inhabitants experience it as too regulated or controlled, and this was a common theme voiced by members of the creative class. I interviewed Faheema, a South Asian street artist born and raised in Dubai, about her perceptions of art, culture, and the changing city. Faheema expressed a nostalgia for a childhood that she feels was less regulated and more exciting, and therefore better, than the childhood experiences she sees happening today. She says:

> I think what's nice about allowing a little bit of chaos to exist in public spaces is there's the potential for surprises. . . . Whereas I think if public spaces are

too regulated and too clean and too tidy, you miss the opportunity for people to have those little magical encounters, and for there to be coincidences or unexpected surprises. . . . And I think that's the challenge in Dubai, [its] public space is vulnerable, it's vulnerable to crime, it's vulnerable to vandalism, it's vulnerable. But you know that's kind of what gives the city a little bit of its soul and character as well as the chaos.

Sanitized and regulated urban spaces have been frequently criticized for being restrictive: for excluding low-income inhabitants and limiting the types of activities that city dwellers can engage in.[28] Faheema expressed a gentle critique to this regulation and a longing for a less-controlled life where she can leave her mark on the city. As opposed to Canada, where she currently lives and where she says that the skateboarding community plays a role in the planning of skateboarding parks, Dubai has no such community involvement. Faheema raises the point of whether Dubai's newly built areas are used as community spaces, and to what extent they can be spaces of belonging when users can neither participate in their making nor make changes to them. When my interlocutors label Dubai as too sterile, superficial, or "glitzy," they are therefore also showing their dissatisfaction with the city's development trajectory, which is exclusive and highly regulated. They are longing for spaces that are less controlled, less sanitized, and more inclusive of different segments of society.

Adam, an inhabitant of old Dubai, shared Kareema's frustrations about how certain people and spaces in the city are being neglected by or erased from Dubai's official representation. Born and raised—and still living—in old Dubai, he felt that this part of the city has been absent from official representations as well as activities that go on in the city (most of which take place in new Dubai). Regarding the Dubai International Film Festival, he argued that such film festivals should not be limited to certain parts of the city: "For me to drive halfway across the city and pay that much money just to watch one single movie. I mean, what are you celebrating here?" he said.

Making an argument about access, Adam raises points similar to Kareema and Faheema. For instance, he argued that Dubai's indie cinema is inaccessible given that a ticket is sold for fourteen dollars—this is not affordable to a large proportion of Dubai's population, many of whom are working class. However, some of his ideas about access and segregation also pit Dubai against a supposedly more inclusive West. He contrasted Dubai with New York City, which he imagines as a more egalitarian place in terms of its art and independent movie scene: "It's not like how it would be in New York or something where everyone can really enjoy it."

Authenticity is associated not only with the West (which is depicted as a place of "real" culture and history), as we can see in Adam's example, but also with low-income spaces that get fetishized (denoting poverty, struggle, or "humbleness" as opposed to "superficiality") and interlinked with Orientalist fantasies (denoting a supposedly more "traditional" life not marred by globalization). These discourses of authenticity take place not only in Dubai but globally, particularly among the middle and upper classes. A fitting example of this is related by Brammer, a Mexican American journalist, who criticized people's quests for "authentic" Mexican culture in the US (and specifically concerning Mexican restaurants):

> What makes [a Mexican restaurant] "authentic"? . . . [M]ost of the hallmarks seem to be about pain: dirty floors, plastic chairs, anything that aesthetically connotes struggle. The cooks and waiters ought to have accents. There should probably be a framed photo of someone's dead grandpa. . . . If the joint has no air conditioning, if it's off the beaten path, if the voyeur into struggle has to "work" to find it, then the experience is supposedly richer for it. It makes the voyeur better, more worldly for having brushed up against it.[29]

While they dismiss other forms of mass consumption, some seekers of authenticity can be voyeuristic, looking to consume images of poverty, struggle, or "tradition." In doing so, certain places and people are fetishized in the process. For example, a film director says: "I kept looking for an authentic aspect of Dubai until I found this old souk. Amazing people with beautiful stories, finally." Here, a *souq* is depicted as an authentic aspect of Dubai, perhaps due to Orientalist ideas that imagine "traditional" spaces as constituting authenticity in an Arab country. But there is also a class aspect to this discussion, wherein low-income inhabitants are exoticized as more "real" than other people, making those who recognize their realness more "real" as well.

Another example is Satwa 3000, a Swiss art collective in Dubai whose members differentiate themselves from the mainstream by their association with low-income areas of Dubai, such as Satwa. Their ad describes them as a "Swiss art collective based in the UAE, which, since 2015, has been remixing the sights and sounds of the *real* Dubai" (emphasis added). Similarly, a Twitter search about Satwa shows a long-term resident of Dubai saying that Satwa is the "only authentic area" in Dubai: "Oh you know satwa! It's still the same. The only authentic area in dubai [*sic*]." Another post reads: "Statistically speaking Satwa is highest in rape crimes. But still, the only authentic place in Dubai! I luv it [*sic*]!"

Since there are no public records about crime rates concerning neighborhoods in Dubai, the statement about Satwa having the highest rape rates appears to be mostly based on (exoticized) narratives of danger. In his discussion about blues music bars in Chicago, Grazian observes that what was perceived to be "authentic" blues music in Chicago was often caricatured with supposed characteristics of what being Black and working class looks and sounds like. He describes the stereotypical depiction people have of blues bars, saying:

> Authentic blues clubs are ramshackle joints with broken front doors and rattling sound systems. . . . They only hire authentic looking blues musicians, who are generally uneducated American black men afflicted by blindness, or else they walk on a wooden leg or with a second handcrutch; as they are defiantly poor. . . . Their audiences are usually black as well, with the occasional white customer surfacing only if they are also sufficiently old, poor, drunk, or blind.[30]

Low-income communities (and people from certain ethnic backgrounds, in some cases) therefore become fetishized as authentic in contrast to the sanitized city which the middle and upper classes have easy access to. At times, the line between fetishizing poverty or "humbleness" and seeking a less-controlled urbanity is blurred. Faheema remembered her carefree childhood days, which she says cannot take place among Dubai's youth anymore due to increased regulations: getting drunk as a young teenager at the beach or teaching herself how to skateboard in parking lots. Today there are government-made skate parks that she felt do not hold the same informality and joy. Skate parks are supposed "to be *dirty* and it's where kids go to get in *trouble* sometimes, you know, but in Dubai it's just very *blank*," she said wistfully. She added:

With Dubai we've tried to make it so world class and clean and polished that we've actually drowned out all those things that gave it so much texture and character. You know when streets were dirtier and windows weren't double glazed and you heard those noises outside. . . . [I'm] really nostalgic about old Dubai. My brothers and I are always like: Why are the streets just not a *little bit* dirty. . . . I don't know if it's because my brother is an artist as well, so we like a little bit of personality and texture and a little bit of dirt and grime and traces of human beings. . . . I used to spend a lot of time going on long drives outside of Dubai . . . in, like, Umm Al Quwain [one of the northern emirates of the UAE], which is just nice, it's *dirty*. There's garbage *everywhere*. And there are these old garages where they fix cars everywhere and I just, I love going on these little drives partly because it reconnects me to how Dubai used to be.

Similarly, academic discourse highlights the informality found in low-income areas of Gulf cities as examples of "real" urbanity where different communities can create meaningful experiences.[31] For instance, Elsheshtawy depicts low-income spaces that are less regulated as examples of a "true urbanity, [where] a certain form of resistance, emerges at the margins of the space, in its surrounding alleyways, away from the prying eyes of authorities."[32] While it highlights how certain forms of (less-regulated) urbanity work better for larger segments of society, this academic writing similarly engages a binary of fake/authentic spaces. Referring to lower-income areas of Dubai, Elsheshtawy argues that the city should, "in its strive to become a global center, uncover 'the real Dubai' which does exist along the shores of the Creek and its marketplaces."[33]

Such discourse presents inhabitants as only being able to make meanings *beyond* the spectacle, but rarely ever *within* it—unless they are (at least) subtly resisting.[34] But the "city can never be the top-down imposition of an autocrat. Even the most centralized political system requires a tremendous network of individuals to come together to produce any idea as a material reality."[35] As I show in chapters 2 and 3, many inhabitants adapt themselves to the spectacles and adapt the spectacles to fit their needs. They experience belonging, make meanings, and engage in cultural contestations in spaces considered sanitized and "glitzy," such as shopping malls and new developments—places where they go to see each other and to be seen, and places where social norms are performed and negotiated. In that sense, discourses of authenticity reproduce not only binaries of fake/authentic but also of belonging/exclusion, controlled/free, binaries which elide the ways in which inhabitants have complex and ambivalent relationships with the city. In doing so, they also fetishize and exoticize places that are considered the antithesis of fakeness, often low-income spaces and communities.

ERASING THE "LOCAL" IN FAVOR OF THE "FOREIGN"

Most of the stuff that Brand Dubai does [is international]—City Walk is all [painted by] internationals. The street art in Karama is a bunch of Malaysian artists. . . . It's a very small percentage that are painted by local artists. . . . This amazing artist was [invited to] Dubai . . . their street art is in, like, the Hall of Fame and their work is amazing, but when they come to the city to tell stories about local people. . . . How much experience do they have to really be able to tell that story? The thing about Dubai is there's a really unique opportunity for cultures to have this conversation between the past and the present . . . between expats and Emiratis, and I think we're just not tapping into that potential at the moment. . . . And I think the biggest unfortunate thing about flying in international artists is that you're not allowing that dialogue to happen.

In the quote above, Faheema describes how international street artists were getting more opportunities to paint the city than local (Emirati or non-Emirati) artists. One of the common frustrations that the people I spoke to of various backgrounds had was that different entities, ranging from educational to art entities, favored bringing in foreign "expertise" rather than utilizing locals' expertise ("local" here referring to both citizens and long-term residents of the UAE). This critique, part of the broader discourse of authenticity, expresses concerns about globalization, "transplant" institutions, and the city's reliance on the "foreign." One of these concerns is that local talents, projects. and institutions are being marginalized in favor of big names (be they people, brands, or institutions) that add little value or meaning to the communities and people who live there, whether it was reflected in importing Western museums or foreign consultants to work on government policies.

Similar critiques can be seen in other Gulf states as well where citizens and long-term residents condemn their countries' reliance on foreign consultants in designing major government projects. Such opinions can also be found on social media and in major newspapers, condemning Gulf states' dependence on outsiders who have little knowledge about the settings they are in. In that sense, Gulf states (and Dubai) risk neglecting their local talent by commissioning "big-name" outsiders to be the artists, designers, architects, and consultants in charge of the making of the city.[36]

In a similar vein, some inhabitants of Gulf cities feel frustrated by the attention given to "transplant" institutions (often Western ones) in place of local ones. At times, these institutions are depicted as inauthentic, as they are neither "authentically local" nor seen as authentic as the head-quarter institutions in the West. Popular examples of "inauthentic" transplant institutions include cultural and educational institutions in the Gulf, particularly projects such as the Louvre and Guggenheim in Abu Dhabi or Georgetown University in Qatar.[37] There are many local frustrations in relation to all these kinds of institutions.

For instance, AlShehabi, a well-known Bahraini academic, wrote on Twitter: "A faculty member in an elite US university branch campus in the Gulf was telling me he plans to 'decolonise' the campus & curriculum. I appreciate the sentiment, but short of shutting it down, how do you decolonize something whose core concept, identity, & mission is imperial?"[38] His critique differs from those of academics in institutions in the West in that it is a postcolonial (as opposed to Orientalist) critique. It is meant to convey a dissatisfaction with the way transplant institutions do not embed themselves with the local environments.

As AlShehabi notes, many branch campuses have been unsuccessful and certainly not all of them have high standards in terms of quality of teaching and research production. Another significant issue that AlShehabi emphasizes concerns local talent, as Faheema described earlier. AlShehabi says: "How does it make sense to talk of 'decolonising' when most of these branch campuses don't even have a single local who is a full-time faculty member? How serious is 'decolonising' when English is imposed as the only language of teaching in Arab countries?"[39] These realities point out the hollowness of decolonizing narratives put forward by some institutions that have accompanied spectacular development in the Gulf. For instance, there are very few Emirati faculty members at New York University Abu Dhabi (NYUAD), the American University of Dubai, and various other private institutions in the UAE. Twitter posts and informal discussions criticize the fact that highly qualified *khaleeji* applicants do not get hired in private universities in the Gulf, as well as the microaggressions experienced by the very small number of "local hires" at these institutions. These discussions highlight frustrations at the way the "local" is being erased in favor of a transplanted import.

Alongside searching for the local, some find that these transplant institutions can never be as good as "the real thing." Abbas Lawati, a GCC citizen living in Dubai, argues that Gulf cities like Dubai are nowhere near the equivalents of Arab cities like Beirut and Egypt, explaining:

> In an effort to develop at a breakneck speed and become competitive with Western hubs, they [Gulf cities like Dubai] have become replicas of those cities with little more of their own to offer foreign visitors and tourists than the clichéd desert safaris packaged with belly-dance shows. . . . In the academic arena, in order to gain fast access to the global stage, these cities have in recent years begun large-scale importing of big-name Western academic institutions that may boast glitzy and high-tech campuses, but cannot guarantee the academic freedom of their Western counterparts. . . . In contrast with the traditional Arab centers that exported literature, art, science and ideas to the world, there is little in these Gulf cities that can be considered organic. They have produced few if any literary giants, scientists, academics or innovators.[40]

Lawati highlights various grievances. Many faculty members in the Gulf are apprehensive about the types of research they can do or the content they can teach. A range of people noted how censorship affected the quality of their work, be it in arts or research. Adam, for instance, described how he became dissatisfied with the Emirates Literature Festival as it became less and less political over time. For people like Adam, these efforts become seen as empty endeavors performed for PR purposes: they are "inauthentic" and superficial events that do not allow for real creativity to flourish. Censorship indeed hampers many efforts that attempt to engage in various topics, restricting many people and leaving them anxious about the types of work they can (or cannot) produce. In that sense, cities like Dubai are seen as "inauthentic" for trying to be "too Western" by importing transplant institutions and relying on foreign knowledge rather than local expertise. Yet they are also viewed as inauthentic for being the "opposite of Western" in other matters deemed more important, such as in regard to academic freedom. Discourses of authenticity are thus used to highlight grievances that inhabitants have with a globalization that neglects or marginalizes the local.

However, some of these discourses on authenticity can also romanticize certain "local" institutions and dismiss "foreign" ones. Indeed, labels of local/foreign can produce exclusionary binaries if not critically examined. Does the term "local" include only citizens (as is often used in the UAE)? Specific "types" of citizens? Does it also include long-term residents? Only Arab residents? As an example, Elsheshtawy argues that some of the UAE's modernist buildings were built by foreign architects who have a "top-down version of an expatriate architect's fantasy about what constitutes Emirati identity" and that buildings such as the new central bus station in Abu Dhabi fail to connect with the city and its inhabitants.[41] He advocates instead for preserving "an Emirati vernacular."[42] But as Kubo points out, Elsheshtawy's position relies on a problematic foreign/local dichotomy.[43] For example, Elsheshtawy cites the Cultural Foundation as an example of successful space built by an Arab architect, but Kubo maintains that this architect never lived in the UAE and that his relationship to it is no different than that of the other architects whose buildings Elsheshtawy deems unworthy of preservation. The definition of "Emirati vernacular" is also problematic: South Asia has a centuries-long history of influencing Dubai and other Gulf cities, and assuming that an Arab architect's visions are more "authentic" erases that reality. Furthermore, prioritizing the architect elides the experiences of residents, who may or may not find social value in buildings built by "foreign" architects that deviate from an "Emirati vernacular."

This dichotomy of local/foreign feeds into the dominant narrative that globalized spaces (such as shopping malls or new developments) are non-places because they can exist anywhere.[44] Not only in folk narratives but also in academic ones, they are deemed unworthy of acknowledgment as significant parts of the city's urban landscape and history, rarely viewed as spaces of local social and cultural interactions and negotiations. Alongside globalized spaces such as shopping malls and new developments, transplant cultural and educational institutions have been depicted by some of the creative classes as similarly problematic, perhaps inauthentic, as I showed in the earlier section.

Lawati's earlier quote contrasted cities such as Dubai with Beirut or Cairo, the latter two being examples of more authentic development and culture that is local rather than imported (or as AlShehabi describes it, imperial). AlShehabi, in his critique of American branch campuses in the Gulf, writes, "The region is not a tabula rasa. There is a rich tradition that focuses on resistance, liberation, anticolonialism, anti-imperialism."[45] In reality, some notable anticolonial efforts in the Middle East, such as in the Levant, have been products of imperial institutions such as the American University in Beirut. These anticolonial efforts, however, are not seen as tarnished by inauthenticity or influenced by imperial legacies, despite their history. Indeed, rejecting these transplant institutions simply as products of imperialism risks erasing "local agency in shaping educational encounters, however uneven they may be."[46]

There is another binary implicit (sometimes explicit) in the discourses of authenticity above: liberalism and illiberalism. Lawati is not alone in pointing out that transplant institutions are inferior to the "real thing" because of certain missing factors—including liberalism. Academics in Western institutions look down on American branch campus universities in the Gulf as inferior to the main campuses, incapable of adding value or having a meaningful presence—particularly because of their perceived illiberalism.[47] Similarly, for some of my interlocutors, the Gulf states' academic and cultural endeavors cannot be "real" because they exist in an illiberal context that is contrasted to a "liberal" Western one (although in Lawati's case, Beirut and Cairo are depicted as liberal and contrasted to the illiberal Gulf). Lawati's essay is intended as a constructive criticism. Yet discourses of authenticity may unintentionally reproduce a familiar Orientalist narrative about the region, which does not allow us to hear about experiences on the ground: Vora argues that scholars who have worked in transplant universities in the Gulf experienced both marginalization and comfort, both self-censorship and intellectual community, both surveillance and activism—all of which produce conversations of much value.[48] "Yet scholars embedded in these locations are rarely considered to have political or intellectual positions of value, precisely because of these connections—they make us not objective enough, apologists rather than experts."[49]

Similarly, having taught for three years at a public university (precisely because I wanted to be part of a "local" institution), I found some of

Lawati's ideas detached from the realities I experienced. While I want to be careful not to stereotype public institutions, my experience also pushed me to search for alternative spaces of learning. I found myself losing motivation in an institution where I was told what textbooks to teach; where there was little teaching autonomy; and where my students were not allowed to be taken on a field trip for a few hours except through long, bureaucratic processes that took weeks if not months of planning. As much as the "transplant" university has its drawbacks, it also offers alternatives for some inhabitants in ways that are not evident through a local/foreign, inclusive/exclusive, fake/authentic binary.

Abdulkhaleq Abdulla, a retired Emirati academic, said about the NYUAD campus: "It's an illusion. It's a bubble there, an isolated entity that has absolutely nothing to do with the society. A few people are sitting in that nice beautiful place. Is that a knowledge economy? If so, then there is a misunderstanding of what a knowledge economy is about."[50] On one hand, Abdulla is correct in depicting such spaces as bubbles that do not sufficiently engage with many segments of society. However, by using labels such as "illusions," these critiques not only dismiss various realities on the ground but cement the stereotypes of superficiality. Similar to AlShehabi, Gulf scholars (like Western academics, and like my interlocutors in this chapter, who can all be considered part of the creative class) themselves inadvertently participate in reproducing the common dichotomies of fake/authentic, albeit from different angles.

Moreover, depicting this bubble to be specific to transplant institutions sometimes leads to romanticizing local institutions (which are implicitly positioned as the authentic binary opposite of Western branch campuses), even when they suffer from some of the very same issues that transplant universities do. Public national universities held events that were rarely if ever open to the public (and were much more closed off than private institutions) and did not engage with local communities aside from having Emirati students (and a *few* Emirati faculty members). Surveillance, particularly of female students, was not uncommon: students' "guardians" receive a text message every time a woman enters or leaves campus, for example. Many of these restrictions are based on assuaging parents' concerns about female modesty and therefore reflect the preferences of some segments of society. Nevertheless, they remain suffocating for others. Public institutions also lack diversity in terms of students' religion and nationality as the absolute majority are Emiratis.[51] Yet they were not entirely exclusionary or bubbled.

Public universities were gender segregated, yet *this* is what makes them accessible to many Emirati women from conservative families in ways that transplant universities are not. Public universities bring Emiratis of different socioeconomic backgrounds together in ways that other private institutions do not (they also accept students with *marsoom*, those who do not yet have Emirati passports or citizenship or who are stateless).[52] Even if they lack certain forms of diversity, Emirati students still get exposed to some forms of difference, ranging from the exposure of public and private school students to each other, or to Emiratis of different citizenship status. In reality, both transplant and public/national institutions engage in various forms of inclusion and exclusion that blur the dichotomies presented in discourses of authenticity about the local/foreign.

AUTHENTICITY AND SOCIAL DISTINCTION

In the above sections, I focused on the creative class's displeasure with Dubai's spectacular developments, and what they considered to be fake, superficial, or inauthentic about the city. Many of those discussed here expressed serious concerns about the city's developmental trajectory. Yet seekers of authenticity do not engage in discourses of superficiality/realness *only* as an expression of discontent. Rather, the quest for authenticity is sometimes intertwined with practices of social distinction. The quest for authenticity can be a means for individuals to differentiate themselves from the so-called masses whom they consider to be dazzled by the city, a way to present themselves as culturally and socially distinct from (and more aware than) mainstream society.

As we passed by an Italian ice cream shop, an Emirati Lebanese acquaintance told me she did not like seeing the shop in Dubai. It did not "fit there" the way it fit in Italy. The vibe and the atmosphere were different, she argued. This was not the first time I heard such comments. Some UAE citizens and residents who regularly traveled were disappointed when foreign retailers opened shops in Dubai. They argued that the shop or restaurant was a transplant, removed from its original habitus and environment and placed in an entirely different one, and was therefore "inauthentic" in Dubai. When I asked my acquaintance what places she enjoyed in Dubai, she mentioned a South African restaurant—which she then acknowledged might be because she had never been to South Africa. In most cases, rejection of the "transplant" institution came from individuals who had access to the "original." A few even claimed that some of their favorite imported chains were ruined for them after they were brought to Dubai because the emirate tarnished the vibe they associated with that place that they first experienced abroad. These individuals had the economic and cultural capital that allowed them to travel to places like Europe and experience an Italian ice cream shop there. When they make such comments, their intention is not necessarily to convey their elevated social status. Nevertheless, taste often indicates practices of social distinction. Whether through food, leisure activities, or places they inhabit, people's taste is one way they distinguish themselves from others.[53] These uses of the discourse of authenticity communicate a variety of meanings such as privilege and distinction.

There are various ways in which these practices of social distinction manifest. Some of them are subtle, and not necessarily conscious practices of distinction. Others are more overt. Some are clearly Orientalist. Others are less so, and enveloped with other concerns about the social issues I described earlier. Many of my interviewees in Dubai, for instance, still felt a sense of connection and love toward the city; and many, though not all, were wary of the ways outsiders tended to stereotype Gulf spaces by exoticizing them. Meanwhile, among Western academics and journalists, feelings of connection and love are rarer, and stereotyping common. Practices of distinction here operate when critical authors depict places like Dubai as inferior to the West, often by discussing illiberalism and "fake modernity."[54] There are various examples of these narratives in Western accounts (including among not only conservatives but also those who consider themselves progressives), which depict these spectacular urban spaces as just a "mirage."[55] For instance, Simon Jenkins, in *The Guardian*, describes Dubai as a place that is built on grandeur but is not meant to last:

> Just as visitors to the Middle East see half-built, mostly abandoned concrete housing blocks and barracks littering the landscape of Syria and Jordan, so

the towers of Dubai will become casualties not of human greed but of archi-tectural folly. Their lifts and services, expensive to maintain, will collapse. Their colossal facades will shed glass. Sand will drift round their trunkless legs. Animals will inhabit their basements. Thousands of residential proper-ties, if occupied at all, will be squatted by a migratory poor, like the hotel towers of the Spanish littoral or Corbusier's blockhouses of Chandigarh in India. Refugees will colonise the camps where Indian workers have lived as they built Dubai. Gangs will seize the gated estates and random anarchy will rule the soulless boulevards.[56]

As opposed to "real cities," fake cities are depicted as temporary. Such discourses are used to "keep these polities and their people 'in their place.'"[57] Smith demonstrates something similar in his reading of twenti-eth-century Western media depictions of the Gulf, arguing that Gulf citi-zens are viewed as "developed" in terms of access to wealth and material possessions, "but not in all those intangible ways, such as proper humility and a properly neoliberal attitude towards business and government."[58] Inherently classist and often racist understandings of the failures of taste of the "nouveau riche" map onto territories, and in this case the territory is the Gulf, seen as a place that has economic but not appropriate cultural capital.[59]

Practices of distinction are therefore evident in binaries about liberal-ism and illiberalism, which elide those forms of liberalism and illiberalism that exist everywhere. When liberals decry the US under Trump as a "banana republic" or an "African dictatorship," they not only engage in an Orientalist narrative but also contribute to the imaginary of the US as "immune to illiberal political formations."[60] By depicting authoritarian-ism as an Orientalist "other," it is seen as foreign to the West.[61] In that sense, practices of distinction are evident here on a geographic scale.

Yet these practices are not only relegated to the West. Centner shows that people from Istanbul and Beirut portrayed their cities as "real" ones in contrast to Dubai, the latter which they depicted as a cultureless place.[62] Similarly, these narratives are not absent among inhabitants of the Gulf themselves. Among my interlocutors, these practices of distinction among the creative class were ways for them to distinguish themselves from mainstream society whom they found to be too dazzled by the city's glitz. We can find this in the academic literature as well. Elsheshtawy, in his explanation about leaving the UAE for the US (the latter which he feels is a more permanent and "real" place), says that

> I left for a place that embodies a sense of history, and where cities are not just looked at as a disposable commodity. I went to a place where freedom is a quality that still holds some meaning, however imperfect it maybe. It is not a slogan disguised under woolly words such as 'tolerance' and 'happiness' [in reference to the UAE's Ministers of State for Tolerance and Happiness and other similar initiatives]. And ultimately, there is only so much one can take of gazing at glittering skyscrapers or partaking in the consumerist delights of shopping malls. Eventually one must awake from what can very easily turn into a *numbingly dull existence* and face *the real world*. The illusion of permanence will then finally dissipate.[63]

Like some of those I spoke to, Elsheshtawy uses discourses of authenticity to refer to the sense of alienation he felt in the UAE. While one can be sympathetic to his experience of estrangement in the place he lived in, it is also true that his work produces dichotomies of liberalism/illiberalism and of superior/inferior places. In the supposedly inferior places, inhabitants appear as victims who lack agency (except those he refers to as resisting). These risk not only being self-Orientalizing but can also be practices of distinction, wherein segments of society disassociate themselves from the "masses" who they feel are less socially and politically aware than themselves.

The quest for authenticity allows its seekers to see themselves as successful "cutting-edge pleasure seekers," thus differentiating themselves from others through their perceived cultural awareness.[64] Adam, who felt alienated by the city's changes, enjoyed going to creative events, ranging from watching indie movies to attending literary talks. His opposition to the city's rapid changes and spectacular spaces was partially due to his memories of the city which he felt nostalgic toward. However, his views of "superficiality" and "authenticity" also highlighted that these were ways for him to engage in practices of social distinction. Adam differentiated himself from people who were impressed by the new developments in Dubai, which he argued all looked the same: "Pleeeaaaase give me a break, no. We don't need this. . . . Why does it have to be another largest." Asking him whether his friends and family shared his sentiments, Adam answered that his friends and family liked the new developments he despised, saying: "I think what they liked . . . their impressions when something new comes out, 'Wow, there's no end to the ambitions of this city' . . . I mean, they're more simple-minded folks than me, I'm too complex."

Adam felt that an ideal space had a "deeper meaning," that it should enhance his life intellectually or socially. Yet his reference to "simple-minded" versus "complex" folks reiterated a common pattern where some seekers of authenticity often associated parts of the city and their users with superficiality. The quest for authenticity here is also a way for some individuals to make statements about themselves as being distinct from others, as morally or intellectually superior. As Grazian argues in a different context, quests for authenticity afford "bragging rights, which accompany any consumed experience of authenticity," resulting in certain individuals being viewed as hip and cosmopolitan—status symbols for them.[65]

Talking about cultural events in Dubai, Adam compared them to those in his imaginary of the West: "Kudos to the whole Dubai spirit, to the government initiative . . . opening opera houses, art galleries. But . . . what kind of crowd comes to these places [?] They don't have the taste. . . . They [creative scenes in Dubai] lack depth. The crowd as well." By rejecting the "superficial" cultural scene in Dubai and the "Dubai crowds" who supposedly lack taste, Adam associates himself with the Western "intellectual" NYC audience whom he looks up to. Just as faculty working in American branch campuses in the Gulf are stereotyped as having nothing of value to offer intellectually, audiences in Dubai are imagined as lacking in cultural capital, causing the "vibe" of that place to become less appealing to those who seek a certain authenticity based on their imaginaries of another place. Through these critiques, people engage in (Orientalist) practices of distinction by distancing themselves from Dubai and associating themselves with people in geographies that they view as superior. Adam says:

> What I like about New York is the fact that there's more flexibility in doing things and there are more people to talk to. More people of your wavelength. . . . They're sure of themselves. . . . They're a bit politically active, they're less superficial. . . . Most of the friendships here are based on very superficial reasons. It's not about intellectual bonding. I'm not saying that all relationships are intellectually bankrupt here, but the fact is that everything has an expiry date here. . . . Perhaps in the West . . . people are still in

touch with their childhood school friends. . . . So, my longest friend is someone I met fifteen years ago. . . . He was new in Dubai. . . . He didn't speak
English that well. . . . Although I would have never gone for that friendship,
because he's definitely not at my intellectual wavelength, but then, the fact
that he had been very selfless, contrary to what Dubai is. . . . Very self-less,
very inviting to his place . . . meeting with the family.

Adam notes something important: because of a system that views residents as temporary and makes permanence difficult (if not impossible for
many), people are constantly moving and changing in Dubai. This makes
many friendships come with an expiry date, as he noted (although one
would wonder if things are not similar in other major cities). However, his
depiction of his longest friendship as something not on his "intellectual
wavelength" also highlights practices of distinction in his quest for authenticity. By distancing himself from friendships in Dubai that he labels
superficial, he construes himself as socially distinct and superior to the
"Dubai crowd."

Referring to others as "the masses" was one way that some individuals
in the creative class separated themselves from others. Sarah, an artist
raised in Dubai, held a side business taking people on tours in the city, an
activity she was passionate about as she hoped to show visitors sights
other than typical tourist attractions. As opposed to bus tours going to the
Burj Khalifah and the Dubai Mall, her tours took people to the "authentic"
parts of the city. When I asked her about the people who came on her
tours, she said: "Most of them are well traveled and kind of know how cities work, and they know how politics is, and know there is always a lot
more than what is presented to them. . . . The masses want the top five,
because that's the advertisement that brought them to Dubai. And there's
the others that want more. They want to learn more, they want to know
more." By using the term "the masses," people differentiate themselves (or
their peers) from others, and specifically contrast themselves as more culturally, socially, or politically "aware" individuals. "The masses" are
depicted to be driven by mainstream advertisements and mass consumption. The more "informed" pursuers of authenticity are juxtaposed to the
implicitly passive and superficial masses. Authenticity thus allows people
to create a sense of distinction from others because "it confers an aura of
moral superiority."[66]

Comparing Dubai to the West, or comparing Dubai to older parts of the city, was therefore sometimes a way to show where one stands and serves as a practice of distinction. Of course, some comparisons were also meant to be fruitful. Dabya, for instance, compared Dubai's art scene to Sharjah's (the neighboring emirate), explaining that Sharjah's art events were better because they attract community audiences rather than just elites and are therefore accessible spaces offering more meaningful work. Indeed, Dubai's policymakers' preoccupation with world-class art events can result in missed opportunities to engage various members of society. Making comparisons to other places allows some people to critique Dubai's policymakers' preoccupation with hosting flashy cultural events that result in classed forms of exclusion. However, this kind of critique can also go hand in hand with more self-serving ones.

Rafia, an Emirati woman in her twenties, described disliking going to the city's shopping malls or new developments where she encountered people who she felt were trivial and engaged in meaningless and superficial interactions, such as gossiping and showing off their handbags or material objects. These comments are not uncommon and are constantly repeated by various interlocutors. Sameer, for instance, described some of his Emirati friends whom he considers to be too sheltered and detached from society as people who can only be seen in places like the mall or a Starbucks (rather than the street, e.g.). By contrasting his residence and places of socialization with those of mall-goers, he is highlighting his distinction from those he considers to be more superficial. These practices are not specific to Dubai. Zukin quotes a British novelist, Hari Kunzru, who moved to the Hackney neighborhood of London as a means of distancing himself from mainstream society and its forms of mass consumption. He argues that he moved "for reasons that I guess are not dissimilar to a lot of the bike-riders, creative slackers, live-workers and thrift-store princesses I nod to on the street: because it is full of weird places and eccentric people and has a grubby glamour to it that has not yet been stamped out and flattened into the same cloned corporate hell-hole as the rest of Britain."[67]

Therefore, associating oneself with alternative segments of society is a way to present oneself as more authentic, as distinct from mainstream society, which is seen as socially, politically, or culturally inferior. Benz describes a similar interest with grit by gentrifying residents of a low-income Los

Angeles neighborhood. Like other creatives described above, these individuals worked in the arts, technology, the film-industry, or high-end bars but gained social status through their proximity to poverty and "urban mascots" (whom she defines as a "public character who is a veteran resident of the area" and who "presents himself or herself as a safe, nonthreatening, and predicable embodiment of poverty").[68] Those who had limited relationships and experiences with poverty and urban mascots, on the other hand, were considered inexperienced or naïve. By shunning certain spaces as superficial and valorizing others as authentic, people create an image of themselves as authentic as well.

CONCLUSION

When I spoke to family, friends, and those who participated in my research about the constant depictions in the media and academia of Dubai as "fake," they often replied that outsiders viewed Dubai as fake because they only saw the malls and Burj Khalifah. They argued that outsiders never bothered to venture to old parts of the city and the *souqs* and were ignorant of the authentic places Dubai offers. Certainly, there is much more to Dubai than the malls and the Burj, and people are correct to note that many critics make no effort to know different parts of the city. Yet, this response illuminates something important: Dubai's inhabitants cite spaces and practices they rarely use as authentic, such as going to the old *souq* to buy spices. By doing so, they (indirectly) dismiss their everyday lived experiences as inauthentic based on a stereotypical expectation of authenticity. However, these concerns do not necessarily stop others from using and enjoying these very same spaces, as I show in ensuing chapters focused on adaptive agents.

Although different individuals discuss Dubai's authenticity in various ways, individuals of the "creative class" more often prioritized this as a personal concern. Unlike adaptive agents who more easily acclimatize to the city's changes, these individuals are more critical, sometimes advocating for changes in the neoliberal city that might cause some academics to label them as "resistors." A primary way these individuals inhabit the spectacular city is by raising concerns that speak to their active critical engagement with it. Their concerns include the sense of loss and displacement that result out of the city rapidly changing; the city's preoccupation with "glitz and glamour," which leads to the emirate ignoring (or making invisible) certain spaces, people, and meaningful opportunities; and frustration with the city's reliance on "outsiders," be it reliance on foreign institutions, consultants, or architects, or the exclusion of its local talents.

Yet by using discourses of authenticity to refer to their grievances, they (sometimes inadvertently) promote moralizing narratives about the region, similar to Western academic and media discourses that promote exceptionalist understandings of Dubai rooted in a long tradition of denigrating non-Western people and places. The quest for authenticity is also entangled with the quest for social distinction, a way to present oneself as more socially, culturally, and politically aware than the "masses" who are consumed by Dubai's shiny new developments. Such narratives may participate in clouding our ability to see how other residents—residents dismissed as "the masses"—exert various forms of adaptive agency in their own interactions with the spectacular city.

2 Negotiating Belonging in Dubai's Glitzy, Neoliberal Spaces

In a newspaper editorial, Reem Al-Kamali, an Emirati journalist, wrote an homage to Bin Souqat Center, a neighborhood mall in Dubai. Al-Kamali describes the mall as a place where prominent members of Emirati society congregate:

> [Bin Souqat Mall] became a home for important Emirati figures in the country who held important positions in the past. Some of these faces were constantly in newspapers in the 1980s and 1990s, and now meet on a regular basis every morning and evening in the mall's coffee shops. . . . What is beautiful is that Bin Souqat, the owner of the mall, joins these men in their gathering and wanders back and forth in the malls' long hallways before going up to his office on the upper floor, or to his official *majlis* behind the mall. Although he has recently been absent because his health is not as it should be, the mall's visitors are still continuously meeting each other there, and their longing brings them there for these chance encounters.[1]

Al-Kamali's depiction of life in Bin Souqat Mall resembles many Emiratis' depictions of the good old days of the *freej* (neighborhood), when neighbors could chance upon one another and socialize. In place of the community life of the *freej*, spectacular spaces like shopping malls, coffee shops, and new developments have become sites for memories and belonging for some of the city's middle-class inhabitants. These spectacular settings provide opportunities to encounter other members of society, interact, people watch, chitchat, and keep up to date with the social life of one's community. They also provide a space where Dubai's inhabitants encounter and negotiate ever-changing cultural and social norms, especially around notions of gender roles and multiculturalism, all of which are being continually shaped by happenings at malls and other glitzy places.

As de Certeau argues, people's actions in everyday life defy the idea that they are passive consumers of a culture that has been imposed on them; instead, people actively construct the meanings of the places they spend time in by using "tactics" to adapt those spaces to their needs.[2] My interlocutors bear out de Certeau's argument: they used "tactics" of use, maneuvering, and inversion to make Dubai's shopping malls and other spectacular settings spaces of interaction and belonging. However, while "tactics" have classically been understood as radical acts by the marginalized against the elite, my work supports a less domination-focused use of this concept.[3] While scholars sometimes romanticize the reappropriation of space when they describe it as an act of resistance, "tactics" are not necessarily "bottom-up" actions against "top-down" planning, but can also denote users' active participation in the making of a city.[4] I argue that middle-class inhabitants act as adaptive agents to reappropriate space not as an act of resistance but as an act of convenience: they adapt the space to fit their needs and desires for social connection and community.

This chapter explores how citizens and residents inhabit one aspect of their city's spectacle that is often associated with its perceived "inauthenticity": its neoliberal urban developments, specifically those built to facilitate shopping. It elaborates on how the tactics middle-class Dubai inhabitants use to relate to these spaces are processes of adaptation. These processes of adaptation have not given places like shopping malls the community feel of the beloved *freej*, according to my older interlocutors. But they have served to domesticate the spectacle, making it useful well beyond the original intents of its developers for acts of informal socializing and community formation, as well as group surveillance and personal expression. My interlocutors therefore *inhabit the spectacle* by adapting themselves to it and adapting the spectacle to their own daily purposes, becoming active users in the making of their changing city. They are neither resisting nor fully supporting the spectacle but exhibiting another sense of agency—agency as adaptation.

Seeing how inhabitants make meanings within commerce-oriented public spaces therefore provides us a different understanding of belonging and agency than the one depicted in dominant discourses. For many scholars, the alienating nature of places like malls is an unavoidable effect of their position in the capitalist political economy.[5] Some describe shopping malls as gilded cages where the only form of exchange is economic.[6] Scholars observe that because malls are privatized spaces, they can restrict the behavior of users based on profit margins—for example, people cannot even sit in an empty restaurant without ordering anything.[7] To these scholars, even if malls can be sites of social interaction, the nature of that social interaction is relatively meaningless. For example, before a version of this chapter was published as a journal article, a peer reviewer commented on it, saying, "People can be social beings in malls . . . but is that all that 'community' and social 'belonging' entails? And if so, then arguably 'neoliberal' urbanism has achieved its ultimate goal: the polity has been deradicalized and we truly have become the society of the spectacle." Likewise, after he had given a public lecture at NYUAD about the alienating facets of spectacles, I asked Alawadi why he did not consider shopping malls as places where people could go to socialize, interact, and create a sense of togetherness.[8] To this he jokingly replied, "We need to change the way you think about malls." Perhaps not unrelatedly, this dismissive attitude toward malls may be due to them being associated with women and younger people, in addition to tourists. Rather than depicting these neoliberal developments simply as alienating spaces, it is more fruitful to understand how the intersections of race, class, and gender influence the terms of inclusion and exclusion in such spaces—as the politics of belonging is situated temporally, intersectionally, and spatially.[9]

If malls are solely instruments of neoliberal power, as the common discourse goes, then the city's residents have only three options for relating to them: they can *support* these spectacular developments in a full embrace of neoliberal consumerism; they can *succumb* to them as alienated, oppressed masses; or they can *resist* them by challenging the neoliberal values the malls promote. This analysis implicitly maps inhabitants of the city into categories of resistors/oppressed/supporters, while also implicitly privileging resistance as the only meaningful option. Yet, most of Dubai's inhabitants I interviewed did not map onto these options. Most inhabited the spectacle by adapting themselves to the changing city, creating a sense of belonging and making meanings in places such as its shopping centers. They used these spectacular and so-called inauthentic spaces as places to relax, get together with friends, create family memories, get the latest news about their social world, engage in courtship, and negotiate social norms—similarly to some of the ways people once used the *freej*. They did these things not as acts of resistance to neoliberal consumerism, nor as its avid supporters or oppressed subjects, but simply as creative social agents using the publicly accessible places at their disposal to meet their dynamic social needs.

CULTIVATING INFORMALITY

Dubai's spectacular developments have earned their "alienating" label in part due to their outward aesthetic formality. In this context, a casual observer may be surprised to see the degree to which residents routinely "make themselves at home" in these spaces. Yet, I came across a variety of scenes of informality during my fieldwork. On one of these early days of my research, I was standing on the first floor of Dubai Mall, looking down to watch as people entered and left the mall. I saw a group of young South Asian girls practicing dance moves in the middle of the mall (figure 3). In the usually quiet luxury section of the mall, where brands like Gucci and Christian Dior are housed, a Chinese woman was playing Chinese pop music with her friends as they stood videotaping her. A South Asian man gave his wife a foot massage as she rested her leg on his lap while they relaxed on two of the mall's chairs.

Meanwhile, outside the Dubai Mall, in front of a big fountain surrounded by expensive hotels, is an open space where people wander, watch the fountain, eat at the restaurants, or simply sit on the benches (or the floor). In figure 4, a group of women are seen relaxing in this space with their shoes off, one of them stretching her legs on the benches, using the spectacular space as an informal one.

Throughout my fieldwork, I continued to see examples of residents inhabiting the spectacle amid Dubai's glitzy developments by engaging

Figure 3. Girls dancing together in Dubai Mall.

Figure 4. Women relaxing outside Dubai Mall.

Figure 5. A man watching TV on his phone using the Wi-Fi at the canal.

with them informally. One of the city's newer spectacles is a canal that was built by razing a section of a park. The project was criticized by many people who were saddened by the loss of a functional space where they went to exercise or take their children, as well as by those who were frustrated at a city constantly changing without regard for their memories. The canal project is not yet completed as there is no retail along the walking paths, and it is unclear how the space will be used once retail opens. However, the walking pathway is open, and residents are already reappropriating the space. For example, I found a group of young Emirati men sitting on the walking pathway with their shoes off while playing cards.

I also found many working-class South Asian men using the canal as a space of leisure. While I walked there, I could hear Bollywood songs and TV shows as people used the free WiFi and charging stations to watch TV, chat with friends and family on their phone, and listen to music. I saw men who had taken off their shoes and were stretching their legs, or watching a football game using the free WiFi (as can be seen in figure 5).

The instances of informality these photos convey are, I argue, one tactic that Dubai's residents of various backgrounds use to adapt themselves to their spectacular city and adapt their city's spectacles to their own purposes. By using the mall and the canal as spaces to relax, take off their shoes, give one another foot rubs, dance, play music, chat on the phone, and watch TV, they inhabit the spectacle through routine acts of informality, personalizing their city's spaces and coconstructing their meaning. The malls, in their use, are not just alienating consumer spaces; they are spaces for everyday life.

The power-centered framework of supporter/oppressed/resister sometimes leads scholars to interpret the ordinary acts of informality like these as subtle forms of resistance against the neoliberal order. Elsheshtawy, for example, describes "small gestures" of informality as acts of not only inhabitation but also defiance and subversion:

> The *khaliji* [Gulf] city is characterized by a high degree of control that frowns upon any sign of disorder. It is dismissive of informality. Numerous regulations aim at preserving its "beautiful appearance." City residents, however, are able to circumvent this by laying claim to the city, in a sense occupying its spaces in clear defiance of rules and regulations. It is an attempt to establish a home, to ascertain their right to the city. Informality becomes a way to proclaim an alternative order which subverts the rigidity of the formal.[10]

Here, informality is understood to be "gestures" meant to communicate an assertion of rights. While some inhabitants are indeed making claims to their right to the city through these acts, this narrative also romanticizes acts of resistance and risks imposing it on "those for whom this is not a meaningful category."[11] As the photos suggest, the acts of informality I observed throughout my fieldwork were routine, ordinary examples of adaptive agents acting out of their own convenience. They reflect the everyday practices of adaptive agents who are malleable to the city's changing urban landscape and who make meanings within its amenities. By making themselves at home in the mall and along the canal, residents were not necessarily supporting, resisting, or succumbing to neoliberal domination, but they were certainly participating in the making of their city—and making it a space of belonging. This appears especially true for my own interlocutors, middle- and upper-middle-class citizens and residents who generally expressed feeling entitled to and welcome in most of the city's new public and commercial developments.

SEEING AND BEING SEEN

In other instances, and for certain groups, spectacular spaces can be ideal places to see one another and to be seen, functioning akin to events like weddings, which one middle-aged Emirati woman I spoke to, Jameela, likened to a social newspaper whose pages keep readers up to date with news of the community. With varying degrees of positivity and critique, this is how many people I interviewed viewed shopping centers and the businesses they contain—as similar to older forms of social events such as weddings, where people congregate to show off and observe one another.

As spaces to see and be seen, spectacular developments become ideal spaces to engage in flânerie. For Walter Benjamin, the flâneur is a (male) wanderer of the modern city who observes it and the people within it, and who experiences both attachment and detachment to scenes of urban modernity.[12] Anke Reichenbach brings the concept to the Emirates' shopping malls, arguing they have important social value for Emirati *women* as ideal sites to engage in flânerie.[13] Elsewhere in the Gulf, similar patterns emerge: Le Renard describes the mall as a place for Saudi women to walk and wander, and many of her interlocutors' stories and narratives were based on observations they had in malls.[14] Bagheri cites a similar example of flânerie in malls in Iran.[15] The streets or other such public spaces are not considered "safe" or appropriate for some women, including Emirati women as well as middle- and upper-middle-class Arab and South Asian women and women from conservative families. Therefore, as Reichenbach argues, they become ideal spaces for women to engage in flânerie.[16] Many of the people I interviewed used the malls for this purpose, just as I had done as a teenager growing up in Dubai. Indeed, shopping malls were one of the few (if not only) public places that were available to me as a teenager. I went there with family, with friends, or alone. Like many of those whose experiences I documented in my research, I spent hours and hours circling the mall with my friends, talking, shopping, and people watching.

While different people frequent different kinds of events and sites, most people did describe having regular venues where they went to see other members of their community and to be seen by them, and many of these were located in newly developed areas. Borrowing Jameela's phrase, I argue that much like attending weddings, spaces in the city such as shopping malls function as contemporary "social newspapers" of society, especially for Emiratis. In the absence of the community life of the *freej* that older interlocutors remembered, these places provide a space for Emiratis (and some non-Emiratis) to bump into other members of their community and to feel connected and up to date. In these glitzy spaces, they people watch, chitchat, and encounter different people. While Augé referred to shopping malls as nonplaces where people are anonymous and faceless, places like shopping malls in Dubai were the very places where some went to quite literally "show their face" and to be seen by society.[17]

For my Emirati interlocutors, places where they go to see and be seen typically feature a high proportion of Emiratis relative to other groups, either as a majority or simply a visible minority (the national dress makes them more visible to one another). For example, figures 6 and 7 were taken inside Dubai Mall; the first shows a mix of ethnicities including a few Emiratis, and the second shows an Emirati-dominated section of the mall—an ideal place where some Emiratis go for social encounters with one another.

In figure 7, Emirati men and some Emirati women congregate near a Kuwaiti-owned coffee shop in Dubai Mall. Part of its popularity is possibly due to it being a *khaleeji* franchise—another popular café in a similar area of the mall is an Emirati-owned franchise—but other, Western chains are similarly popular among Emiratis, such as Parker's Restaurant and L'eto Caffe. Elsewhere in the city, another favored spot is Design District (also known as D3), a new mixed-use development with offices, restaurants, design spaces, and cafés that seem especially attractive to young Emiratis. The presence of many Emirati men in a coffee shop leads some of my Emirati interlocutors to compare it to a *majlis* (or *meelas*, in Emirati dialect).[18] A *meelas* is a detached building next to the main house found in many Gulf countries, mostly used by males to socialize and discuss

Figure 6. Near the main entrance of Dubai Mall, a few Emiratis among a mix of
nationalities. The 3-D figure in the middle represents another "spectacular"
development project that is being advertised in the mall.

different topics, ranging from business to social issues, although there are
some women who attend the (women's) *meelas* as well. The *meelas* existed
in the pre-oil era and is still used today. Most of my interviewees considered the coffee shop as a *meelas* to be a familiar metaphor. When I
explained that part of my research included looking at how people used
spaces, and how some individuals used coffee shops as a *meelas*, almost all
Emirati respondents told me about a father, uncle, or another male relative—often an elder one, but not necessarily—who patronized a specific
coffee shop (often in a mall) with the same group of people on a regular or
everyday basis. Even if the person I was interviewing did not personally
know these groups of men, they generally knew *of* them and would tell me
about a group of retired government officials, footballers, or elder intellectuals that assembled daily in their neighborhood mall. When I told
Maitha, an Emirati woman in her early twenties, about the coffee shop

Figure 7. Emiratis congregating near a coffee shop in Dubai Mall.

and *meelas* comparison, she told me about the coffee shops in D3 that she often went to:

> I see people going to D3 with the same guys from their *meelas*. It's just like, they keep up the same conversation [from the *meelas*]. They just move, they just change locations for *taghyeer jaw* [change of scenery]. . . . I think, literally, people just want to look around. I guess you go out to see people, I don't think it's a bad thing, I go there knowing that. . . . I was at the Lighthouse café having breakfast, and after there, I went to pick up coffee from Frame [café]. People who were at the Lighthouse, they walked with me [in the same direction] to Frame and had coffee as well. It was so funny, literally, we have the same routine.

Shopping mall coffee shops do not necessarily replace a *meelas*: the *meelas* requires the owners to engage in some upkeep, such as cleaning and restocking coffee and some foods, as opposed to the socializing that takes place outside. While it allows some people to socialize and interact, it is not as public as a coffee shop and so does not allow people to see and be seen in the same way, or to "change scenery," as Maitha put it. But it was widely agreed among those with whom I discussed the topic that the coffee shop seemed to represent a related way of socializing. These coffee shops with a *meelas* vibe can be found in big and small shopping malls and developments, as well as stand-alone shops in the street, such as those dotting the popular Jumeirah Road. Wherever they are, one of their functions is to enable people to observe other members of society.

Maitha was clearly aware of her surroundings—she noticed who sat with whom in the coffee shop and where they went after they finished their breakfast. The otherwise unknown people she encountered at the café have similar routines to hers, migrating from place to place at similar times and with similar purposes. Similar scenes can be found all over the city. At a coffee shop in a small shopping mall near my house, a group of older Emirati men congregated daily. Because I did not wear a *sheila* (hair cover) and *'abaya* (a long and flowing, usually black cloak), they did not know I was Emirati, but they saw me sitting with Emirati women on several occasions. They later told me that they decided I must be an interior designer meeting with my clients. Setting aside their curious assumption, this example demonstrates how my interlocutors use spaces of consumption to carefully observe other members of society, including me.

Lefebvre argues that urban spaces are designed not only by city planners and developers but also by the perceptions, discourses, and practices of inhabitants.[19] Although entering a busy café and calling out "hello" to the people sitting there would normally be considered odd (at least in most big cities), it is reportedly not uncommon for Emirati men to greet café customers with "*al-salam alaykum*" ("hello" in Arabic) as they enter Emirati-dominated coffee shops, much as they would when entering a *meelas*. The presence of many other Emiratis (particularly Emirati men) replicated for them the atmosphere of a *meelas*, encouraging them to reproduce some of the *meelas*'s social codes in a commercial space.

In some cases, the use of the café as a *meelas* imbues it with a sense of familiarity and connection, not only for these groups of men but also for other patrons who have grown used to seeing the same familiar faces there. At the beginning of this chapter, I quoted Al-Kamali describing scenes in Bin Souqat Mall. Her descriptions are similar to the way many

Emiratis depict the good old days of the *freej*, when neighbors could chance upon one another and socialize without ceremony. Spaces like shopping malls, coffee shops, and new developments provide opportunities for many Emiratis and some non-Emiratis to socialize regularly without necessarily having to schedule to do so, as can be seen in figure 8. Humorously, one Twitter post reads: "Some guys make me feel that Dubai Mall takes attendance and that they need to attend daily, and if they don't go they feel guilty. And the same thing with Mercato [mall], they have to be sitting in Starbucks."[20]

Those I spoke to usually decided whether to spend their time in a particular café or mall based as much on their sense of who else might be there as on its location and offerings. In fact, when they mentioned urban change, they often spoke not about physical structures but rather clienteles. For instance, in a Twitter post, an Emirati noted the absence of other Emirati patrons at Deira City Center, an older shopping mall in Dubai that had formerly been popular among Emirati customers and was now mostly used by South and Southeast Asians. He joked that the only Emirati in the mall was its owner (Al Futtaim). "I passed by Deira City Center, oh the memories. The only citizen I saw there was Al Futtaim loooll. My, how things change. I wonder if the same would happen in Mirdif City Center?" (Mirdif City Center is currently dominated by Emiratis due to its location.)[21]

While most of the examples in this section have centered on seeing and being seen among the Emirati community, newly developed commercial spaces can be used by different groups for similar purposes. For example, Shireena, a Filipina Pakistani woman in her thirties, remembered her teenage years in Burjuman Center, an older mall in Dubai. She said:

> I think especially if you're expat, because like, your parents are mostly working and they can't take you places. So you have to figure out a way to amuse yourself, you know what I mean? And a form of amusement was walking in the mall over and over and over again [laughing] . . . . We would just hang out in the food courts. It sounds really sad. . . . We would just hang out and meet other people. Back then we were like, so into Hip Hop and R&B. . . . So I remember me and my sister going to Burjuman [center] . . . wearing our pants the other way around, thinking we were so cool. And the guys are like, "yaa, whoa man." I think about it now and I can die of embarrassment.

Figure 8. Emiratis bumping into each other and saying hello among tourists taking selfies in Dubai Mall.

Similarly, Ahmed, an Indian man in his forties, recalled dressing up as a teenager to go to Al Ghurair Center, one of the first malls in Dubai. He claimed that you could find all of Dubai in that one place on the weekend, which is why he was interested in going there.

While many, especially Emiratis, feel a sense of familiarity in spaces where they bump into other members of their community, some people avidly avoid such spaces or feel annoyed in them for the same reasons. For example, an Emirati man tweeted about his discomfort in a particular coffee shop because of its clientele: "In regard to the guys in the Starbucks in Mercato, as soon as you enter they all look at you. Don't tell me I entered your *meelas*."[22] Because such cafés are places where Emiratis congregate, members of the Emirati community are highly visible to one another, and some people feel that they are constantly under observation in them. Sometimes Emirati women used the word *meelas* to signify Emirati male-dominated spaces where they felt under watch. In particular, a number of the women I spoke with said that they felt uncomfortable in these spaces because they can make women feel as if they are on display. I personally did not feel as watched as they did, because I did not "appear" to be Emirati, but I knew what they meant as, ironically, I felt more under scrutiny in certain *khaleeji*-dominated areas of London than in Dubai because I was more visibly *khaleeji* to other members of the community there. I still remember the distinct feeling of being watched when I went to an Iraqi restaurant in Knightsbridge many years ago and saw everyone turning their heads to see who was entering the shop, which they continued to do every time the door opened. This experience is depicted well by a satirical photo and caption posted on Twitter: A large group of male students are looking at the camera. The post reads: "A girl enters Home Bakery" (an Emirati-owned café dominated by Emiratis).[23]

Some of my interlocutors view these spaces where people go to see and be seen negatively as spaces where trivial people congregate to fill their empty lives with meaningless things. They criticize such people for not having any hobbies other than dressing up, looking at one another, flirting, and gossiping. They feel that they are constantly being judged when they go to such places and that they have to perfect their make-up, clothes, jewelry, perfume, hair, and other aspects of their appearance to fit in, as mallgoers scrutinize small things like what type of shoes or bag one is wearing. They claim that most users of these spaces are stiff and arrogant, checking one another out with prying eyes, without bothering to smile or appear friendly. They do not feel that such spaces allow them a real sense of connectedness but rather propagate nosy and unkind talk. For instance, some Emiratis I spoke to criticized practices of courtship (which can range from consensual flirting to harassment) they saw in malls, viewing these as "inappropriate" or "trashy" compared to other more "civilized" ways of courtship that they engaged in at coed university settings, volunteering, certain workplaces, or while studying abroad. While recognizing the very real concern with harassment, it is important to also point out that the courtship that takes place in malls (such as men following women and sharing their numbers with them) can be consensual, and for *some* people who go to gender-segregated schools or who may not have access to the types of coed environments described above, it is a way to meet others of the opposite sex. In any case, the panoply of critiques I heard related to some mall socializing practices (which many of my mall and coffee-shop-going interlocutors here also criticize) highlight various practices of social distinction. They also show how these spaces, functioning as places to see and be seen, play an important role in how Dubai's adaptive agents use sites of spectacle to actively engage with their communities and society more broadly.[24] This can further be seen in examining how Dubai's spectacular developments provide a terrain on and through which residents negotiate social mores and norms.

In general, it is the perceived exclusivity of certain places that makes them ideal spaces for segments of society who want to be around others of a similar class, background, nationality, or lifestyle. While Emiratis certainly can be found in a variety of places, many people I spoke to claim that they find more Emiratis in the luxury areas of the mall. Some even argued that luxury (such as wearing branded clothes or driving expensive cars) has become a defining factor of Emirati identity. Therefore, social distinction may be one of the very reasons that Emiratis choose to congregate in spectacular new developments. Not all Emirati-dominated spaces are necessarily luxury spaces, however. Emiratis create an atmosphere of a *meelas* in places that range from a luxury Fauchon café to a Starbucks coffee shop (the latter which is frequented by middle-class users of various backgrounds).

How can we discuss the exclusivity of many of Dubai's new development projects, and the related politics of belonging they may engender, without depicting them as universally alienating or presenting those who use them as "passive" citizens? Take Elsheshtawy's description of City Walk, a new mixed-use development used by many Emiratis, which he portrays as a

> space that ultimately alienates and repels. . . . Geared towards a transnational clientele it aims to rectify issues related to previous planning debacles which interiorized the urban experience. . . . City Walk is an isolated space, disconnected from its surroundings . . . These images capture a placeless, and anonymous urbanity. *People are reduced to mere spectators. They are disengaged.* In such settings there is no place for the capricious, the unintended or the informal—the very stuff that defines cityness. *Instead we can only sit on the bench provided for us by the developers and watch in awe as the spectacle unfolds before our eyes.*[25]

Elsheshtawy's accompanying photographs of an empty City Walk reflect an important point about new mixed-use developments and their sustainability as an oversupply of them come into the market. Some are empty on weekdays or entire months of the year or lose popularity to newer ones. The Box Park development, for instance, has become mostly vacant after the nearby City Walk was built. During the hottest months and on some weekdays, City Walk can be empty, which Elsheshtawy's photographs reflect. However, City Walk is crowded and popular on weekends, as well as weekdays in the cooler months, particularly among Emiratis (as can be seen in figure 9). The depiction of inhabitants who "can only sit on the bench" and "watch in awe as the spectacle unfolds before our eyes" underlines how such discourse strips agency from urban denizens, as only acts of resistance are seen to constitute a form of agency. Yet my research shows that many inhabitants do not experience meaningful relationships to the spectacular city primarily through acts of resistance. They adapt to the changing city in varying ways, engaging in socializing practices that are significant for *them,* and often exerting considerable geographic mobility as they do so.

Similarly, the large number of Emiratis in a place like City Walk is what makes it the opposite of a "transnational" and "anonymous urbanity" for many citizens. City Walk was the first place where I ever walked in the street—not in a mall or a pedestrianized development—surrounded by

Figure 9. Seeing and being seen at City Walk.

UAE nationals. By contrast, in the streets of Dubai I often encountered Westerners or South Asians, but not Emiratis. Some Emiratis have positive associations with privatized spaces in which they can be around other citizens. For example, a woman compared Mirdif City Center, a large mall dominated by Emiratis, to the atmosphere of a neighborhood, saying: "Mirdif City Center = A *freej* [neighborhood] that's full of locals."[26] For some Emiratis, choosing Emirati-dominated spaces may be a deliberate act that indicates their preferences for a less "foreign" society.[27] This does not represent the view of all my interlocutors who seek out Emirati-dominated spaces, however. For instance, some Emiratis enjoy spending time both in Emirati-dominated areas and those where Emiratis are largely absent, as I show in chapter 3. Finally, it is also important to note that some Emiratis who come to Dubai from elsewhere actively seek out the spectacularity of commercial sites that bring goods and people from around the world together in one place. Aidha, an Emirati man in his thirties from Abu Dhabi, when asked what he did when he came to Dubai, said:

> For me, almost every time I go to Dubai, I have to visit KinoKunia (Bookworld) in Dubai Mall; It is one of the biggest bookstores in the world, and for me, it is not only intellectual but almost a "spiritual" experience. . . . I do not think a Catholic visiting the Vatican or a Muslim in Mecca will get more satisfaction than I do in this huge bookshop in Dubai mall. . . . I buy books every time, and I sit at a coffee shop putting the books in front me while having coffee and watching this amazing "stream of humanity" passing by. People from literally every corner of the world. I love watching them passing by; veiled women, and women in shorts, young and old, men and women, from every race and creed. I feel happiness every time I go there.

As this example shows, Emiratis, who were the main focus of this section, can frequent Dubai's new developments to experience different kinds of definitions of community.

NEGOTIATING CHANGING SOCIAL NORMS

As spaces to observe and contemplate society, spectacular developments such as shopping centers are ideal sites for social contestations and cultural negotiations to take place. Assaf is one of the few to have directly discussed this role of malls in the context of the Gulf; she argues that conflicts that arise out of rubbing shoulders with the "other" are precisely what makes malls public spaces.[28] She gave the example of two Twitter campaigns that were initiated by Emiratis advocating for more modest dress codes to be enforced in malls (after these women saw Westerners dressed in revealing outfits there). In the following examples, I show similar forms of social contestations that happen in these settings, ranging from the negotiation of dress codes to women's presence in public spaces.[29]

Some of these social contestations *can* be described as someone intentionally intending to subvert social norms, while others may not. Yet I want to argue against assigning more meaning or value to actions that are transgressive as opposed to those that may appear "passive." What all these examples represent is adaptive agents negotiating the terms of social belonging in Dubai's spectacular spaces. They are all meaningful to how middle-class residents create a sense of belonging in these spaces while also participating in shaping a broader politics of belonging that influences different terms of social inclusion and exclusion in Dubai. As adaptive agents, they may vehemently resist some social norms and passionately support the status quo in other ways while being indifferent to a host of other things. Of course, even those who do *not* "resist" may still in effect challenge the status quo through their actions.

For example, there were some points in time when Emirati women wearing a colored 'abaya (the long—and usually black—cloak worn by women) was controversial (it still is for some families). Were the women who were wearing colored 'abayas in public doing so to challenge the status quo? The answer can vary tremendously: some women wear the colored 'abayas because they want to challenge the status quo, some of them do it simply because they find it fashionable, and some might *not* consider it transgressive if they come from families or social circles which approve of it. Whatever the intentions of these actions may be, shopping malls serve as focal points for discussion of this pattern. For example, a Saudi Twitter user wrote: "Go to any mall here [in Saudi] and see the colors of the 'abayas, five years ago they did not wear colored 'abayas."[30] Their phrase "go to any mall here and see" encapsulates how malls are ideal places to observe social norms in a society. These places are stages for certain encounters to take place, and friends, family, and strangers debate these encounters and what they signify.

Examples of social contestations taking place in and through spectacular spaces are evident in everyday conversations as well as on social media. For example, an Emirati Twitter user criticized some people's racist actions toward Chinese tourists that he observed in the mall during the beginning of the COVID-19 pandemic: "The situation in Dubai Mall is uncivil, if you are afraid of Chinese tourists then stay at home.... But embarrassing them by your moves and words and your exaggerated fear, that is the epitome of rudeness."[31] Meanwhile, in 2017, passersby recorded three seventeen-year-old Emirati boys performing dangerous stunts with their car on the roads of City Walk, as onlookers stood nearby. The next day, Sheikh Mohammed bin Rashid, ruler of Dubai, ordered the boys to clean the streets on which they performed their stunts.[32] Community service was not a common form of discipline, so performing community service in City Walk in particular, under the gaze of many Emiratis, made this punitive act even more visible, and invited the community to debate what they saw. One Emirati Twitter user said: "As I am sitting in one of the cafés in City Walk, in front of me were three young men, wearing janitor's outfits and cleaning supplies, while all eyes are on them!!" He went on to criticize the behavior of people who filmed the boys without their permission or made "degrading" comments to them.

These spectacular spaces equally afford opportunities to negotiate gender relations.[33] Hanin, an Arab woman, recounted her memories in the mall as a teenager. In one memory, she had romantic escapades with her first boyfriend in the cinema. Hanin also made use of other luxury places. She and her boyfriend went to walk on the private beaches at the Palm, a popular coastal development. Hanin was not allowed to date, and she knew they would not bump into anyone they knew there. But because they were not residents of the Palm, they had to sneak in, and security guards would occasionally chase after them. In a Twitter post, an Arab user recalled similar memories: "Secretly dating in the café that used to be in Debenhams ... in Deira City Center where I spent most of my teen age days! Memories."[34]

Other members of society do not view such actions favorably. A young Emirati Twitter user said: "It's the first time I like Mercato [mall] coz [*sic*] no locals [Emiratis] sitting in a café flirting . . . the mall was almost empty! #thankyouRamadan."[35] Such comments indicate that these commercialized landscapes in new Dubai are important stages where inhabitants encounter difference, places where they observe and negotiate social and gender norms.

When families and friends discuss something out of the ordinary that they had observed, or transgressive behavior they came across, they frequently observed the act in a mall, coffee shop, or similar kind of place. Related discussions are found on Twitter, Instagram, and Snapchat. For instance, in a mall in Qatar, an older male social media influencer recorded himself walking into a cosmetics shop. Looking at a lipstick advertisement depicting a group of women and a man, he argued that men should not advertise cosmetics and that this man's actions were corrupting the youth.[36] He called for the posters to be removed, and the shop complied. Assaf argues that these sorts of conflicts, which arise out of rubbing shoulders with the "other," here in the form of an advertisement from a global cosmetics brand, are precisely what make malls public spaces.[37] While a shopping mall is not the embodiment of an ideal public space as many philosophers have imagined this concept, my interlocutors adapt to their environments in ways that allow them to *view* and use the mall as a public space of some sort.

Spectacular spaces become sites where a variety of behaviors, activities, and rituals can be seen at once by many other people. For this reason, they have the power to affect social mores and discussions around them. Behavior that critics might consider daring or immoral can become commonplace as more individuals practice it in such public places over time. For instance, in previous decades in the UAE, some would find it controversial if they saw a young woman sitting in a coffee shop either alone or with friends without her family present. Suaad, an Emirati woman in her forties, recalls from her teenage and early adulthood years in Dubai that

if I was standing alone in front of Wafi [mall], not at a very late hour [laughing]. But if it was like, let's say six o'clock in the evening, and you're not with somebody. . . . If people saw you like that, they'll be like, "Aah, someone saw you in Wafi, you were alone, weren't you? What were you doing?" So again, the culture was . . . like . . . "you're not to be seen." And that went on for a good [while], like even in the nineties also, you know?

Figure 10. Home Bakery in Dubai Design District.

This quote highlights that these social and gender norms in the UAE have drastically changed, and it not coincidentally puts a shopping center at the heart of such changes. One reason for this change is precisely that different segments of society saw the presence of more and more women in these malls, coffee shops, and developments that catered to their consumer interests—until their presence became normalized over time. My Emirati female interlocutors, as well as some Arab and South Asian women, described not being allowed to go out as teenagers or young women without older family members accompanying them. Although the same rules may still apply for some conservative families today, for the majority it has undoubtedly changed (see figures 10 and 11).

Malls are places where changes in social norms are enacted and become observable to my interlocutors engaged in flânerie. In an interview, Suaad gave me an example of transformations to family dynamics that she observed in people's behavior in malls:

> Like for example now, when you go to Dubai Mall, and it's nice I've seen it in my daughter's generation, they're all with their husbands and kids, whereas in the past, the woman used to go off on her own and the man was sitting in the coffee shop somewhere else. And [the man] was like, "No, don't come say hello to me, my friends will see you," or whatever. That's all changed now. It's like, my son-in-law's friend will say hello to him and say hello to my daughter too.

For social norms to change, individuals had to behave in novel ways including, on some occasions, transgressively. Often, the discussions, or gossip, about what changes one observed at a mall or coffee shop take place in family living rooms or among friends. However, we can also find examples of these debates on social media, which offer a window onto the ways inhabitants actively engage with spectacular sites through processes of social contestation and cultural negotiation.

In a Twitter post, an influential Emirati woman bemoaned the behavior of Emirati youth who, she says, were sipping their coffees at the Mercato Mall Starbucks during prayer time.[38] Another Mercato Mall customer complained on Twitter of another sighting she deemed inappropriate: "You [a woman] sit in Starbucks in Mercato between all these men? Excuse me but you have no shame."[39] The two Twitter users I quoted here explicitly mention the (same) place where they observed behavior they considered indecent, at a Starbucks. There are various other examples of this dynamic. Another Twitter user writes about seeing an Emirati model whom she criticizes for not dressing "appropriately," and that she's instead dressed "like she's English."[40] Yet another described "indecent" behavior in a coffee shop in a shopping area in Jumeirah: "An old woman from a Gulf country, [wearing] *abaya* and *niqab* [and smoking] shisha!!!"[41] While these comments appear to be from and about other Emiratis (or *khalijis*), there are clear differences in the way these individuals negotiate modesty, religion, and gender norms. The common thread is that these privatized and "inauthentic" places—including American and global chain coffee shops—become important social and cultural spaces where norms are negotiated, by both individuals and a broader community.

As the city's spectacular developments allow individuals with different ideals and subjectivities to come across one another, they impact evolving sociospatial dynamics within groups of similar class and ethnic backgrounds and between those of different groups.[42] While some may use

Figure 11. A woman sitting in a male-dominated environment at Home Bakery in Dubai Design District.

Dubai's malls and other glitzy spaces to engage resistive behavior, or to police this kind of behavior, many middle-class inhabitants engage with these spectacular spaces in less dramatic ways, adapting their behavior to create new norms, or in other cases to engage in negotiations about social changes they see taking place in them.

Other parallels can be found in other societies where individuals have used spaces of consumption to perform different subjectivities and to challenge dominant social norms. Upper-middle-class Egyptian women use upscale coffee shops in Cairo to engage in behaviors that are impermissible elsewhere in the city, ranging from the way they dress to mixed-gender socializing.[43] In Pune, Indian youth use cafés to engage in behavior that their families or more traditional members of society frown upon: smoking, drinking, and premarital relationships.[44] While cafés in Pune are geared toward youth who want to escape family and societal control, in Dubai, glitzy spaces bring together a variety of people with different value systems and allow them to practice different norms in sight of others. This makes them important cultural sites and meaningful spaces of belonging where social changes and contestations over these changes also unfold.

MAKING MEMORIES

Because of these various meanings inhabitants make in the spectacular city, "inauthentic" places become not only important social and cultural sites for them but also places of memories and attachments. Many older citizens and residents I interviewed feel nostalgic at times not only toward the "old Dubai" but also toward some of the big shopping malls and developments. This nostalgia illustrates the extent to which social interactions and cultural experiences people have had in such places have been meaningful to them as individuals and as members of communities that may have in part taken shape amid Dubai's spectacular developments. Commercialized urban spaces that appear impersonal on the outside can host deep-seated memories and attachments.

For example, Farah, an Indian woman who grew up in Dubai, described her connections to Al-Ghurair Center, one of the oldest malls in Dubai. Farah said:

To me Al-Ghurair [Center] was the ONLY mall. I visited it weekends as a child, as a teenager with my friends. The cheesy 80s music always playing in the background, the Indian-owned Choitrams supermarket serving Indian snacks, a very nice family-friendly entertainment place with something for everyone. I remember the hours spent in Sindbad game arcade. The getting off from school bus on the last day of high school with school mates for a Baskin-Robbins ice cream treat. I guess it was a finale that even our high school prom was held in Ghurair, so in essence I realize it has touched every phase of my growing-up life and makes me realize it's time to pay some homage and revisit, but having said that I have, but the last time I was there it has hurted [*sic*] my good memories so let's keep it at that. I think the population explosion makes the place less pleasurable now than it used to be.

Younger individuals like Hassan, who had recently turned thirty, remembered their childhood in later malls such as Deira City Center. In a Twitter post, Hassan showed his toy car collection that he accumulated through shopping visits to Deira City Center when he was a child.[45]

Hassan said that Deira City Center in the 1990s was like Dubai Mall today. Indeed, it was bustling with people, not just children like Hassan, but teenagers and adults from all over the city (and beyond it). When he was a child, Hassan's father used to take him to Magic Planet, an arcade popular among children and teenagers. Hassan had vivid memories there: he would get his hand stamped at the door of the arcade as he went inside to play in the "kid's cage" (or at least that was what he and his peers called it) until he got dizzy. Hassan still remembers the layout of the mall: His parents used to take him for ice cream at Baskin-Robbins in the narrow hallway next to Carrefour (which at that time had another name, he recalls); and there was a food court where his mom used to enjoy eating Asian food, in a place called Panda. While many Emiratis today avoid going to malls during Eid because of the crowds, it was not necessarily so in the past. Hassan remembered going there with his Eid money to purchase a Disney movie. But like many other Emiratis, Deira City Center is not a place he visits much anymore now that other malls have opened. The last time Hassan went to Deira City Center was a year ago. When he entered the parking lot, he remembered parts of his childhood there, such as a parking sign near IKEA reading "customers only" but written in incorrect Arabic, which his mother used to laugh at every time she went there.

While scholars of Dubai have tended to focus on the connections and nostalgia people have for older parts of the city (a topic explored further in chapter 5), my research reveals many people expressing similar emotions about places such as malls.[46] Indeed, the older malls in Dubai held memories and nostalgia for some of my interlocutors, similar to the way neighborhoods, streets, and parks held memories for them. For example, as one Twitter post by a young Emirati put it: "Walking around Deira City Center is like taking a walk through your childhood. The memories won't stop stimulating my brain."[47] In such nostalgic accounts, we see people remembering the small and mundane everyday memories of their youth, such as their favorite games or funny moments with their families, in reminiscences tied to their experiences frequenting what were once spectacular new commercial spaces. When de Certeau discussed how ordinary inhabitants re-create the city through walking in it, he referred to the mundane and everyday interactions and uses of a space that "contradict or neutralize the rigor and formal patterns of urban organization."[48] Similarly, in shopping malls, the mundane and everyday uses of these spaces, as well as their leisurely uses, allow people to experience them as much more than just sites of commercial exchange. For some interlocutors, malls are places that house significant childhood memories, and they reminisced about them as nostalgically as older people recalled their own childhood memories in the *freej* in the "good old days."

Another telling example can be seen with Ali, who remembered his childhood in the older malls as vibrant and exciting, an experience he contrasted to those of children today:

> For us, people who grew up in the 90s had a very different view of Dubai. We witnessed the growth and, yes I do visit these new malls like Dubai Mall and such, but again it's just a mall. . . . I don't think people from the future generations will have the same thrill we did. They kinda grew up in the city after the major developments. . . . We were happy for McDonald's for example. It was something new. "Exotic." Now well, you order it anytime you want.

In this example, a globalized chain—a prime example of what Augé might refer to as a nonplace—becomes a place from the "good old days." In locations such as Magic Planet (in Diedre City Center), Ali says, "We did really socialize. And create memories," leading him to muse that "I think we had the best childhood." For Ali, a large and globalized mall with Western chains and brands is nonetheless a site of memories from a simpler childhood, one that he wishes current generations could experience.

Scholars have often recorded these narratives of wistfulness in relation to the old town and noncommercial spaces and interpret that wistfulness as a sign of personal connection, belonging, and the significance of these places. Yet here we see people expressing the same feelings about shopping malls, which suggests that their perceived "inauthenticity" does not keep them from also serving as significant sites for inhabitants—sites of memories. This not only highlights that these spaces are meaningful parts of the city and its inhabitants' social histories, but also the adaptive agency of Dubai's citizens and residents who inhabit the spectacular city and form connections to it in ways similar to those they have done in other parts of the city deemed more "authentic." For example, the Emirati social media influencer, Abdulla AlNeaimi, posted a photo of Deira City Center, saying: "In Deira City Centre. . . . Recalling memories and days that are gone. . . . When it used to be the most important mall, and the most popular. . . . A strange feeling, with some sadness, and a lot of longing. Anyway, what do you think of the Huawei phone photos? :D"[49]

It is important to note that while older malls my interlocutors mentioned still exist today, many have changed not only physically by adding extensions but also in terms of clientele. While people feel nostalgic about these places, they rarely go back to them; and when they do, they may feel uneasy, as Farah shows, because of how their demographic has changed. Sometimes this discomfort is overtly based on perceptions that the character of a place has changed its potential to be a site of belonging for them. Practices of social distinction are evident here: some interviewees term malls that used to be popular among their elite or middle-class communities as now "low class," or in a condescending and racist manner refer to them as "just for Indians" or "just for Filipinos." Changes in demographics might alienate some inhabitants even if they do not view a group as "lower" than them in the status hierarchy. For example, some might refer to the newer places in the city as those "just for Westerners" to highlight that they feel out of place there. This indicates that the ways inhabitants experience what the literature on "nonplaces," such as malls, portrays as nameless and faceless landscapes are influenced by the people they see in these places. However, because people of different backgrounds can be found in most places of new Dubai (such as Dubai Mall), the diversity of people present there allows the place to not be seen as "just for" one group, as some might deridingly refer to other places, and therefore a place that may hold future memories of belonging.

Inhabitants' relationships with urban spaces are complex, but what is clear is that spectacular spaces obtain important social meanings as inhabitants use them to make memories. By this, I mean not only that they have socially meaningful experiences of belonging in places such as malls in their contemporary lives, as we have seen above, but also that they invest spectacular developments from past years (particularly those they frequented as children) with great personal and collective significance. Nostalgic accounts expressed in conversation and on social media, including many containing expressions of discomfort and anxiety about other demographics using these spaces, provide insight into the significance middle-class citizens and long-term residents of Dubai give to malls and other commerce-oriented developments as repositories of memories that can be mined to produce feelings of attachment and belonging to the spectacular city.

CONCLUSION

As we have seen in this chapter, residents of many backgrounds who frequent Dubai's shopping malls, coffee shops, and other new developments utilize various tactics to adapt these master-planned and often commerce-oriented spectacular spaces to their personal social needs. For middle-class citizens and residents, these sites provide rich opportunities for them to see other members of society, people watch, gossip, and keep up to date with the social life of their community; to observe and negotiate changing social mores and cultural norms; and to make and revisit memories that emphasize feelings of attachment to the city. It is partly the myriad connections they enable that make these spectacular spaces resonant and meaningful. In contrast to stereotypes of anonymous and faceless non-places, they provide inhabitants with opportunities to see and engage with members of their own communities who they might not otherwise encounter, which appears to be especially valued by Emiratis because of their minority demographic status. In some cases, as the accounts of many women indicate, as do the memories of those who remember spending their youth leisure hours in malls in the late twentieth century, such spaces may have even provided paths to socializing in public that were not available before they were constructed.

Of course, everyday practices of inhabiting spectacular spaces such as malls also produce sources of friction for middle-class citizens and residents, especially because these sites reveal not only economic transformations but also social and cultural changes Dubai has undergone. While it is certainly the case that many middle-class residents do not welcome all of these changes, such as shifting demographic patterns or changing gender norms (and people vary in this respect), it is important to note how they actively negotiate them within and through expressing ambivalence or criticality about spectacular spaces from the positionality of engaged urban denizens who actively frequent, surveil, recall memories of, and render judgements about these sites. The following chapter delves more deeply into the ways Dubai's citizens and middle-class residents exhibit adaptive agency in the ways they encounter and respond to different forms of demographic and cultural diversity that accompany spectacular development.

3 Globalization and Diversity at a Cosmopolitan Crossroads

Divya's father arrived in Dubai by ship in the 1970s. He came as a laborer and worked his way up the social ladder. Divya grew up in old Dubai. She was fortunate to go to a school funded by wealthy Indians who subsidized its cost. Divya later got accepted to a major Western university and went to study abroad, before returning to Dubai as a lawyer and moving to the new part of the city. When I asked her how she feels about the older parts of the city that she grew up in, Divya returned the question, asking how *I* felt there. I admitted that I was not entirely comfortable there and that I felt out of place and stared at. Divya seemed satisfied with that answer, saying that she was stared at even more than I was because she was part of that community, an Indian woman whom they viewed as having become too "Westernized." Going to old Dubai also reminded her of times she did not want to remember. She felt that old Dubai was poor and dirty.[1] Divya's comment expresses her social mobility and class aspirations: old Dubai is a place she left behind and feels uncomfortable in now, while new Dubai reflects the cosmopolite that she is today. She grew up in a very conservative community and said that she worried about people judging her and spreading rumors about her when she went back to that part of the city. Interestingly, her depiction of feeling watched mirrors the experiences of some Emirati women in Emirati-dominated spaces, as I show later in this chapter.

Like Divya, Maryam is also an Indian woman who grew up in old Dubai—but one with an entirely different relationship to that place. Although there have been times in her life when she had wanted to leave, she now feels rather differently, contrasting it positively with the new Dubai, which she resentfully describes as a place filled with "newbies and wannabees" who recently arrived in the city and who have little attachment to it. Maryam feels that her life, her part of the city, and her neighborhood have been rendered invisible or irrelevant: by officials who are more focused on new Dubai and its new inhabitants, and by the (often Western) middle classes and upper-middle classes who live and socialize there. Other inhabitants of old Dubai similarly felt marginalized, both physically as new Dubai became the new center of the city, and metaphorically, as their urban history was omitted from official accounts.[2] Dubai was a hub for commerce and business, a cosmopolitan space of some sorts long before it became the spectacular city that it is known as today. But as it grew, a larger number of nationalities and a more diverse ethnic and national makeup constituted the city's demographic, and these changes have been palpable for long-term inhabitants.

Like Maryam, it was not uncommon for those I interviewed, especially Emiratis, to make passing comments about how Dubai caters to Westerners and tourists. Similarly, it was not uncommon to hear their disapproval of how some (often Westerners) were behaving (or dressed) in public and descriptions of feeling out of place in areas of the city where these groups dominate. And yet, these very people also enjoyed going to places that at times they deemed "too Western." They found them to be posh and indicative of good taste, even if they avoided them at certain times of the night when the behavior there would be too debaucherous. These seeming contradictions were, in fact, quite common reactions to what is officially touted as Dubai's cosmopolitanism—that is, the ways spectacular developments brought in a larger influx of people from various backgrounds and places who have helped define the character of new Dubai and influenced the city's self-branding and development trajectory.

The nature of Dubai's superdiversity, and whether this diversity is the same as cosmopolitanism, is a source of widespread contestation. For some, the superdiversity Dubai exhibits, which was forged through and is visible in its spectacular development, is a characteristic that points to Dubai's supposed inauthenticity and superficiality. According to this logic, the "local" culture (whether this is understood as Emiratis and Emirati culture or also the cultures of long-term residents) has been razed to give way to "foreign" people and influences, including tourists. For others, it is not that they consider diversity itself "inauthentic" but that they consider Dubai to be too segregated and exclusionary to be a site of "real" cosmopolitanism, a quality that cities like London or New York are usually seen to possess. In such understandings, citizens (as minorities whose culture is not dominant) are assumed to be alienated, and residents excluded since they cannot be citizens (or if they are highly privileged, are segregated in their own bubbles). However, centering the perspectives and experiences of inhabitants illuminates a more complex story about how they engage with diversity and attendant ideals and discourses of cosmopolitanism that have accompanied the city's spectacular development. As I show in this chapter, binaries between belonging/exclusion, foreign/local, and diverse/segregated that structure some discussions of cosmopolitanism (or its lack) in Dubai do not adequately capture some realities of Dubai's spectacular spaces as they are experienced by my interviewees. Focusing not only on the ways inhabitants of spectacle interact with those from other places and cultures but also on the discourse around diversity highlights the ways they seek to shape how cosmopolitanism as a set of ideals and practices is expressed in Dubai. Figure 12 is a great visual example of inhabitants adapting to a spectacle that is foreign, or even too Western, for their tastes.

This chapter thus begins by problematizing some of the ways that cosmopolitanism has been understood in the context of Dubai, particularly in relation to discourses on "real" versus "fake" cosmopolitanism. The next section then demonstrates that for a more nuanced analysis of cosmopolitanism and segregation in Dubai, there is a need to explore the *various* forms of cosmopolitanism that take place in the city, which can vary along dynamic spatial and temporal axes as new forms of diversity take shape. The rest of the chapter explores how inhabitants navigate these cosmopolitanisms and adapt to (or reject) them in various ways. Adaptive agents, I show, do not necessarily feel fully alienated, nor fully supportive, of a

Figure 12. Adapting to the "cosmopolitan" spectacle.

cosmopolitanism created in part through spectacular development. They adapt themselves to the cosmopolitanisms that exist in their urban environs, while also working to define and exert their own preferred forms of cosmopolitanism, some of which represent new formulations of this ideal crafted in response to local circumstances. In the last section, I analyze how middle-class inhabitants of Dubai's preferred forms of cosmopolitanism impact how they relate to the older and lower-income parts of the city, shedding light on cosmopolitanism's operations as a reifier of class hierarchies not only in Dubai but also in middle-class and elite circles globally.

BEYOND "FAKE" VERSUS "REAL" COSMOPOLITANISM

While Dubai presents itself as a diverse, cosmopolitan city, it is certain forms of diversity that officials promote.[3] For instance, in global events such as the Dubai Art Fair, "authorities project a selective, discretionary representation of diversity."[4] Dubai's official cosmopolitanism is classed, often privileges Westerners, and does not allow for citizenship (or permanent residency status) for non-Emiratis, minus a few exceptions.[5] This form of cosmopolitanism is globally apparent rather than specific to Dubai; however, the authenticity of Dubai's cosmopolitanism attracts wide critique because of perceptions that true cosmopolitanism cannot exist due to the degree of segregation there. An example from this narrative is Bayat's depiction of Dubai:

> The cosmopolitan Dubai turns out *to be no more* than a "city-state" of relatively gated communities" marked by sharp communal and spatial boundaries, with labor camps (of south Asian migrants) and the segregated milieu of parochial jet-setters, or the "cosmopolitan" ghettos of the western elite expatriates who remain bounded within the physical safety and cultural purity of their own reclusive collectives.[6]

Similarly, the Bahraini academic Omar AlShehabi describes the newly built major developments in Gulf cities as such:

> Their most important feature is the emergence of the phenomenon of "closed society" or what can be called "the city within the city." Where a society is created out of separate "cantons," in which each group lives in complete isolation from the rest of the parties, is not linked to each other by any national, cultural or political affiliation, and its overarching goal is nothing but economic growth.[7]

In such accounts, Dubai is implicitly depicted as a place of fake diversity because inhabitants do not engage with difference as they are all depicted as living in segregated enclaves, working in parallel to advance a neoliberal agenda.

Indeed, multiple forms of segregation do exist in Dubai. Many of the city's low-income residents live in specific parts of the city that cater to them, often in old Dubai rather than the spectacular new Dubai. The most prevalent reference to segregation in the city often refers to "bachelors" from abroad who cannot sponsor their families, many of whom live in male-dominated, low-income neighborhoods.[8] However, lines are not clear cut: old Dubai is diverse economically and culturally in certain ways, as middle-class South Asian inhabitants live there with their families alongside single men and women who cannot afford to sponsor their families. Meanwhile, "glitzy new Dubai" caters to wealthier residents. Although, again, there is a type of diversity, as these residents include Emiratis, Arabs, South Asians, East Asians, and Westerners from places such as Europe, North America, and Australia.

Aside from classed segregation, there are also other forms of segregation that are often used to understand Dubai: for instance, the citizen/noncitizen binary. The fact that it is almost impossible for noncitizens to be naturalized can support the idea of Dubai as not a "real" cosmopolitan city. However, it is also important to note the untypical demographic reality in which those who do have citizenship in Dubai, Emiratis, make up a fairly small minority of the total population, meaning that the vast majority of people residing long term in the city are not Emirati.

These patterns of segregation mentioned above, ranging from class to citizenship, are indeed very real, and they create regimes of hierarchy and exclusion. Yet to use the rubric of exceptional segregation to categorize Dubai's cosmopolitanism as "fake" in comparison to other globalized cities is problematic because it can overexceptionalize the city's patterns of segregation while blinding us to intercultural interactions that may take place more frequently or deeply in the city. In cities in the West, for instance, intense residential segregation can also exist, with richer areas more culturally homogenous than they are in Dubai. There, there are also many who have a legal status and rights to permanency this status entails but who experience marginalization and exclusion in other ways.

Moreover, as scholars have shown, cosmopolitanism, not just in the Gulf but internationally, often manifests as a "classed phenomenon, as it is bound up with notions of knowledge, cultural capital and education: being worldly, being able to navigate between and within different cultures, requires confidence, skill and money."[9] Yet, values normally associated with cosmopolitanism, such as diversity and familiarity with different cultures, exist in low-income communities too.[10] Some scholars, for instance, have noted this about old Dubai, which they describe as possessing an Indian Ocean cosmopolitanism.[11] Elsheshtawy, likewise, says that in lower-income neighborhoods a "form of cosmopolitanism is asserted ... that goes against the official cheery version of 'happy existence' but it is one that occurs from below, initiated and sustained by the marginalized and

Figure 13. Jumeirah Beach Residence.

excluded—a cosmopolitanism-from-below."[12] Highlighting the forms of cosmopolitanism that take place in the city's low-income spaces is a much-needed task, especially as these places are neglected in the official narratives and mainstream representations of cosmopolitanism in Dubai. Yet, working-class areas in Dubai can get fetishized as the only ones possessing real cosmopolitanism, an argument that can overidealize poverty or undertheorize the ways cosmopolitanism exists in new Dubai.

Ultimately, to focus on determining whether Dubai's cosmopolitanism is "real" or "fake" can detract from broader understandings of how this discourse and ideal can itself be used to create separations and hierarchies between different groups of people while inherently valuing those with more resources over those who lack such resources. It can also fail to acknowledge the porosity of some of the boundaries that separate groups within Dubai's landscape, including the ones between old Dubai and new Dubai's spectacular spaces. In figures 13 and 14, for instance, we see parts

Figure 14. Jumeirah Beach Residence.

of new Dubai that some of my interlocutors (and the academic discourse) associate with Westerners, such as Jumeirah Beach Residence (JBR), are used by different people—some of whom may be middle class and elites and some of whom may not be.

What I propose here, then, is to expand our understanding of cosmopolitanism in Dubai, not only beyond depictions of it as a segregated space but also beyond a binary of fake/authentic cosmopolitanism that fails to challenge the broader discourse of authenticity of which it is a part and that works to overexceptionalize Dubai.

PARALLEL AND INTERSECTING COSMOPOLITANISMS IN NEW DUBAI

Raisa, a twenty-two-year-old Emirati woman, was standing with her husband and friends in the valet area of a popular five-star hotel in Jumeirah. It was 11:00 p.m. and they were waiting for their cars after having had dinner at one of the hotel's restaurants. The hotel was frequented by both Emiratis and wealthy residents and tourists, but today—at least in the valet area—it was different. Raisa noticed they were surrounded by Westerners dressed in their evening wear, while she and her friends felt out of place in their 'abayas and kandoras. Raisa said it was the first time she had felt odd in her own country.

Raisa and her husband, Abdulla, were no strangers to socializing in spaces where they encountered people of different nationalities. Their favorite restaurants were at Dubai International Financial Center (DIFC), where a minority of Emiratis and a much larger group of Westerners, Arabs, South Asians, and other upper-middle-classes went to socialize, dine, and/or drink at upscale places such as Zuma or BOCA. The restaurants in posh hotels and DIFC differed from the ones found in shopping malls or on the streets because they served alcohol, had a larger Western clientele, and were significantly more exclusive. Many of these restaurants became similar to lounges in the evening, playing the loud music one might find at a bar or nightclub. Because DIFC is known for its nightlife, some women also go there in evening wear, as they would to the hotel in Jumeirah where Raisa found them. In these spaces, Raisa, her husband,

and her friends may have been minorities, as Emiratis usually are, but they were still there.[13] Raisa felt comfortable there.

Places like DIFC may be considered cosmopolitan enclaves wherein practices of consumption allow their users to engage with limited forms of difference—what one might refer to as an economically homogenous form of cosmopolitanism.[14] This is a good example of the type of cosmopolitanism that takes place in these upscale parts of the city: one can find people of different ethnicities and nationalities but other forms of difference are excluded—in particular, low-income residents and those without certain forms of cultural capital. An upper-middle-class Emirati, an Indian, and a European might cross paths at a restaurant in DIFC, and they may be friends. On the other hand, a low-income taxi driver, for instance, will rarely be part of *this* cosmopolitan bubble.[15]

While Raisa and Abdulla have the cultural capital that allows them to feel at home in these upscale restaurants and hotels, even *they* may sometimes feel excluded when the cosmopolitanism that takes place there becomes too white or Western. In the context of Dubai, it is not inevitably the group often regarded as the most privileged (Emiratis) that is doing the "tolerating of otherness" in places like DIFC, or in the valet area where Raisa felt uncomfortable. Instead, as Yuval-Davis has argued, the politics of belonging—and therefore the carving of who belongs and who does not—is inflected by temporal and spatial variables and operates intersectionally.[16]

At times, white and/or Western forms of cosmopolitanism dominate in certain settings in Dubai. The privileging of Western cosmopolitanism in spectacular spaces is part of what makes some otherwise privileged urbanites uncomfortable in some parts of new Dubai, even as the exclusivity of these spaces also makes them inaccessible to low-income and some middle-class inhabitants. But what makes the cosmopolitanism be perceived as Western or not? This varies among people and contextually. For example, Raisa did not normally feel uncomfortable in the hotel, but she did on a specific day when she saw that she and her friends stood out among a sea of people dressed very differently from them. For many of my interlocutors, a place being too Western could refer to the dominance of certain ethnic and national backgrounds, and especially of white people. But it could also be associated with certain social norms that they connected with the West, such as "revealing" clothing for women (miniskirts, very low-cut tops or tube tops, etc.); public displays of affection; at times, alcohol consumption, and so on, with some of these denoting Westernness more than others for different people I interviewed. How residents feel around this type of Westerncentric cosmopolitanism that is common in elite spaces of the spectacular city depends on a range of factors, including their familiarity with it, but it not infrequently produces feelings of discomfort when spaces are seen as "too Western."

Another type of cosmopolitanism that exists in Dubai might be referred to as a "mixed cosmopolitanism." Adnan, a Lebanese in his thirties who grew up in the UAE, describes a cosmopolitan "mix" of people who he grew up with and which he believes represents the culture of Dubai:

> When I go to Lebanon . . . I just want to leave, I can't relate. . . . *Khalas*, I grew up differently. . . . My culture, it's a mix of Lebanese, and Emirati, and Palestinian and even Indian, and everything, all of it is mixed together [*killo mkharbat bi'alb ba'du*], you know what I mean? And I think that's the unique culture of Dubai. Not necessarily the Emirati culture of Dubai, but the culture of Dubai of the majority of people who have been here for a long time. . . . The only Lebanese friend I have is the one with me from school. When we sit with people who grew up in Lebanon and came here to work, I feel as if I'm sitting with someone from a culture I don't know about.

Whether coincidentally or not, he only mentions non-Western countries when discussing the influences he has been around. This does not mean the absence of Western influences, as many of those who went to schools or universities in this "mixed" environment, as Adnan and Raisa did, speak English with their friends and can be comfortable in "Western" and elite cosmopolitan settings—although many (or most) of their close friends are non-Western. This type of environment is one some participants in my research described as a "mix of East and West."

Encounters, as well as expressions of personal identification, with this type of "mixed" type of cosmopolitanism are common among middle-class people who grew up in Dubai, both citizens and noncitizens. This type of cosmopolitanism is rarely addressed in the academic discourse, however, which either focuses on Dubai as a segregated space catering to elites and Westerners, or on cosmopolitanisms in working-class neighborhoods.[17]

The "mixed environment" that Adnan refers to, and which is familiar to him, is an experience shared by many in his peer group, especially those who went to school in the UAE. As Adnan noted, this mixed environment may not represent the "Emirati environments" of Dubai (although in some cases Emiratis also grow up in such environments), but they do represent many others living like him. In reality, this was not too different from the experiences of some younger Emiratis, who also grew up in a similar "mixed" environment as Adnan, but who found certain parts of the UAE to be "too Emirati." These individuals, therefore, were accustomed to a certain kind of cosmopolitanism based on mixedness; notably, this cosmopolitanism did not make them feel at home everywhere, and certainly not in places that they felt were too homogeneous.

Some of my other interlocutors, however, were able to feel some sense of home both in the mixed cultural environments of Dubai *and* in their home countries, which might also be understood in relationship to cosmopolitanism. Those who spent whole summers in their country of citizenship sometimes had familiarity and comfort in both places. For some Emiratis who grew up in "mixed" environments, similar parallels emerge. For instance, when I asked Bayan, an Emirati woman in her early thirties, about her trip to Kuwait, one of the things she commented on was the high ratio of Kuwaitis to non-Kuwaitis. On one hand, she viewed this positively, saying that it was nice to go out and see so many citizens, a contrast to many places in Dubai. Yet when I asked her to compare her experiences in both cities, Bayan said that she couldn't imagine living in a place where there were so many Emiratis. Bayan went to an Emirati-only university for her undergraduate degree and was not necessarily uncomfortable in such settings but found herself to be more at ease in leisure spaces where there were many non-Emiratis, and where she therefore felt less watched. While some citizens prefer going to some places where they can see other Emiratis, others may more often opt for spaces characterized by a cosmopolitanism of mixing people from different national backgrounds to which they have become accustomed through certain schools, universities, or the workplace. Meanwhile, several of my Emirati interlocutors generally felt comfortable in both "very Emirati" and "cosmopolitan environments," similar to some noncitizens who felt comfortable both in their country of citizenship and in the UAE's "mixed" environment.

To be sure, not all of Dubai's middle-class inhabitants in my study grew up in such "mixed" environments. Adnan said that people "can live in ten different ways in Dubai," and perhaps what makes Dubai home to some is the ability to remain within their own communities rather than "mixing." What this points to is that the city allows various forms of cosmopolitanism that emerge from specific class-, nationality-, and ethnicity-based clusters or enclaves to exist. While these clusters or enclaves can be regarded negatively as examples of segregation, they have positive implications for some inhabitants who feel they make Dubai a tenable place to live for international residents. This too, I argue, can be seen as an iteration of cosmopolitanism.

For instance, many Indians in Dubai preferred living there over moving to Western countries because they felt no pressure to integrate and give up their own identity.[18] Vora's study of Indians in Dubai shows that some chose Dubai because, among other reasons, they knew they did not have to integrate with Emirati society there, something they felt they more or less had to do if they immigrated to the West.[19] In some ways, Dubai provides them with some freedom to maintain their cultural practices, including exercising more "traditional" ideas about morality, in a way that they may be unable to do in other states. However, this freedom is based on the absence of a track to citizenship and permanent residency (with a few exceptions for a handpicked elite) and is what allows them to *not* integrate as they would be expected to in the West. This reflects a certain trade-off for them, as Vora describes, as they are seen as temporary and therefore their integration is deemed unnecessary.

The experiences of non-Western residents in Dubai are different from Western residents of Dubai, the latter who also do not feel they have to integrate in Dubai—or elsewhere. Geopolitical power dynamics mean that non-Western immigrants are often expected to assimilate to Western societies if they immigrate there, while Westerners are less likely to behave as "immigrants" (but rather as "expats") in many of the places they immigrate to. Westerners may therefore feel more entitled to *not* integrate, not only in Dubai but elsewhere as well. Not integrating with Emirati society, therefore, can have entirely different contexts and meanings, as well as consequences, for different groups, yet not having to integrate to Emirati norms can be conducive to certain manifestations of cosmopolitanism for residents of Dubai who move there from elsewhere.

Ultimately, many of the people I spoke to grew up being exposed to different forms of cosmopolitanisms, making them feel more at ease in settings where they are around people of different national backgrounds. But some of them also recognized the difference between the diversity of newcomers and the diversity of various groups who had been living in the UAE for a long time. For instance, one older Indian man who came to Dubai as a young man described the arrival of many Chinese to Dubai negatively, depicting them as untrustworthy. While some of these attitudes may well be xenophobic, they often also indicate how older (including noncitizen) inhabitants of the city regard newcomers. The city was cosmopolitan before Dubai became the global and spectacular city it is known as today. Yet my interlocutors viewed that cosmopolitanism differently from the newer forms of diversity in the city, which they more often associate with foreignness.

Fatima, an Indian Muslim woman in her twenties, was born and raised in Dubai, and lived in the same house throughout her life in the city. The neighborhood she lived in was at some point dominated by Emiratis, but many left and rented out their villas. Fatima seemed to have good relationships with her older neighbors but told me how some of the newcomers lacked an understanding of acceptable customs and norms. She gave the example of an unpleasant situation that transpired with their European neighbors: Fatima's family had parked their car in front of their new European neighbor's house. Instead of asking Fatima's family to remove their car, their neighbors called the police to report this incident, which Fatima was understandably upset about. This example captures how some newcomers do not engage with the dominant social codes that others have built in these spaces. While many Emiratis may use this very example to demonstrate how residents (in general) are not aware of local customs, long-term residents use it to differentiate themselves from short-term residents. Fatima's European neighbors moving in indicated an unwelcome shift in social codes not only because of their background but also because they were newcomers who did not understand the appropriate community behaviors (or did not care about them). My non-Emirati interlocutors therefore sometimes shared similar attitudes toward the city's cosmopolitanism, and similar experiences to "outsiders" that some of my Emirati interlocutors did.

In sum, the cosmopolitanisms that upper-middle-class inhabitants experience in Dubai can be multinational, multiracial, and multireligious, but different groups and classes are not included on equal footing in popular understandings of cosmopolitanism. This is reflected in the ways they discussed Dubai's diversity. Many of them cited diversity as their reason for loving the city. They explained how Dubai's multiculturalism made them aware of difference and helped them become more open to varied ways of thinking. Similar to them, I always considered myself to have grown up in a highly diverse environment: my university in Dubai had Emiratis, Arabs, Iranians, Indians, Pakistanis, Russians, Kazakhs, and a variety of other nationalities. But even when I had friends of different socioeconomic backgrounds, this diversity was still limited to people who *could* afford university and work in middle-class jobs after graduation. I raise this here not to imply that Dubai's diversity is "superficial," as some academics have presented it, but to point out the classed dimensions of discourses of cosmopolitanism that emerge from the city.

ADAPTIVE COSMOPOLITAN SUBJECTIVITIES

How do middle- and upper-middle-class Dubai citizens and noncitizens relate to the various dimensions of cosmopolitanism in Dubai, a cosmopolitanism created in part through neoliberal and spectacular development? As adaptive agents, most experienced ambivalent feelings toward Dubai's spectacular diversity and the kinds of cosmopolitanisms that have accompanied the city's development. In response, residents actively engage with the diversity and shifting norms wrought by Dubai's spectacular development by forging adaptive cosmopolitan subjectivities that center their own cultural perspectives and personal agendas. In doing so, they sometimes express critiques of Dubai's official cosmopolitanism or the attitudes and practices of other groups, especially tourists and newcomers. At other times, they utilize cosmopolitan ideals and geographies to enable new social and cultural practices for themselves.

Raisa, an Emirati woman in her twenties, discussed Dubai's shifting social and physical geography:

I have people, for example my aunt, she says sometimes, "Don't take me near the Palm and Marina [areas of new Dubai often associated with Westerners], I want to see the old soul of Dubai." . . . But for me, I love [the new places]. If I go to Marina, I won't wear my 'abaya and my *sheila* because I feel I'm not in Dubai anymore. It's not that I don't feel comfortable enough [to wear it], but you *genuinely* don't feel you're in Dubai. . . . Sometimes you feel sad, as in, where are we [Emiratis]? But then again, we're 900,000 out of 10 million [in the UAE]. . . . So this is expected, it's not necessarily a bad thing . . . but [when] you go to places and you don't see any [Emiratis] *at all*, that's where you feel, where am I? . . . Sometimes, from time to time, I feel it's nice. Other times . . . it feels odd.

At first glance, Raisa and her husband appear to fit the characteristic of "flexible citizens," which Kanna describes as Emiratis who "engage in an active, often creative alignment of Emirati and neoliberal values."[20] Raisa and Abdullah both worked in multinational organizations and spoke positively about the "year of tolerance," which the UAE declared in 2019, expressing a belief in Dubai as a place inclusive and tolerant of all. While Kanna argues that flexible citizens are cosmopolitan and endorse neoliberal ideas, he explains that they also embrace some "traditional" aspects of their Emirati identity to varying degrees. Kanna also depicts citizens with "neoorthodox" tendencies, those who are critical of the city's rapid development and the influx of foreigners, like Raisa's aunt appears in this vignette. However, he finds that flexible citizens generally reject neoorthodox voices, regarding them as "stifling and rigid." Kanna contends that a neoorthodox criticism, such as of the demographic imbalance, also represents veiled criticism of Dubai's developmental model. Although Kanna provides some nuances for our understanding of flexible citizens who also have some reservations about the city's development trajectory, we nevertheless get an understanding of these people as generally enthusiastic supporters of the state project, while those with neoorthodox tendencies appear to be antagonists. However, in my analysis, all these individuals are adaptive agents with varying levels of ambivalence to the top-down development project, rather than supporters/antagonists.

Aside from the fact that Abdulla himself had "neoorthodox" tendencies and voiced nostalgia for an older way of life, most people I interviewed similarly had a complex relationship to the different dimensions of cosmopolitanism in new Dubai. Mizna, a middle-aged Emirati woman, argued that Dubai's developments were being built for Westerners and foreigners while citizens were being sidelined and alienated in their own land. However, Mizna also enjoyed taking the metro (which is not often used by Emiratis) instead of her car to go to Western-dominated areas in the city, saying that she thoroughly enjoyed these places because she felt like she wasn't in Dubai anymore. A similar sentiment was shared by other middle-aged Emirati women regarding Western-dominated spaces. While they heavily criticized women in skimpy outfits or the presence of alcohol, they also expressed their enjoyment of going to these very places as they considered them to be "higher class" and because it made them feel that "they're in Europe." In that sense, they are adaptive agents with varying degrees of ambivalence who accommodate themselves in various ways to the city's different cosmopolitan and exclusionary dimensions. They were not necessarily always cheerleaders for Dubai's changes and cosmopolitanism (they were not always "flexible citizens") nor did they feel totally alienated by them, but rather they felt included and excluded, supportive and critical, of the city's cosmopolitanism in complex ways. They experienced ambivalent forms of belonging as they adapted to (rather than resisted) the city's changes and its cosmopolitanism. That adaptation is a form of agency in itself that gets elided in discourses that favor resistance as the most meaningful way for residents to engage with top-down development.

My discussions with others reflected these layered and complex relationships with the globalized city. When I asked Muna, an Emirati researcher in her thirties, about how she and the women she knew felt about going to the beach, her answer illuminated attitudes toward modesty and women's dress that made it difficult to entertain common categorizations (of Emiratis and non-Emiratis):

> I think because there are options that are ladies-only, like for example Wild Wadi Ladies' night and Dubai Ladies' Club [private beaches]—if they [Emirati women] really care about modesty, they would go to these places. There are some people, they don't care about modesty but they care about reputation, so for them, they would hide under the cloak of anonymity and they would go to places that are more Western-oriented and where they won't see anyone they know, and yes, of course, some of them wear bikinis

and some of them wear slightly more conservative [swimsuits]. . . . But by the way, the Ladies' Club nowadays, it's not really so private anymore; there are so many projects around it that directly look over it, so I think most of the people now who go there, honestly, they're not so bothered with no one seeing them, they just don't want to be around men. It's just a more conservative option. There are so many jet skis and there are so many boats nearby that people can really see your figure and what you're wearing from a distance. But I see a lot of Emiratis there, and a lot of Arabs there [wearing swimsuits], and also a lot of people who . . . prefer staying in their *hijab* and long clothes.

The variety of preferences that Muna recounts demonstrates that these women experience the city's waterfront developments in a variety of ways. Those who choose not to wear swimsuits at Dubai Ladies' Club because of the lack of privacy and those who cannot afford to go to private beach clubs, for instance, may find that the city does not cater to them as much as it does to Western forms of cosmopolitanism. Would they be those individuals with, if we use Kanna's analysis, higher neoorthodox tendencies? The answer is not clear. The quote above exemplifies the complexity of my interlocutors' attitudes toward the city's urban spaces, even among individuals who may otherwise be considered cosmopolitan, flexible citizens or more "traditional" individuals with neoorthodox tendencies. In doing so, it allows us to see inhabitants' subjectivities beyond a triptych of oppressed/resistors/supporters of Dubai's developmental model.

In general, however, being in a place that they perceived as "too Western" was often uncomfortable for some Emiratis and non-Western inhabitants. Raisa's experience of feeling out of place was shared by many of my other Emirati interlocutors. Muna gave a similar example about the public beach. Speaking about how she felt seeing women in bathing suits, she said: "Sometimes I get a little bit shocked when I see butts, and stuff like that, in front of me, like when people are wearing very small swimsuits." However, she clarified that it was not necessarily their swimsuits that made her uncomfortable but rather seeing them in contradistinction with her wearing her *'abaya*: "I feel uncomfortable when I'm wearing my *'abaya* around all of these people that are super, super naked."

Other Emiratis I spoke to recounted similar experiences of their discomfort in a place where they felt they stood out while wearing the national dress. A middle-aged Emirati man I spoke to, for example, recounted tourists taking photos of him at a luxury development as he and his friends were the only ones wearing a national dress there. Visually, the national dress can cement the difference between citizens and noncitizens.[21] Because of its visibility, non-Emiratis clearly notice who is Emirati or not, and vice versa, leading Emiratis to potentially feel out of place or marginalized in some contexts in new Dubai while they can be very comfortable in cosmopolitan spaces in other circumstances. For example, most of them feel at ease with the cosmopolitanism in places like Dubai Mall, which includes a mix of Arabs, South Asians, East Asians, Westerners, and Emiratis.

Dubai's inhabitants make many iterative decisions about how to respond to shifting cultural and social norms. The public beach provides a good example of this, demonstrating my interviewees' ambivalent forms of belonging, exclusion, and adaptation to emerging markers of Dubai's globalized cosmopolitanism. The majority of Emiratis in my study use the public beach as a space for leisure—but not for swimming. I realized it was not always this way: Maysoon, an Emirati friend, surprised me by saying that her female relatives used to go to the beach and enter the sea in their clothes (the *jellabiya*, essentially a long dress), something they would not do today when most of the women surrounding them were dressed in swimsuits. I myself had never experienced swimming at the public beach, nor did I remember seeing women from my social circles doing so. Maysoon's comment made me realize that there was something I had missed out on. Like her, I felt a bit frustrated that this experience was lost for me. Non-Emiratis also recalled changes over time here. Shireena, a Filipina Pakistani woman, similarly mentioned the transformations that she felt took place in the public beach:

> I remember the wave of Russians that came through, that changed Dubai overnight. . . . I remember I was fifteen, we went to the beach. It's now La Mer, before it was just an open beach [laughing]. . . . And you know, back then, like, we didn't go to the beach in swimming costumes, right? Like, we would wear, like, tights, a shirt or whatever, you know. I mean, I make fun of these people now [laughing] . . . I don't make fun of them. . . . It's just, it's funny, but this was us back then. . . . I remember, you know, the waves of Russians coming in, and they'd be in the shower, and they'd be topless taking a shower.[22]

Shireena's memory shows how new forms of diversity in the city can be experienced as forms of "Westernization" of local public space.[23] The beach scene that Shireena describes *prior* to the influx of Russians and/or Westerners was still cosmopolitan. There were not only Emiratis there, but other non-Westerners such as Shireena and her friends, who were South Asian and Arab. While these individuals did not wear the same types of dress as Emiratis did, they did share the similarity of dressing more modestly. Maysoon said that the women in her family went to the beach and swam with their clothes on, which did not seem out of place among other (non-Emirati) women entering the water also fully clothed. As a larger number of Westerners came to Dubai, the type of cosmopolitanism in that place changed, and with it the social norms of that place. Like many other Emirati women, the women in Maysoon's family now felt strange swimming in their clothes, a feeling that spans the citizen/noncitizen binary.

Some women, like Shireena, appear to have with time altered their own dress codes to adjust to the city's continually globalizing social scene. Their changes reflect a form of adaptation or drastic shift in social norms that *some* inhabitants engage in. Others may continue to go to the beach and enjoy swimming there in modest dress. But for many Emiratis, these options are not socially acceptable, and their use of the public beach is often limited to walking or exercising there (but not swimming). Adaptation in the form of participating in new norms is therefore not always feasible for all inhabitants, nor is it desired even if feasible. Yet people find different ways to form relationships with their city. Because some of them felt they stood out wearing the 'abaya on the beach (in addition to it being less convenient to exercise in), they sometimes went there wearing hoodies. "Even when the weather is hot . . . [the hoodie] is like the negotiated outfit that's not a 'abaya but not unconservative, so you'd see a lot of teenagers and young women . . . maybe 20s and 30s, wearing hoodies even if the weather is hot because it gives them more mobility," Muna said. Wearing hoodies can therefore be understood as a form of adaptation to the different social norms of a place. What this indicates is that the changing population dynamics in the city also lead to changing social norms among inhabitants, even those that appear minuscule: Emirati women, as well as potentially some women from more conservative backgrounds who used to go swimming in their clothes, stopped feeling comfortable doing so as the demographics and dynamics of the beach changed. Meanwhile, it became more socially acceptable for young Emirati women to wear something *other* than the national (or traditional) dress at the beach, a practice that may be otherwise be considered taboo in other spaces or other times.

Muna contrasted the walking path on the beach to the walking path in Khawaneej, the latter being a place where many Emiratis live and where women rarely wear a hoodie even when engaging in the same activities they would on the beach. Wearing a hoodie to feel less out of place, however, is not necessarily something they are "pressured" to do to fit in. Many simply find that the hoodie is the "appropriate" thing to wear at the beach, just as getting dressed up and wearing the 'abaya* is the "appropriate" form of dress for the mall. Meanwhile, many women still do go to the beach and walk there wearing the 'abaya*—this is more common especially with the opening of upscale food trucks on the beach, some of which are very popular with Emiratis.

For many, such patterns of negotiation are ongoing. Abdulla shared many similarities with his wife in his relationship to the city. Unlike his wife, however, he was more socially conservative, noting that Raisa's family members were more liberal than his. He said, for instance, that she spent time with her male cousins without wearing the *sheila*, while he and his own cousins were segregated by gender and sat in different rooms when they gathered as a family on Fridays. Abdulla worked at a multinational corporation and was surrounded by different nationalities at school and at work. He also enjoyed some of the same spaces in the city that Raisa did, such as DIFC. Perhaps more than her, however, he had several negative experiences in the city that made him feel as if he was no longer in Dubai. A recent event he recalled was when he and Raisa went to Arabian Ranches, a mixed-use development where many Westerners live. They were invited for a Christmas party and were the only Emiratis—even the only Arabs—there. Abdulla found Arabian Ranches to be very white and therefore more alienating than places like DIFC. Abdulla is relatively adaptable to the changing city, experiencing both belonging *and* exclusion within it. In overwhelmingly Western spaces, he felt somewhat excluded. What becomes clear in these examples is that many feel discomfort in places that are dominated by a *certain* group and their social norms (whether this group is Westerners, South Asians, or another group that they feel is different from them). This indicates that it is also the cultural *homogeneity* of a space when it is not their own group (e.g., its Westernness or its South Asianness rather than its cosmopolitanism) that makes them feel out of place.

Although some of the Westerners that Abdulla and Raisa met at Arabian Ranches had been in the UAE for a long time, Abdulla could tell they stuck to their own bubble. Some of them gushed that he and Raisa were the first Emiratis they had conversed with. When I asked him if he liked going to such places, Abdulla said that what he enjoyed doing was introducing his culture to people who did not know about it. He believed it was his responsibility as a good citizen to do so, to establish good relationships with residents and to challenge their misconceptions about Emiratis. Many Emiratis who grew up and worked in Dubai's multicultural environment felt similar to Abdulla, particularly because they encountered the stereotypes some residents had of them on a more regular basis.

By taking on this responsibility to change people's stereotypes about Emiratis, however, people like Abdulla may feel pressured to compromise their preferences sometimes, to an extent. The people he met at the Christmas party, for instance, wanted to take photos with him and Raisa. This was not something he was fully comfortable doing, as many Emiratis (and *khaleejis*) do not consider it appropriate to have their photos shared by strangers. Women especially are expected to be private about their photos, and a large number of them do not share pictures showing their faces on their private Instagram accounts, even when it is only their friends who can access them. Despite his slight misgivings, however, Abdulla agreed to take photos with them so that he could show them that he, as an Emirati, was open to them. His response represents how he feels pressured by the types of cosmopolitanism that he encounters to act in certain ways so as to be seen as a "reasonable" (i.e., an "open-minded," cosmopolitan) Emirati.

Abdulla had been in other uncomfortable settings from a young age. He attended a British school in Dubai at which, for many years, he was the only Emirati student. He said that he felt somewhat alienated there and that he found people he met at university (abroad) and in his workplace (in Dubai) much more accommodating and interested in his culture than his schoolmates had been. He reflected that they may have been too young for such openness and added that their lifestyles and attitudes also made it difficult for him to develop close friendships with them. "They would go out for drinks and such and I couldn't go," he said.

Abdulla recalled a time when he invited them for dinner with him at Chili's, and when the bill came, tried to pay. This was an ordinary thing for him, as inviting friends for a meal and then fighting over the bill is the culturally appropriate behavior in the environment that he grew up in. His British friends were surprised, however, and kept asking him why he has "so much money." Basic cultural norms that Abdulla grew up with were deemed strange or alien when Abdulla practiced them in that environment, with his friends assuming that because he was from the UAE, he had more money. "My dad told me not to spend time with them anymore," he said. These interactions again highlight that it was the dominance of British social norms (or more accurately, the *lack* of cosmopolitanism) that made him feel excluded. Abdulla was not necessarily always critical of Dubai's cosmopolitanism and its effects on local social norms. Rather, he felt ambivalent, being supportive and subtly critical at different times. He attempted to adapt himself to the city's cosmopolitanism as it was expressed by diverse residents, experiencing various forms of inclusion and exclusion, as well as a sense of personal responsibility for mediating difference in some spaces.

That inhabitants adapt themselves ambivalently yet actively to cosmopolitanisms on display in the spectacular city as a result of its developmental trajectory moves us away from narratives that depict them as simply estranged from the spectacular city, as helplessly watching the spectacle unfold, or as resisting it. It shows us inhabitants going on with their daily lives and adapting their different needs to the options available to them, highlighting that agency can be understood not just as resistance but also as adaptation to spectacles of diversity that they negotiate in tandem with their own ideas about what constitutes cosmopolitan values and practices.

LOCALIZING COSMOPOLITANISM

Middle-class inhabitants also recall various ways that cosmopolitan spaces built to cater in large part to Westerners and nonresidents can become integrated with more localized ideas about what cosmopolitan does or should mean. Most adaptive agents therefore experience an ambivalent form of belonging to the city's changing urban and demographic landscape, and to the new forms of diversity that appear there. They create a sense of belonging through adapting to the city's changes and the changing social norms. Some attempt to fully change themselves to fit a place, while others may adapt themselves to some parts of it, and in doing so experience varying levels of inclusion and exclusion (an ambivalent belonging). Through inhabiting spectacle, they also adapt the city to themselves at times. For instance, places that they have an ambivalent belonging to and that they feel are "too Western" may at times change and become more "Arab" or Emirati." Some of these "Western" places even become spaces where Emiratis go to see and be seen by the Emirati community. Abdulla, who spoke about feeling out of place in spaces in the city where he did not see any Emiratis also avoided certain places where too many Emiratis congregated:

> I avoid some places like Naseem [hotel] and certain times in Dubai Mall because there is so much gossip. When I first got engaged and I went with Raisa to a restaurant, people messaged my mom and told her, "We saw Abdulla with a girl," and they sent her my photo. There's so much gossip, and I don't like it, and I don't like to go to these places. And I tell Raisa not to go because people will gossip, but she doesn't care.

Perhaps what is most interesting here is that Abdulla and Raisa were seen together in one of the restaurants dominated by Westerners and cosmopolitan elites (similar to those at DIFC), which indicates that these venues have become part of some Emiratis' lives and started reproducing some of the same features of other Emirati-dominated spaces. This highlights that not only do inhabitants adapt themselves to the city and its various spaces and forms of cosmopolitanisms, but the city is also sometimes shaped by these inhabitants. In the above case, a place that was considered too Western became a place where certain forms of Emirati socializing habits were being re-created.

Similarly, Muna recalled a time when she became aware of these changing social dynamics: "I remember the first time I was [in Caramel lounge] with my sister, I saw the bar, that it was exposed, and that there were a lot of drinks in the area, and I was telling Sumaya [her sister], "Oh, is it 'ady, [normal]? Like, [Emiratis] are ok with it now?" Muna expected Emiratis not to go to places where alcohol was so visibly displayed. Many Emiratis prefer not to go to these places, and even some of those who go may still be critical of the exhibition of alcohol and women dressing in revealing outfits (particularly parents, for instance, who may be dragged there by younger family members). This was even more so the case when these types of establishments were still new. With time, however, things changed. "There were all sorts of people including Emiratis wearing *'abaya* and *sheila*" [at Caramel]. And I think with Zuma and Petite Maison, and Caramel, they become 'it spots' and somehow that makes it okay for anyone to go there, like it's not *'aib* [shameful] anymore for some people because it's an 'it spot,'" Muna said. She saw not only younger Emiratis in these establishments but families as well, although the latter tended not to go to the lounges like Caramel but rather to the upscale restaurants in hotels: "It's not just couples or a group of girls or a group of guys [who go there]. It's like a whole family with an older dad and traditional-looking mom going there with their children," she said.[24] As opposed to other places such as Marina where some Emiratis go to avoid being seen by other members of the Emirati community, places like Caramel or Zuma that were once associated with Westerners or cosmopolitan elites become ones where some Emiratis also go to see and be seen: they are not spaces to hide but rather to display oneself to other Emiratis. They come to have different meanings among citizens over time. These places also become sites for the negotiation of social norms related to ideas of cosmopolitanism (albeit among a smaller group), as can be seen by Muna's discussion.

The fact that some Emirati women, including those wearing the *sheila* and *'abaya*, go to lounges with exposed bars and loud music is something of a more recent development. In her book about women in Abu-Dhabi, Bristol-Rhys said that the spaces catering to Westerners and tourists like hotel restaurants were not acceptable spaces for Emirati women.[25] Perhaps this is reflective of the attitudes from a decade ago, as well as possibly a reflection of different attitudes and behaviors in different emirates. To be sure, these spaces are certainly not enjoyed by or even attended by all Emiratis. Some women may face repercussions from their families for going there, and there are Emiratis who cannot afford them. Others may not face the above-mentioned restrictions but nonetheless feel uncomfortable in such places. However, because these are neither bars nor nightclubs (although some of them may have similar atmospheres in the evening with loud music and dim lighting), they are regarded as more respectable. While Emiratis who attend nightclubs or bars normally attempt to keep this socializing practice private, attending restaurants like the one Muna described is not generally something Emiratis are secretive about. Many of them post photos of these places on Instagram and Snapchat, indicating that these are places they want to be seen in or associated with. They are no longer taboo for some segments of Emirati society but rather spaces in which to display social distinction—for example, a certain form of cosmopolitanism. This is not to say that many people, including those who go to these restaurants and lounges, do not complain that the city is too "Westernized." Rather, it demonstrates that these places become embedded with new or different meanings over time and that inhabitants play important roles in influencing the roles they hold in society.

Many of my interviewees also selectively choose when and how to engage with demographically diverse spaces in relationship to which cosmopolitan values they are looking to encounter, and this can include seeking out Westerner-dominated spaces to avoid surveillance or finding other kinds of belonging. For instance, consider Raisa again:

Depending on my mood, sometimes I get this feeling that I really don't want to go to Dubai Mall because I will see everyone [Emiratis]. I always comment on my sister because she says, "Ewww, I don't want to go there, it's all locals [Emiratis]," and I say, "Why, then what are *you*?" . . . But I get what she means, you want to escape. . . . I think I've never been to [Galleria Mall] in my life without saying hello to people [Emiratis]. And it's fine we don't mind it. But there are days where I'm not in the mood. . . . Because when I go there, I need to make sure I'm dressed up, I need to make sure that I look presentable. Other times, I'm not in the mood. I remember once going to Marina in a hoodie and sneakers, and I'm enjoying myself. That's something I wouldn't be able to do here [City Walk]. . . . I remember I went ziplining once. . . . You know the Dubai Mall zipline . . . it ends in Dubai Mall. I was wearing my *sheila* but I was wearing jeans [without the *'abaya*]. So when I got out at Dubai Mall, I was *really* uncomfortable. I mean, personally I'm fine with it, I'm not even *mit-hajba* [does not fully cover her hair but wears a loose hair cover]. . . . But me being in Dubai Mall and not dressed, I thought a lot, maybe someone will see me, maybe someone will say something, maybe, you know. So, I've done also the same zipline in Marina [an area associated with Westerners]. Here is when I was in my hoodie and I don't care and I was comfortable, and I enjoyed that ten times more. . . . [But] in Dubai Mall, we immediately got our *'abayas*.

Raisa, who earlier commented about feeling excluded in a Western-dominated space in Dubai, expressed her preference for them at other times when she did not want to encounter members of her community. The comment her sister made about not wanting to go somewhere because "it's all locals" is not uncommon. Like Raisa, some of the other Emiratis I spoke to wanted to go to spaces associated with Westerners, such as the Marina area, to get a sense of anonymity and comfort. This was a way for them to go out without feeling the need to dress up or behave in a certain way, particularly as they felt scrutinized in Emirati-dominated spaces. For those who did not want to wear the *sheila* and *'abaya* but knew they would be criticized either (or both) by family or society, going to Western-dominated spaces, which feature some different norms of attire and comportment, allowed them to do so without fear of being caught or chastised. It permitted them a sense of freedom because in those places you "don't feel like you're in Dubai anymore" and therefore are unburdened by the social norms you have to abide by elsewhere in the city. Similarly, Emirati women who do not feel comfortable smoking *sheesha* in Emirati-dominated spaces, for instance, choose to go to certain hotels or to areas of the city where a large number of the people there are Westerners and/or tourists.

Even if they do not intend to engage in transgressive acts, these spaces provide not only Emiratis but also other women (and men) from more conservative backgrounds and with extended family networks in Dubai the opportunity to get away from environments they find suffocating, even if it is just a place where they know they will not bump into people and have to constantly say hello. Wilson argues that one of the attractions of the modern city, for women as much as anyone, is the possibility for people to lose themselves in the crowd.[26] While modern cities can be solitary, they provide anonymity for inhabitants.[27] In that sense, some of the Western-dominated areas of Dubai (but not the city as a whole) offer anonymity for my interlocutors. On top of that, being in either cosmopolitan or Western parts of new Dubai meant being part of a different world: they enjoyed the feeling of having an international experience in their own city, they liked the anonymity and not having to say hello to everyone, and many of them felt that these places were high end or "high class."

In the previous chapter, I wrote about Emiratis who avoid Emirati-dominated spaces because they felt that they were centered on *khaga* (showing off) and appearances. In places like the Marina, however, many felt that no one knew who they were, and no one cared either. Indeed, the possibility of going somewhere and not constantly bumping into people they know and stopping to say hello was reason enough for some of them to enjoy these developments. Bayan talked about how anxious she was when she passed a coffee shop where all she "could see was white" (men wearing the national dress), saying that she probably would have not felt this way if these men were of different nationalities. This is a very common reaction among Emirati women to spaces dominated specifically by Emirati men, and therefore this is an axis along which they can judge the cosmopolitanism of different spaces at different times in the spectacular city.

Parallels are found in other settings. Nonheterosexual Bangladeshi British men in London frequent some of the coffee shops dominated by white cosmopolites in their gentrifying neighborhood in Spitalfields, as the atmosphere there lends itself to providing "cover for men from less privileged social groups" from their own communities.[28] Meanwhile, young British Muslim women from South Asian backgrounds wanted to move to the middle-class and white suburbs of the city because it allowed them to "occupy social, cultural, and spatial position on the margins of the community, which affords some freedom from perceived social strictures and conventions."[29] These British South Asian men and women, however, are also marginalized in majority white spaces. White middle-class cosmopolites have gentrified the areas that the Bangladeshi diaspora live in, while the British South Asian women faced racism from neighbors. In fact, racism was one reason that many of these individuals preferred to remain in their own communities. Yet, some of them found pleasures outside of it at times for various reasons. Exclusionary spaces, therefore, may be used in various ways for different purposes, and people may create ambivalent forms of belonging within them. In that sense, cosmopolitan environments, even exclusionary ones that are experienced as Western, can provide useful escape from some of the constraints found in more homogenous environments, or even in "mixed" ones.

Non-Emiratis also discussed sometimes preferring spaces where one is not likely to encounter members from one's own community. Hana and Lubna, two Arab (non-Emirati) women in their twenties, felt uncomfortable in "very Arab" middle-class spaces of the city, which they felt were "low class"—not in terms of economic capital but perhaps cultural capital. Hana said:

> There is an area in Garhoud with *sheesha* cafes and restaurants, like lined up next to each other. And . . . the restaurants, they might be good, the food might be good. But I don't like the kinds of people who go there. . . . It's like a lower-class downtown. . . . It's too Arab. It's very, very Arab. . . . It's like you're sitting in an *ahwa, ahwat Shabab* [coffeehouse, men's coffeehouse]. . . . It's just uncomfortable for us. . . . Maybe because we're too boujie. . . . Like the one time I went there with my friends, a guy actually got up and talked to one of my friends. And that's not normal, like if I'm sitting here right now and a guy will come here and talk to me right now. Impossible. No guy will come and talk to me right now. But over there . . . [t]hey'll talk about us, they'll 100 percent talk about us. Because we look like we don't belong . . . . The only thing I can say is that it's a lower class. Like, not in a "I'm wealthy and they're not way." Because we could all probably be the same. [W]hen I go to Egypt, I want to go to places like that. Because it's fun there. . . . It's an experience there. But here . . . I feel because we're all [Arabs], they feel they have the right to judge [here]. So they would think, oh my God, what is she wearing? Or why is she sitting with a guy? Or what is she doing here at 12:00 a.m., as girls.

While Hana and Lubna found the "lower-class" *sheeshas* to be "very Arab," the types of spaces in the city that they enjoyed had a more cosmopolitan clientele, including many Westerners. The Arab versus Western distinction became more apparent when Hana later said that she went to a nice place but immediately felt uncomfortable when an Arab singer started performing. When I asked how she would feel about a Western musician playing the guitar at the place we were in, she laughed and said that she would love it. Hana and Lubna were not the only interlocutors who expressed an idea of Western cultural capital (or traits they associated with Western culture) as desirable, more sophisticated and "higher class." Their attitudes point to (cultural) class aspirations that connect them to what may be understood as more modern (or global cosmopolitan) lifestyles.

This is not to deny that some practical considerations made Hana and Lubna uncomfortable in Garhoud. Being in a "very Arab" place made them feel more watched, similar to the way some of my Emirati interlocutors felt in Emirati-dominated spaces. They expected to be judged there or to be on the receiving end of unwanted attention. They associated places with a more cosmopolitan—which for them also equated to more Western—culture with more appropriate social interactions, where people did not gossip or observe one another, where men were unlikely to approach them, and where privacy was respected. This has parallels to what Krishnan points out in India, where some middle-class women use the term "local" to refer to someone they deem "backward" and "uneducated," even if they are referring to individuals who are with them in college instead of people who are of an entirely different class.[30] While stereotypes certainly play a role here, Hana's and Lubna's attitudes about these places were also based on negative experiences they had in certain "very Arab" settings. Therefore, Hana and Lubna did not choose their spaces of socializing based *only* on (cultural) class aspirations, but also on practical considerations as women who faced various forms of gendered discomfort in certain spaces of the city.

Nevertheless, in my research I found that spaces with a dominant Western presence were often considered more prestigious and classier, which influences local assessments of their cosmopolitanness as compared to places associated with non-Western, non-Emirati populations. This perception was even shared by middle-aged Emirati and *khaleeji* women who criticized Westerners for "immorality." They linked certain behavior, such as order and organization, with Westerners, while viewing chaos and disorder as Arab traits. Sara, a Jordanian woman in her forties, noted something similar: she described the culture shock her own children went through when they went to a summer camp in Jordan. Although Sara said she placed them in the poshest summer camp there, she said her children did not fit in and begged her not to leave them there:

My kids are very polite and respectful. And they share and they wait for their turn. But the kids in Jordan, they're not like that. We joke about it, like our kids are more soft. In Jordan, no one waits for the queue. . . . The strongest person is the one who's going to get to play on the slide. In Jordan, in Lebanon . . . they still do that because that's a cultural thing. And our schools in Dubai, [they're] dominated by Westerners. And they have that culture of having queues and stuff. So our kids have learned from them. My kids are used to, you know, when they get into cars, they have to buckle up. This is very important for them. In Jordan no one does that. So for them, you know, they missed that order. . . . They see chaos in Jordan. Once, I put my daughter in the bus in Jordan. It was a bigger culture shock as well. Because there they sing some sort of songs that bring her a shock. For example, you know, she was trying to understand but because her Arabic is not very good, but it was something about Chinese, Japanese. You know, they were making fun of types of Asians . . . and also, you know, like very low-class kind of songs. So she didn't know how to fit in and make friends. So she stood out. And my daughter is not tough, you know. So she didn't survive that rough life.

An Arab researcher living in the Gulf pointed out to me that it was common for Levantine and Egyptian Arabs to condescendingly refer to Arabs raised in the Gulf as "too soft"—too spoiled, naïve, or unable to navigate the world competently. On the other hand, being "too rough," as Sara implies the children in Jordan are, comes with negative implications of being disorganized or *hamaji* (barbaric). When Sara says that her daughters are "too soft" for Jordan, she is referring to a sort of cultural capital they exude: Waiting for queues or being "organized" was associated with a more "Western" (Sara referred to her daughters' classmates as European) cultural norms, which Arabs in mainly Arab environments are depicted to not have. This highlights how the middle- and upper-middle-class cosmopolitanism that Sara's children inhabit, which has been shaped by norms in Dubai, might be closed off to *other* forms of difference. However, we can clearly see that in the Jordanian summer camp as well, racial difference is stigmatized and results in overtly racist tropes and practices (some of which Sara refers to as low class).

By raising the point that Sara's environment is *also* exclusive I do not mean to discount the experiences Sara's children had in Jordan nor claim that her children's alienation there is exaggerated or unwarranted. Indeed, Sara's children were likely discriminated against for being "too spoiled," which led them to have negative experiences in the camp. Rather, I raise this point about cultural capital to highlight the breadth and limitations of cosmopolitanism in new Dubai. Having grown up among people of a variety of backgrounds, Sara's children had access to certain forms of diversity but not others, such as that at the summer camp in Jordan. This is not to romanticize the diversity (or lack thereof) in the Jordanian school nor to dismiss the overtly racist and culturally inappropriate language that exists within it, which Sara finds troubling (although this does not mean racism—and certainly classism—does not exist in the ethnically diverse schools Sara's children attended).

In these examples above, we find that the sought-after forms of cultural capital were often linked to "Westerners" (even things such as standing in queues). Yet people like Sara chose to stay in Dubai, rather than go to the West, because they felt it provided them a balance of "East and West" (somewhat similar to the mixed environment Adnan described). Dubai is an aspirational place that allows them to be part of a more "modern" society (which they depict as lacking in their own countries) while still being in an Arab milieu. The "best of East and West" has become a cliched way for policymakers and advertising strategists to refer to the city. Reiterated often among my interlocutors, a topic I discuss in the next chapter, this formulation of cosmopolitanism influences how people experience the spectacular city as a global crossroads.

Indeed, Sara told me that the diverse cultural and social opportunities she finds in Dubai are major reasons why she loves the city. She appreciated exposing herself and her children to arts and culture without needing to travel to do so, something she felt she would need to do if she lived in another Arab country. Taking her children to see plays such as *Mary Poppins* (originally British) or the Cirque du Soleil (originally French Canadian) were the types of activities that they had access to throughout the year. She compared her children to their cousins in Jordan, saying that the opportunities in Dubai have allowed her children to be more "cultured." For instance, Sara's daughter participated in the Special Olympics Games for athletes with disabilities (originally founded in the US) in Abu Dhabi. She argued that had her daughter not been in the UAE attending the school that she did, she would not have had that opportunity. "Now my kids can go to the world and say, 'I sang in the Special Olympics of the UAE and there were like, 30 million people watching it on TV.' They met with this football player and . . . she stood and she asked him a question. She's eight years old. And I have . . . her on camera asking him a question," she said.

Many of the events Sara extols are free: annual art week events; the Emirates Literature Festival, which included both free and paid events; and Dubai Design Week, where her children attended a workshop about electricity taught through Play-Doh. "The things for free, sorry, no Arab country gives as much free things for people as Dubai does," she said. Referring to City Walk and Meeras, a Dubai-based holding company, she said that she liked them because "they're creating ways for us to walk," including in the summer. "There's so much free stuff when you walk . . . I mean they bring shows, and sometimes arts, and sometimes they do 3D arts in the street."

Sara also enjoyed taking her children to the mixed-use JBR, where some shows take place on the streets, ranging from children's entertainment to free concerts. "JBR has always arts on the floor. . . . In Marina Walk [a mixed-use development] a few days ago . . . there was a concert. My girls, they went crazy. They sat, and there was one singer after another, and they were standing and listening, they were mesmerized." As someone with these class aspirations, Sara felt positive about Dubai's cultural scene. It provided her children with a set of experiences, as well as cultural capital, that she felt they would otherwise not have access to in other Arab countries and therefore offered them the opportunity for further upward mobility both economically and culturally. Although they are free, these events and opportunities are not necessarily accessible to many segments of society, however. Sara's positive associations with opportunities Dubai provides for cosmopolitanism therefore highlight *cultural* class aspirations for a global cosmopolitan lifestyle—ones that are available to a certain segment of society who themselves have access to certain forms of cultural capital already.

Some of the areas in Dubai that my interlocutors consider "too Western" are experienced as exclusive at times but inclusive at other times. For some inhabitants, these places offer them a cosmopolitan/"modern" experience within their own city. For one, they liked the anonymity they provided, ranging from allowing them to behave in ways they would not in other parts of the city, to simply not having to constantly stop and say hello. For some of them, the city also gave them an "international" experience and opportunities while still remaining in their city or in an Arab milieu, fulfilling their aspirations of living what they perceived as a more cosmopolitan lifestyle.

CRITIQUING THE ERASURE OF LOCAL NORMS

My interlocutors adapted themselves to the changing city, and at times adapted the city to them in the process, but that did not mean that they did not feel marginalized or excluded from it. For my Emirati interlocutors, this was particularly evident in the ways they felt some people were making no effort to integrate themselves to an Arab and Muslim country. Among both my Emirati and non-Emirati interlocutors, the individuals who were seen to be either not respecting the country's cultural norms or who were seen as the "newbies and wannabees" were often Westerners and/or white people (although there were many times criticism was directed at other inhabitants who were *not* white or Western).

Above, I noted that not being expected to integrate with the Emirati community (or even with other nationalities or groups) has different implications for different groups and can be less tenable for some than others. In the examples below that surround the topic of cultural norms, we find that many of the examples also focus on the experiences my interlocutors had with Western tourists and residents, and how it influenced their critiques of cosmopolitanism as a practice and ideal.

Abdulla spoke about his experience with cosmopolitanism in the city, saying that he wanted to meet others halfway in regard to their cultural background. "I can go in between, I can compromise, I can go to Zuma or a lounge or something [places that serve alcohol and play loud music], but not to a nightclub," he explained. While he feels marginalized in some settings, particularly in those where the forms of cosmopolitanism center on Western (or highly socially liberal) attitudes and behaviors, Abdulla is generally adaptable to the dynamics of the neoliberal city. He does not always feel that he fully and completely belongs everywhere in Dubai, yet he is not necessarily alienated by it. He enjoys the cosmopolitanism in his workplace, where he feels his colleagues are interested in learning about his culture and vice versa. Like Raisa, he views Dubai as a tolerant and multicultural city, something he is proud to be a part of. As opposed to Longva's depictions about Gulf citizens feeling alienated in their own countries, Abdullah is happy to engage in various forms of cosmopolitanism but feels uncomfortable when these cosmopolitanisms *entirely* center on *Western* (or socially liberal) behavior.

For my interlocutors like Abdulla, one of their concerns is to what extent their values were being afforded importance or relegated to the periphery. To what extent were they visible, heard, understood, and respected? These concerns can translate into how they experience the city. Do they feel they have a "right to the city" or that others' values and lifestyles are privileged over their own?

The public beach again provides a fitting example to understand how they navigate these tensions. Many Emiratis, both older and younger, argued that they did not have a problem seeing women in their bathing suits so long as they remained in the designated area of the beach. Beach regulations dictate that individuals cover their bodies if they are not directly on the beach (i.e., if they are not in the sea or on the sand). Crossing on to the walking and jogging pavement or going to the food trucks and cafés on the beach requires cover-ups. Most Emiratis, therefore, told me they were irritated when they saw others disregarding these rules, viewing this as flagrant disrespect for local laws and customs. Not only Emiratis but even other residents commented on women wearing see-through cover-ups in supermarkets or shopping malls during the summer. It was not entirely uncommon to hear some non-Emiratis saying things like: "Why is she dressed this way during Ramadan, it's so disrespectful." While some were angry that women were allowed to dress in skimpy outfits in general, it was particularly when they did not abide by dress codes for particular times and spaces that produced frustration. The distance between the beach and the walking and jogging path is short but obviously has significance for many citizens.

This difference in attitude toward what is appropriate directly at the beach as opposed to the beach's walking paths may stem from a variety of factors. One reason may be that some individuals do not feel comfortable criticizing forms of dress that are officially sanctioned (such as wearing bathing suits on the beach), leading them to focus their energies on denouncing misbehavior that they have legal grounds for critiquing. These concerns speak to a debate about who has a right to these places. Some of my interlocutors might feel that Western (or non-Emirati) indifference to moral codes, especially in places that have more Emiratis, is an encroachment on the rights of its inhabitants, highlighting rather overtly their lack of authority over space.[31] Yet even when Emiratis feel their voices are marginalized, "Westerners" do not necessarily have a say in regard to which laws get implemented. Ultimately, it is the government that sets the rules and paves the road for overwhelming changes. As Kanna argues, therefore, criticism of foreigners' behavior may be an indirect critique of the city's development path.[32] While this may very well be true for some of my interlocutors, I do however want to be careful not to overemphasize these "hidden meanings." Another reason for some Emiratis' frustrations is that disregard toward local laws implies open indifference toward both Emirati social norms and local laws. Some of my interlocutors view dress codes, such as those on the beach, as protecting Emirati (and Muslim) values while also granting people with different social norms certain rights. These regulations are seen to be tolerant and fair. By disregarding them, nonabiding individuals are viewed to be disrespecting not only local social norms but also the generosity of the Emirati law, which some see as usefully mediating different kinds of cosmopolitan values in a diverse space.

Muna, for instance, said she felt conflicted between the idea that women's bodies should not be policed and the feeling she had when she saw some women dressed in ways that blatantly disregard local laws and norms. She explained that she was not upset when she saw tourists dressed immodestly but felt angry when she believed they were residents (for example, if she found them at a supermarket). Tourists may be ignorant of local regulations or social norms, she said, but residents *knew* that this was not how they were supposed to behave—yet they *"really* don't care."

A similar dynamic can be seen in an example provided by Khuloud, an Emirati woman in her twenties. Khuloud did not hide the fact that she drank or went clubbing and was normally not concerned by the sight of women in miniskirts. On the other hand, she recounted seeing a Western woman in a tiny miniskirt and a see-through shirt at a residential mall complex near her house, which she found inappropriate. Khuloud said that her sister politely approached the woman to ask her to adhere to mall guidelines (malls have dress codes that are mostly not enforced), but the woman was dismissive. Khuloud became irritated and contacted the police to complain but was frustrated that they did not seem very interested either.

As I wrote about Khuloud's experiences in this chapter, I found it difficult to explain why someone who regularly socialized in "spaces built for Westerners" or dressed in ways other Emiratis would deem inappropriate was particularly incensed at the woman in the mall. After going back to her with further questions, Khuloud explained that the way this woman was dressed would have been fine in other parts of the city, such as at DIFC, where Khuloud also went to socialize. However, she felt that the woman was transgressing the social norms of a *specific* residential area dominated by Emirati and Arab families. The example Khuloud presents is similar to the one on the beach, where Emiratis accept women wearing bikinis on the beach but not on the adjacent jogging path, where they are supposed to dress more modestly.

My interlocutors like Khuloud were not angered necessarily because the city was "not Muslim enough" or because they worried about the loss of local values—although some of them were.[33] Rather, they may believe that certain types of cosmopolitanisms (and behaviors) should be confined to certain spaces and should not overlap or be considered interchangeable. Khuloud did not dress in miniskirts in her own neighborhood—one main reason being, of course, that she could only dress that way in places where she was more anonymous. But aside from these social and family restrictions, Khuloud also recognized that some forms of dress and certain behaviors would be inappropriate in different contexts and behaved with these considerations in mind. These calculations do not seem to factor into the decision-making of people like the woman she argued with at the mall. This lack of calculation indicates that some (often Westerners, but others as well) do not feel that they need to negotiate the social and cultural norms associated with different places in the city, but rather that they expect the city to cater to them in all its spaces and at all times. For my interlocutors, this highlights a lack of respect for local regulations and/or norms and highlights that Western (or "foreign") social norms are being privileged. It is not what they deem to be true cosmopolitanism but rather a neoimperialistic ethos of one-way nonadaptation.

The people I spoke with therefore saw and articulated context-based nuances of what constituted appropriate behavior in diversely populated spaces that Westerners did not consider, or at any rate did not respect. They saw Westerners as sometimes treating all of Dubai as entirely susceptible to Western norms at all times and in all contexts, in contrast to their own awareness of and attention to factors such as whether it was Ramadan, whether it was an Arab residential area, and the difference between the food truck area of the beach and the rest of the beach. That they wanted Westerners to respect these variations in context reveals an important element of how they conceptualized cosmopolitanism.

CONCLUSION

There are many dimensions to cosmopolitanism in new Dubai: there are new forms of cosmopolitanism taking place; there are cosmopolitanisms that are experienced as too Western by my interlocutors, and others that are experienced as more "mixed"; and there are enclaves and bubbles, as well as temporal dimensions, to take into consideration. Recognizing these dimensions allows us to move away from binaries of certain places as segregated/diverse, western/local, or as places of real/fake cosmopolitanism.

My interlocutors' experiences suggest that the classed nature of Dubai's cosmopolitanism renders it not superficial but, rather, limited in specific ways. Dubai's inhabitants find different bubbles of cosmopolitanism and experience some places as appropriately cosmopolitan during the daytime but too Western at night. This complexity belies popular binaries that designate some places as segregated and others as diverse, or some as simply Western and others local. My interlocutors experience an ambivalent sense of belonging in relation to many of these forms of cosmopolitanism and respond to them with various forms of adaptation. In particular, they speak of their experiences when a setting is dominated by what they see as "Western" behavioral norms—or "Westerners" themselves—in other words, when a so-called cosmopolitan space actually feels insufficiently cosmopolitan as they understand this concept. Sometimes, this domination leaves inhabitants, including Emiratis, marginalized in their own country, while at other times, they seek out such spaces to get away from their own community. As a result, they experience an ambivalent, layered, and intersectional belonging that leaves them feeling included at some times and excluded at others within Dubai's globalized development trajectory. At the same time, many inhabitants work to define cosmopolitanism in concert with their own local and personal values, which influence the ways they engage with and assess the cosmopolitanism in their globalized city.

4 An Appropriately Modern City

Salama was ready to go jogging in the park next to her house in Ajman, one of the UAE's seven emirates. She was dressed in a long-sleeved shirt and long pants, but no *sheila* or *'abaya*. Her mother, who was accompanying her, told Salama to keep her distance from her in case they bumped into anyone they knew—that way, she said jokingly, she could pretend she didn't know Salama. In contrast, Salama's mother didn't mind her daughter jogging in Dubai without covering her hair. Salama was less likely to bump into people from Ajman there, and even if she did, Salama and her mother felt that things were a bit different in Dubai. Salama's brothers also preferred their sister to go jogging in Dubai because they believed that men were less likely to look at or harass her there. The idea that certain social norms or attitudes are different in Dubai marked the attitudes of many of my interlocutors who came from other Gulf Cooperation Council (GCC) states, *khaleejis* or not, as well as Emiratis who lived in different emirates but visit Dubai, all of whom are the focus of this chapter. Some described Dubai as a place where they could lead more "normal" lives than they could live elsewhere. For them, Dubai is a place to pursue opportunities for mobility and modernity that do not necessitate rupture from the religious, social, and familial contexts of the Gulf.

This chapter thus explores how middle-class Gulf residents inhabit an aspect of Dubai's spectacular development—what they commonly describe as its modernity—by focusing on citizens and residents from other GCC states and from neighboring emirates who relocate to Dubai. For these individuals, the city's spectacular developments offer them what might be called an "appropriately modern" lifestyle.[1] It provides them a variety of daily social benefits that they associate with modernity and don't experience in their home countries, but without the racism, prejudice or sense of being different that they'd expect to encounter in the West. In coming to Dubai, they've chosen a context that binds them to family and place yet also offers a comparatively liberal social environment and a city bureaucracy that prioritizes order, efficiency, and responsiveness, benefits associated with modernity that, as upper-middle-class inhabitants, they experience in positive ways that may not apply similarly to less-privileged groups.

In the previous chapters, I demonstrated how middle-class residents of Dubai make meaning within spectacular elements and spaces that are otherwise commonly seen as evidence of the city's "inauthenticity." Dubai's *modernity* is similarly often disparaged as part of its "fakeness." The city is at times portrayed as too modern—hypermodern, in fact—due to aspects we have already been discussing, including its top-down development, architecture, and diversity. For critics, the city is not traditional enough, not Arab enough, not Middle Eastern enough. In some academic and journalistic accounts, this modernity is portrayed as not as "real" as Western modernity. Koch points out that it is a common trope to present the modernity of spectacular and illiberal cities such as Dubai or Astana as a façade, covering up a lack of modernity underneath.[2] As many scholars have shown, such discourses of modernity presume teleological accounts of development toward Western norms that are assumed to be more evolutionarily advanced.

This chapter is thus a more serious attempt to understand how the spectacular city's modernity is perceived and experienced by some of its neighbors, particularly those who aim to take advantage of this quality by locating themselves there. In particular, my research identifies and explores specific attributes of Dubai that those who come from elsewhere in the Gulf most value and find adaptable to the everyday lives they want to lead. Foremost among these are what they perceive as Dubai's optimal "mix of East and West"; its orderliness and effective regulations; and for women in particular, its status as a place where they can be relatively independent without being seen as having strayed too far from social norms common in their families or communities of origin. Although less explicitly named in my interviews, another aspect of modernity they value, my research suggests, is not having to face discrimination based on their race and religion, a freedom Dubai offers them that would not be the case in some other places they considered locating themselves.

Focusing on the experiences and relationships Dubai's neighbors have with and to spectacular development in Dubai is important, as they have been understudied in the literature. There has been ample discussion already about how new Dubai's developments cater to Western lifestyles and tastes.[3] There is good reason for this: many property buyers in Dubai are British, and Western tourists overall constitute almost 40 percent of those staying in hotels in Dubai.[4] Moreover, Western residents are structurally advantaged in Dubai (for instance, with higher salary packages and benefits compared with other nationalities).[5] Yet except for the British, Dubai's top real estate investors have typically been from non-Western countries, including India, Saudi Arabia, and the rest of the UAE.[6] Moreover, Dubai's largest tourist group by nationality is Indian, followed by Saudi, British, Omani, and Chinese tourists,[7] and many Kuwaitis, Bahrainis, and Qataris visit Dubai during holidays. On weekends, Dubai also receives visitors from the other emirates of the UAE. Thus far, there has been disproportionately less scholarship on the ways non-Westerners, particularly from the Arab world and especially the Gulf, engage Dubai's modernity and the ways the city's development relates to their desires and values.

Beyond my interlocutors from the Gulf, many middle-class and wealthy citizens and long-term residents of the UAE find in Dubai the ability to lead a convenient, enjoyable life that they feel is appropriately modern along various dimensions. In Dubai, they can be comfortably middle class, with all the consumer amenities and cultural capital this positionality allows, or upwardly mobile. They can live, work, and socialize in globalized milieus that reflect their own definitions of cosmopolitanism. For women who are *not* from Dubai, it is possible to lead lifestyles that include new possibilities such as living alone and doing activities that might be deemed inappropriate elsewhere, as Salama has shown. And in all these instances, locating oneself within, or relocating to, Dubai can be categorically different from going to other places in the world that might require those from the Gulf to be further minoritized or separated from people, institutions, and values they deem important. Many of my interviewees appreciated that Dubai was close enough to home to allow them to easily visit their families but far enough that they could direct their own daily lives away from family constraints and obligations. And because Dubai was a comparatively easy, safe place to carry out life's ordinary tasks for them—where they did not think they needed networks or influence to be able to complete these tasks—they felt generally respected as members of society. Overall, they experience Dubai as a place that allows them to have a "modern" lifestyle in key economic, consumer, behavioral, and bureaucratic dimensions while simultaneously inhabiting a certain set of ethical (and relatedly for some, also religious) practices that bind them to family and home.

In previous chapters, I have so far described adaptive agents as city inhabitants who are neither supporters nor antagonists to the state development project but who have ambivalent relationships to it and adapt to it in various ways. Similarly, many of those discussed in this chapter come to Dubai to live a life that allows them to distance themselves from *certain* social and familiar practices without being viewed as resistors of social norms by their family and society. *Their* form of adaptative agency means that they physically move from their own countries but do not rebel against all the social norms and values of Gulf society, some of which remain important to their definitions of what it means to live a modern life.

Because my interlocutors in this chapter chose either to move to Dubai or visit it constantly, this chapter reflects views that are quite favorable toward the emirate. But these positive views were not shared uniformly. For example, one Saudi interlocutor raised in London moved to Dubai because he was offered a very high-paying job but planned to return to London in the future. He found Dubai's environment more restrictive than London's and was less concerned with the "mix of East and West" that my other interlocutors sought. Meanwhile, a Western official in Ras Al Khaimah argued that Dubai is often too concerned with "Brand Dubai" to allow for the critical social discussions that take place among policymakers in Ras Al Khaimah. Similarly, a half-Emirati, half-Omani man living in Dubai, but originally from Ras Al Khaimah, argued that Emiratis in the northern emirate are more socially and politically aware than those in Dubai. He also said that his Omani family members found Emiratis to sometimes be arrogant, as they often boasted about the UAE being more "advanced" than Oman. This echoes what Suliman, a Palestinian man who grew up in Sharjah, said: he was getting tired of people from Dubai who "crap on Sharjah" and poke fun at it for being supposedly "less developed" than Dubai. Moreover, even for neighbors who do enjoy Dubai, the city's significance to them may change over time. For instance, some of my Saudi interlocutors who I interviewed in 2019 see more reason to return to Saudi Arabia now with the major changes that took place there. In that sense, the experiences of some of my (particularly Saudi) interlocutors here reflect a certain point in time.

Meanwhile, some participants in my research *from* Dubai (Emiratis and non-Emiratis) were sometimes not as impressed by Dubai's modernity as those who previously lived elsewhere in the Middle East (or in the West). For instance, some of them found that the city's preoccupation with smart governance made things overly complicated. Those who had their own businesses felt constantly inundated by bureaucracy, paperwork they had to get done, and constant requirements to pay fees, which they felt got more complex over time. Outside of bureaucracy, some of my interlocutors who studied abroad (often in the West) complained that Dubai was boring and did not have the same opportunities that life elsewhere provided them. They were unhappy to return to Dubai and often sought ways to travel on vacations. They missed different things. For some of them, it was the academic lectures and arts events that were plentiful in places like London or American student towns. Some of them found that places like London had more entertainment opportunities—more public spaces, such as parks, concerts, museums, neighborhoods to walk in—while Dubai was limited in its venues. Others argued that they could not meet like-minded people in Dubai and that everyone they knew was "superficial." I have explored many of these topics in previous chapters, and here we can further see ways in which inhabitants' relationships to Dubai's spectacular developments are not uniform, including the ways members of relatively privileged groups relate to different aspects of the city's modernity.

"A BALANCE OF EAST AND WEST": A CLICHÉD REALITY?

Zaleekha, a thirty-five-year-old Saudi woman, moved to the UAE when she was eighteen to continue her studies. Her main motivation, however, was to gain a degree of independence without moving too far away. At eighteen, Zaleekha wanted to break off her relationship with her fiancé but felt that her voice was not being heard at home. Her family often reminded her that she was too young to know any better in making life choices. Zaleekha wanted to move to a place where she "could express herself" while remaining in her comfort zone. She explained that Dubai was the right "balance of East and West."

"A balance of East and West," as we saw in the last chapter, has become a clichéd way for policymakers and advertising strategists to market Dubai to the outside world, but many of its non-Western residents choose the city because it gives them access to modern conveniences and some forms of social freedoms they associate with the West while accommodating Arab and Muslim cultural norms. This echoes the experiences of middle-class Indians who move to the Gulf because they find it more modern than their country but choose it over the West because they find it "appropriately" modern.[8] Zaleekha's story was repeated, in various forms, by many of my interlocutors who had chosen to move to Dubai from elsewhere in the Gulf. One of the reasons many of these interlocutors chose Dubai over other cities, particularly Western ones, was the opportunity to move away from family and social pressures while remaining close to home and in a familiar environment. This combination enabled them to live an appropriately modern lifestyle that accommodates Arab (or Muslim or South Asian) cultural life and family embeddedness.

Moving to Dubai can be understood as a balancing act wherein my interlocutors are neither resisting the values they grew up with nor feeling the need to center their own everyday lives around these same values. In that sense, they are adaptive agents who want to lead a more socially liberal lifestyle than at home without wholly rejecting the social norms they grew up with or being perceived as rebels who left their culture behind by immigrating to the West. For those who moved, their families and social circles at home perceived moving to Dubai differently—and more positively—than moving to the West. In fact, for their families as well, Dubai's spectacular developments connote a positive example of modernity and success—one which they are frequently happy for their children to be associated with. Moving to the West, on the other hand, connotes some degree of cutting ties with one's community, which pushes beyond the bounds of acceptability some of these families and communities have drawn.[9]

Many of my *khaleeji* interlocutors could find high-paid jobs in their own countries (although this would usually exclude Bahrain and Oman). Comparing the work she was invited to do in Dubai with her job in Europe, Hayat, a Saudi woman, said that when she came to Dubai, she was excited to be working on something that could have a positive impact in the Arab world. Hayat had received offers for high-ranking and high-paying jobs in Saudi Arabia, but she found the work environment as well as the lifestyle there unsuitable for the type of life she wanted to live, particularly as a Saudi woman married to a Tunisian. Therefore, for some *khaleejis*, Dubai's attraction may include career opportunities, but even when high-status options are not necessarily absent in their own countries, lifestyle and workplace environment can still override other factors. Hayat said:

> We felt like [Dubai's] a nice place because it's close to Tunisia, it's close to Saudi, but it's neither one of those. We're a mixed couple, I mean, if we lived in Saudi he would *yetbahdal* ... 100 percent *rah yetbahdal* [he will be treated badly]. . . . The way that he would get treated as a Tunisian, I think would not be positive. I think there would be a lot of bias against him being married to a citizen. Although I have a lot of friends who have mixed backgrounds [there] . . . . [B]ut there's other stuff . . . I can't control. . . . And the same thing, I didn't want to go to Tunisia. . . . And Dubai to me . . . is a place that seemed to like, offer very different kinds of spaces for people. So . . . if . . . you want to stick to your little expat-y thing and want to sit on the beach wearing a bikini, you can do that. But if you don't, and you want to have a different kind of lifestyle, you can, so we said we'd try it.

Hayat wanted a place where she and her husband could live a comfortable life within the Middle East, and she found it easier it to live with her non-*khaleeji* husband in Dubai than in either of their home countries. Other interlocutors from outside the Gulf shared similar stories. Khaled, a half-British, half-North African man, said his parents chose to move to Dubai because they viewed it as a place of in-betweens. Dima, who is half Arab and half Indian, said her parents had lived in a variety of different places, ranging from Sudan to Canada, but had decided to settle in the UAE: "My father was against living in Canada or the UK, because he's like, my kids will not learn Arabic and they won't know religion the right way," she explained.

Rami, a Jordanian man in his forties who grew up in Kuwait and has permanent residency in Australia, now lives in Dubai. His brothers have acquired American and Canadian citizenships, which guarantees them a safety net in case they lose their jobs or retire (and are therefore required to leave the UAE, although recent laws have changed to allow *wealthy* retirees to remain). While many non-Westerners in the UAE who have the opportunity to become citizens and find good jobs in the West leave, it is not uncommon to find the type of citizenship/residency arrangements that Rami and his brothers practice, whereby they acquire a Western passport and then return to the UAE. "For me, Dubai has been the perfect connection between West and East," he explained. Sometimes it was just the small, everyday things that mattered. He gave as an example the ease with which he could find a prayer room in Dubai's shopping malls, something he had struggled with in the US. In Dubai, many aspects of Rami's culture were normal rather than foreign or peripheral.

Like Rami, some of my interlocutors had acquired Western citizenship, which would seem to offer them more stability given that citizenship is restricted in the UAE and all noncitizens are at risk of having to leave at some point. Most Western countries also offer the stability of social security and free or subsidized healthcare and education. Yet their economically privileged status frees them from dependence on these social programs, and in Dubai they can lead more "normal" lives by *not* being ethnic minorities or immigrants while still being in a cosmopolitan city that caters to people like them. For example, Sara, an upper-middle-class Jordanian woman with young children, said that she and her husband had considered moving to Canada but couldn't bring themselves to complete the immigration paperwork because of the word "immigrant," which she said made them feel sorry for themselves. In the Gulf, where the term "immigrant" is not used (to emphasize that noncitizen residents are "temporary"), Sara felt more comfortable in her status as an upper-middle-class resident (or as someone like her would usually be termed in English, an "expat"). In Dubai, she and her husband had a more privileged status in the socioeconomic hierarchy than she thought they would have in in the West, where she worried they would be marred by what the "immigrant" label connotes. Dubai is a place where they can enjoy greater social freedom and fulfil their class aspirations for living a "modern" life without fearing that their non-Western identities would mark them as different.

Meanwhile, to my *khaleeji* interviewees, Dubai felt like a more stable home for a variety of reasons. Because of similarities in culture, language, food, and family dynamics, *khaleejis* could easily claim a sense of belonging in Dubai even if they had only recently moved there or were just visiting. Many also had Emirati family members due to *khaleeji* intermarriage. The city's legal structure also facilitated this sense of belonging: *khaleejis* weren't required to have a visa to enter Dubai, and they could rent and buy property as easily as an Emirati.[10] Compared with my non-*khaleeji* interlocutors, for whom the UAE was often a contested home, even those *khaleejis* who had lived in the UAE for only a few years found it easier to express a relatively uncontested belonging. For instance, Lamya, a Saudi woman in her late twenties, moved to Dubai after she married her Saudi husband who worked in the emirate. Lamya, like most of my interlocutors in this chapter, can be considered part of the cosmopolitan classes: she grew up in Riyadh, and studied and worked in Europe. She shared her experiences living abroad and contrasted them to living in Dubai:

> I travel every week for my projects, and I come back every Wednesday night. And like, my flight is full of foreign consultants. And, you know, everyone is running, like the minute we land . . . and everyone is queuing. . . . And I feel very privileged to be able to walk at a normal pace and then arrive at the GCC nationals' line. . . . That makes me feel like home. . . . The minute I get into Dubai, I am greeted by the same greetings that we use back home. . . . I talk the same language; I look the same. I mean, I lived in the UK for a long time, and I lived in Switzerland; I never in my life felt that sense of belonging away from home.

Lamya enjoyed an environment that was more socially liberal than in Saudi Arabia and fit in easily in new Dubai, where she was more privileged than she was in the West.

Some may describe people like Lamya as being Westernized. Relatedly, the global cosmopolitanism that she enjoys in Dubai is sometimes associated with middle-class whiteness.[11] Kathiravelu says that "although middle-class developments in Dubai house migrants of many different nationalities, this globally mobile elite class position homogenises . . . . Part of the unmarked nature of whiteness is that it is taken as normal . . . embed[ding] migrants in a space that is discursively and culturally white, but which passes as neutral."[12] While this perspective is insightful, it is also important to keep in mind how Lamya, like others, felt excluded in Western and white spaces in the West. She was discriminated against for being Arab when she lived abroad and contrasted her experiences there with the sense of home she felt in the UAE. Because Dubai is an Arab, Muslim, *khaleeji* space, it allows people like Lamya to feel a fuller sense of belonging than they do in Western cities. By virtue of their class status, Lamya and my other interlocutors are privileged members of society whether they are in the UAE or in the West. But because they are minorities in the West, they are less privileged there than in Dubai and so less able to experience a norm of living an everyday life unencumbered by feelings of unbelonging stemming from their minority status or the everyday forms of marginalization or discrimination this status can bring.

While my interviews have focused on citizens and residents of other GCC states who moved to Dubai, there are also *khaleeji* frequent tourists, as well as non-*khaleejis*, who come to Dubai often because it's a nearby place of appropriate and accessible modernity where they want to spend considerable time. One of my interlocutors noted that Saudis of different backgrounds feel comfortable coming to Dubai for vacations, although *living* there might be an entirely different experience for them if they are not middle class or elites. Houriya, a Saudi woman from a low-income community, said that Saudi "working-class people are the dominant majority visiting Dubai in comparison [to] Europe which is home to middle- or upper-class visitors." She explained that there were various reasons: there was no language barrier; the tickets were cheaper; it is easier to go and come back; Dubai has many festive venues that cater to *khaleejis*; and a lot of people who have unpaid car fines cannot travel outside the Gulf without paying them. Lamya argued that her cousin who works in real estate comes across *khaleejis* with different budgets and lodging preferences—ones who seek high-end lofts in downtown Dubai and others who stay in budget-friendly areas. Those who do not have a large disposable income

[are] here for the *furja* [leisure] and they don't really spend much [money] in Dubai. They drive for ten to fifteen hours from wherever they were.... They usually come in like, really big cars, and they have everything with them, like their plates and pots and coffee and tea.... So the only extra payment they have to do is the rent and like, the gas.... There is cheap rent and there are also really cheap hotels. So next to the area where I live in, Tecom, there are a lot of hotels that are like two- [and] three-star hotels, and you see a lot of Saudi cars parked outside.

A search on the Booking.com website in February 2019 (which can be generally considered a good season for tourism because of the weather) showed a double room in a three-star hotel in "old Dubai" went for as low as £32 on a weekend night. For around £50 or less, one could get a double room for a three- and even four-star hotel in more modest areas of new Dubai. While this is not cheap for a family, it is more affordable than a trip to Europe. However, as Saudi Arabia is now becoming a tourist destination of its own, this is likely changing.

When I asked Lamya about the Saudi tourists she encountered in Dubai, she said they came for a change of pace that wouldn't require them to "change who they are":

A lot of people want that change [travel] but don't want to go too far away, and they want to be comfortable in their own skin. So you have, for example, the *munaqabat* [women wearing *niqab*] and the *muhajabat* [wearing the hijab] and the ones wearing *'abaya 'al ras* [*'abaya* worn on the head, seen as more traditional or conservative]. They want to be who they are and not have to change who they are for the trips, and that's comforting. And the same thing for the men, in the *thoub* [*dishdasha/kandora*] so he doesn't have to change who he is for that trip.

Indeed, in figure 15, women wearing a *niqab* are seen enjoying leisure time at Jumeirah Beach Residence, an area often associated with Westerners. Based on the generalization that Saudi women often wear *'abayas* with sneakers, the women in the photograph appear to be Saudi (and based on my time there and hearing some of them speak, many of them are), highlighting Lamya's point that many come to Dubai to get a change that is at the same time comfortable and familiar in a city they can experience as not only "Western" but also as *khaleeji*.

Figure 15. Jumeirah Beach Residence.

Having said that, some visibly religious people do not always feel welcome in the city. Le Renard says that a few of her Muslim interviewees had
negative experiences in Dubai's job market. "A young man, for instance,
had not obtained a job after the last interview, which took place with the
CEO of the firm to which he applied. The latter believed that his short
beard and the fact that he did not drink alcohol made him unsuitable for

the job."[13] Nevertheless, the city is still seen as more welcoming for Muslims than many places in the West.

Ghada, a Bahraini woman in her late twenties living in Dubai, said that Dubai is a perfect combination of "liberal but not too much and open but not too open." She explained, "People will *not* be suspicious of a woman who took a trip to Dubai and say 'Ooh, she went to Dubai [*rahat Dubai*], what is she doing there?'" This highlights the place of Dubai in (at least some) Arab imaginations as a place that is appropriately modern for their children or family members to be in. In the West, Ghada said, only the socially liberal can find a place for themselves in the cities, but in Dubai both the *khaleeji* woman wearing a *niqab* and the *khaleeji* woman wearing a miniskirt could feel comfortable.

Other short-term residents and even "perpetual visitors" are also able to claim some aspects of belonging to Dubai using different labels such as Arab or Muslim. For instance, in her work on Kenyans who visit Dubai to import clothes and sell them in their own countries, Mangieri discusses connections these individuals make between their own identities to Dubai's.[14] Mangieri quotes one of her female interlocutors who went back and forth to Dubai for business, who said: "I am Kenyan, of course, but I feel almost at home in Dubai. As a Muslim, I can be here and feel at home and as a woman, even alone. It's not like Nairobi, or even Mombasa. . . . This business has given me opportunities."[15] For her, Dubai represents a geography of comfort and cosmopolitanism in the Global South. Similarly, Stephan-Emmrich argues that Tajik businessmen in Dubai "mobilize religion to claim belonging to Dubai as a "Muslim place."[16] While some of these Tajik men are working semi-illegally as street brokers and come to Dubai on tourist visas, they drew on the cosmopolitan aspects of their Muslim identity to "successfully integrate into the Iranian, Afghan, and Arab commercial networks that dominate Dubai's formal and informal business sectors."[17] Stephan-Emmrich quotes a Muslim Tajik who moved from Moscow to work in Dubai:

> Of course, Moscow is a better place [than Dubai] to earn good money. But you are not safe [in Moscow]. The streets are full of criminals and drunken guys. They attack you. . . . But I even didn't trust the police. They don't protect you but take your money! . . . I wanted to return home [from Russia to Tajikistan], but as a Gharmi you cannot live a good life. If you have a good business, they come and destroy everything. They even find you in Russia.

That's why I came to Dubai. I don't have rights here and cannot move up in my job. . . . But (here in Dubai) I am safe, autonomous (*ozod*), and I am respected as a Muslim. You know, *Dubai is a real Muslim place.*[18]

Many other examples point to Dubai having distinct meanings for a variety of non-Western groups. Moghadam shows that Dubai allows "Iranian migrants to permanently weave links with their past and present in Dubai, to stay in Iran while building their life in Dubai."[19] In an article about young Iranians in Dubai, Fattah said that many of them moved to the emirate because they considered it a "free" and safe country in the neighborhood.[20] "None of the other countries near Iran have this. You have everything that you have in Europe and America, but close to home," a young Iranian explained. "You have more freedom here to live as you want," one interviewee said. "Here you can interact with people from other countries. It is interesting for me."[21] This "mix of East and West" therefore provides some sort of "freedom" for a more socially liberal lifestyle that is neither transgressive nor disconnected from home. The freedoms being referred to here are not political freedoms but rather (relative) social freedoms, as well as economic freedom.

Laila reiterated this idea. A Jordanian woman in her early thirties, she grew up in Saudi Arabia. When I asked her about people she knew who had moved to Dubai from Saudi Arabia or Jordan, she said that many had moved there for the same reasons: "The [Westerners] come here to live the glitzy lifestyle; the Arab girls don't come for that." She explained that they came not only to get a degree of independence but also "because it's safe, somewhere Arab and closer to home, and they can build a career and also find someone." Laila, like many of my interlocutors, was attracted to the "glitzy" aspects of the city because she saw them as reflecting Dubai's modernity, which she wanted to be a part of. But being in a global city also had its practical benefits that allowed people like her to live a life that felt "normal" in terms of career opportunities, access to leisure pursuits in public spaces, and socializing opportunities. Laila appreciated the city's multinational nature, which she viewed as an example of modernity. To her, this modern element made her more anonymous among a sea of other outsiders than she would have been in another Arab country. Her everyday life and movements were less watched than they would be in Jordan or Saudi Arabia, but her Arab identity and cultural values were not foreign, nor did they mark her as a minority as they might in the West. It is these themes—the combination of Arab culture and cosmopolitanism, the sense of ease and order, and the sense of independence facilitated by anonymity—that constituted an appropriate modernity for middle-class people from outside Dubai who choose to travel or move to the spectacular city.

THE COMFORT OF ORDER AND REGULATIONS

Lamya, who is Saudi, represents how many find comfort in Dubai's order and regulations, which are widely perceived as another indicator of the city's modernity.

> I was driving to work every day and there was a huge hole [in] the street that could be hazardous .... So, I called RTA [Road and Transport Authority] and told them about it. They asked me to take a picture of it and send the exact location, and within three days the hole was fixed. And that's something that I find amazing, and it's not very easy to happen not in London nor in Riyadh.... You come across a lot of crazy drivers and I call the police to complain.... I feel that as a cit...—like, you know, as a citizen, I consider myself a citizen, and I feel obliged to let the system know when something's wrong.... And [the police] call you [back] ... about the ... plate number. And, usually within a day or within a few hours they tell you a fine has been registered for them.... One day I called the municipality because there was a lot of cats in our neighborhood, like an unbelievable number of cats ... and they sent someone to make sure that all these cats are vaccinated ... Whenever you complain about something, whenever you suggest something, I feel that it's more often than not taken into consideration ... and that's why I love being here ... and I feel ... a huge sense of belonging here.

Saudi Arabia has changed drastically over the past few years, but the last time I spoke to Lamya, she still planned to remain in Dubai. There were many reasons, she said, but among them were order, regulations, and the ease of using public and private services, which she felt catered to her needs and desires as a valued inhabitant of the city. The civic engagement that Lamya participates in (such as calling the RTA) allows her to feel that she has a voice or a stake in her city—a voice that is being heard, which makes her feel like a metaphorical citizen if not a literal one. Lamya's civic engagement here is not, according to many definitions, political, in that it does not primarily aim to change structural dimensions of power. This form of civic engagement adheres to the state's and the emirate's vision for order and efficiency: her calls to the RTA and police assist, rather than push against, the state's efforts. On this occasion, she appears to be a supporter of the (neoliberal) system, while at other times, she criticizes the status quo. Like many adaptive agents, she moves between varying levels of support and critique of the neoliberal city, inhabiting a subjectivity that enables her to live a life that is meaningful to her in the context of an illiberal state whose order and regulations she sees as markers of modernity.

As I noted in the introductory chapter, scholars have criticized the (liberal) assumption that everyone has an innate desire for freedom and seeks to assert their autonomy.[22] For my interlocutors, political freedom, even formal citizenship, is not as important as safety, order, and regulations, aspects that make their everyday lives easier and that, to them, are important aspects of a modern society. As privileged inhabitants, they benefit from these forms of control in many ways that poorer residents cannot; furthermore, they make meanings through their participation in these forms of order. However depoliticized some may consider it to be, Lamya engages in a form of civic participation that makes her feel empowered as a (metaphorical) citizen, which she defines in contrast to its limited formal meaning as someone who belongs, carries out responsibilities to the community, and benefits from its rules and regulations.

This kind of civic engagement can have positive results. It can also be malignant and promote exclusions. For instance, "undesirable" people (often the working poor) are directly or indirectly barred from places where inhabitants, officials, or property and business owners deem them to be disrupting the order of a place, and developers purposely build spaces that exclude them to cater to the elite.[23] Likewise, some might argue that individuals like Lamya are able to enjoy benefitting from Dubai's forms of modernity and order because they appear to display the characteristics of the ideal citizen that the Emirati state aims to cultivate. According to Jones, the ideal Emirati citizen is a neoliberal one adapted to illiberal conditions: economically, socially, and culturally more conscious, active, and hard-working, but shunning political engagement.[24] However, Jones says that the results of social engineering have not worked as planned and have not produced these neoliberal subjects. Nevertheless, the forms of civic engagement that Lamya described oftentimes parallel the state's ideals rather than conflict with them, allowing her to experience these forms of order and regulation positively, as markers of a desirable modernity.

Lamya said it was the small things in Dubai that made a difference to her everyday life: When she was living in Geneva, "in the city of banks and bankers," she had to take a few hours off work to pay her rent at the post office. Meanwhile, she described everything as easier and automated in Dubai, ranging from being able to pay fines and tolls online on her phone, to having transportation that she felt was well-connected and easy to get around in. Like others who reiterated their appreciation for Dubai's order and regulations, this reflects both their practical considerations for convenience as well as their desire to be part of a society that effectively deploys civic management, personal finance, and transportation technologies that save people time and stress.

The Dubai government website states that e-government services were developed to "ease the lives of people and businesses interacting with the government and [to] contribute in establishing Dubai as a leading economic hub."[25] For some critics, the city's development of such infrastructures merely reflects the Dubai government's key interest in enabling certain kinds of "expatriate belonging" through various neoliberal strategies of development.[26] This critique does capture the ways in which residents in Dubai who refer to their positive experiences in dealing with bureaucracy are reacting to the emirate's efforts to provide good "customer service." For example, an American man living in Abu Dhabi said that Dubai conjures up ideal customer service for him: the buses, the metros, and other public services are easy to use, on time, and provide a good service experience.

While services that imagine users as customers can often make everyday life easier, smoother, and more efficient for middle-class and elite citizens and residents, the larger paradigm of neoliberal governance of which they are a part can make other systemic issues, such as labor conditions, take a back seat. This results in some of the well-known ills of the region, such as an absence of minimum wages, meagre living conditions, and the building of isolated labor camps at the edges of the city, which of course can and should also be seen as markers of Dubai's modernity. However, it is also the case that at times, some of these developments that are created to display Dubai as a modern place and ease the paths of middle-class and elite urban denizens turn out to be useful to lower-income and lower-middle-class inhabitants as well. The metro provides an important example. Although the metro only connects certain areas of the city (the suburban areas are not connected at all), Lamya argued that it was still convenient. "At least there's a metro," she said. Indeed, opened in 2009, Dubai's metro remained the only one in the Gulf until 2019, when Doha opened its own. In their work on public transportation in Kuwait, Al Awadhi and Martin argue that facilities "at bus stops and stations are generally poor, as is pedestrian access and associated road crossings."[27] Similarly, Sara finds walking in Dubai easier than in Lebanon and Jordan, where she lived previously: "The infrastructure [in Lebanon], you have to walk on the pavement, not on the sidewalk, because the infrastructure isn't good." Ranging from small conveniences such as paying parking fees online to more major issues such as public transportation, my interlocutors compared the order, regulations, convenience, and safety that they found in Dubai favorable to those in their own countries as well as to Western ones. As privileged individuals, they are likely to be the biggest beneficiaries of this order, but exceptions such as the metro case or not having to take off work to do minor banking or postal tasks can benefit wider populations.

Rami, a Jordanian man who was born and raised in Kuwait but moved to Dubai as an adult, made similar comments. Rami recognized I had a Kuwaiti background (a Kuwaiti mother) as soon as we met, and we spent much of the time talking about his experiences in both places. Rami's response was more detailed than the common comparisons usually made between the UAE and Kuwait, but it reiterated things I had heard before:

Before the [Iraqi] invasion, Kuwait was number one in everything. Unfortunately, since the past 28 years they didn't develop much. . . . Healthcare, schooling system . . . even if you're a businessman, the rules. The UAE is way, way ahead. . . . It's simple, straightforward, there are rules. In the UAE, if I want to do some process and an employee delays me, I am not scared to go and escalate this. In Kuwait, I'd be scared. . . . Because . . . the system there is not clear. [I] will not know if his boss will actually care or not. He will say *wafid* [a resident] complaining about a Kuwaiti. . . . In

Kuwait there are still simple things based on *wasta* [networking]. The UAE doesn't. Especially the easy stuff . . . your daily life, it's easy.

For example, I want to bring my parents to visit me. . . . Straightforward. . . . Bring your job contract, the rent contract, two photos and so on and you apply and then you get an SMS once it's approved. It's simple. . . . In Kuwait, you might go, and . . . someone might not be in the mood to work and doesn't help you. . . . It's not straightforward. . . . There is no pressure on government services to [work well].

I'll give you another example. The police, Dubai Police. They're everywhere, but they never interfere. In Kuwait, the policeman, I'm sorry . . . I'm not saying it's right or wrong . . . it's a culture at the end of the day. . . . In Kuwait he asks about the car, he asks about the license, he asks about the residency. He asks, "Who are you? What are you doing in the street? Why are you walking here?" *Khalas*, that's the culture. In Dubai, the traffic cop has a certain role. Anything related to traffic. He doesn't ask you, "Why are you sitting here? What is your ID?" He only deals with things related to traffic. There are other police who are specialized in security, maybe these will come and ask you "Why are you sitting here." . . . So you see the traffic police they are specialized, they are trained how to treat people, they are polite. Even when they give you a fine . . . they do it with a smile.

As I described in previous chapters, different people experience the city in various ways depending on their race, class, gender, and citizenship positionalities. As an Arab, Rami's experiences with the public service sector are likely to be more positive than a low-income, non-Arabic and non-English speaker. However, as an upper-middle-class Arab man, he experiences Kuwait and Dubai differently. These differences make his everyday life easier and more enjoyable in Dubai; they also make him feel that he has a voice capable of influencing municipal affairs (at the very least, to complain about a government employee who does not help him, which he feels he cannot do in Kuwait). While Kuwait has more formal political freedoms for Kuwaitis, these freedoms do not encompass non-Kuwaitis (who practice self-censorship in Kuwait as they similarly would in the UAE). For someone like Rami, both places are therefore politically illiberal, but Dubai provides him with the opportunities of living a more "modern" life, in part because of what he experiences as the smooth and predictable workings of its order and regulations. In turn, this modern and orderly place provides people like him and Lamya with the feeling of being heard—therefore bolstering the sense of belonging they had to the city and the UAE.

Given that my interlocutors are mostly upper-middle class and all of them speak either English, or English and Arabic, their encounters do not explain how a low-waged worker with limited language skills navigates governance systems associated here with modernity. Vora says that her Indian interlocutors "described numerous incidents in which they felt [that] Europeans and other Arabs [were given] the benefit of the doubt," which they did not receive.[28] As I show in chapters 2, 3, and 5, where I explore topics of belonging and safety in Dubai, these circumstances vary depending on the intersections of race, class, gender, and citizenship. Belonging and exclusion are layered, and some South Asians who felt discriminated against in Dubai also found the city to be welcoming in other ways because of the large presence of South Asians there.[29] Therefore, my interlocutors' experiences of order and safety in this chapter do not necessarily represent the experiences of other inhabitants, especially those from other socioeconomic or ethnic groups. As I also noted in the introduction of this chapter, while my interlocutors who lived in other countries (often Middle Eastern ones, but sometimes also Western ones) spoke very positively of Dubai's bureaucracy, some of the Emirati ones complained that new and increasing regulations led to more bureaucracy and complications. They found some online services cumbersome and argued that there was an increasing amount of paperwork and bureaucratic expectations (that came along with making Dubai a modern place) that they had to complete to get simple tasks done.

For privileged interlocutors like Rami and Lamya who experienced life in other nearby cities, however, aspirations for a modern life (which they associate with order and regulations) means not only having an *easier* life but also feeling like they are respected and heard—respected and heard not in a political sense but in terms of the everyday and mundane. This might be called a civic sense of feeling heard, which is not entirely unrelated to politics, in that it lays out expectations and forms judgements about the broader political system and whether it meets them. My other upper-middle-class interlocutors shared similar experiences as Lamya and Rami. Nada, a Lebanese woman who grew up in Kuwait, came to Dubai when she was twenty-eight-years old. When I asked her about some of the differences between the two cities, Nada talked about her experience doing paperwork in a government office in Dubai:

It's the first time I go to a ministry, I feel like, it's fine. Not like . . . fighting and you need to know someone, or someone giving you a hard time. I used to always have problems with the police in Kuwait. So anything that has to do with government and police, I immediately get the nerves. Here, wowww, really nice, they don't mean any harm, they don't harass you [*ma 'aam yetharkashou feek, yetharashou feek*], just doing their job. . . . The experience with police here was completely the opposite than Kuwait. I never felt like I'm at risk. I always feel like I'm empowered to speak. If someone harassed me, I would in his face say that. I never felt like that in Kuwait. The opposite, in Kuwait, you want to avoid problems. Don't cause a scene with the police. Don't do anything out of the usual. Don't complain.

In reality, some of my noncitizen interlocutors who grew up in Dubai were also being told by their parents or friends that they should not "make problems" with Emiratis, or else they would get deported, as Nada described hearing in Kuwait. Nevertheless, Nada's and Rami's comparisons to Kuwait do indicate they are more comfortable navigating government bureaucracy in Dubai than in Kuwait, perhaps largely also because they are the types of people that policymakers aim to attract to the city. These individuals want to live a modern lifestyle and inhabit a subjectivity that enables them to live within an illiberal state with minimal constraints on their ability to conduct everyday activities. In fact, precisely because the city provides them with the order, regulations, and safety that they seek, they experience it as a place where they can have a say, a place of belonging, a place where they can have a voice of some sort, and thus an aspect of the kind of modern civic experience they desire.

THE COSTS OF ORDER AND MODERNITY

As we saw above, many people I interviewed compared places they had previously lived to Dubai, with Kuwait coming up frequently as a point of contrast. What makes places like Dubai and Kuwait different is due to a variety of reasons beyond the scope of this book, but a brief analysis using this comparison allows us to better understand the costs of Dubai's order and regulation, which many see as an attractive form of modernity. First, as a city that derives its wealth from not only tourism but trade and a financial and media sector, Dubai needs to attract and maintain the presence of its elite noncitizens. Deriving its wealth from oil, it is far less crucial for Kuwait to do the same, although it still relies on noncitizens to staff many occupations. The different economic and political situation of each city drives the way policymakers engage with and treat their inhabitants. Kuwait has a democratic system, in which Kuwaitis can vote for a parliament. Yet at times this seems to also embolden xenophobic attitudes as only one group (citizens) have a say (in contrast to the UAE, where no one officially does).

As I show later, even between Dubai and Abu Dhabi there are different visions regarding citizenship, with Dubai having a more heterogeneous view of the citizenry due to its economic pursuits.[30] To attract white-collar residents to Dubai, the emirate has to pay them handsomely, but it also needs to provide them with a high quality of life. Beyond entertainment and consumption, this also means allowing people's everyday lives to run smoothly—from minimal bureaucracy in opening a business to ease of accessing government services. Brand Dubai and its image thus rely not only on the building of a "pristine" and "shiny" city as some have described it but on an everyday life that is experienced as efficient and easy (at least for middle-class residents).

Kathiravelu says that state-led development and modernization resulted in the city's physical infrastructure being designed in ways that draw foreign private capital. While this push is mostly evident in Dubai, it appears to be a more general strategy in the UAE as a whole.[31] The UAE seeks to cultivate citizens who embrace neoliberal norms such as self-management, entrepreneurialism, creative thinking, and risk taking, while also being apolitical.[32] In Dubai, public services are expected to be similarly fashioned: they are supposed to be efficient, and display entrepreneurialism and creativity or "innovation," which is reflected in the high-tech, smart government initiatives, supporting its outward appeal and reinforcing its legitimacy with the city's inhabitants.

Yet for those who value a greater degree of participation in civil society and more room for (especially political) freedom of expression, living in Europe or North America is a much more favorable option than a place like Dubai. Within the Gulf itself, Kuwait provides liberties that do not exist in other Gulf countries, and which some Kuwaitis and even more politically minded Emiratis indicate as preferable to the way a place like Dubai functions.[33] In terms of freedom of expression and political participation, Kuwait allows the more politically minded not only more space to engage but also more safety when doing so—although this democracy is not similarly accessible to non-Kuwaitis, who constitute 70 percent of Kuwait's population.[34]

For other inhabitants who place less emphasis on democratic participation, or have not felt entitled to such participation anyway in other places, Dubai's development is preferable. Ali describes a discussion with a South Asian person in Dubai that elaborates on this point:

> At a friend's house early in my stay, I suggested that not having a democracy, not having certain civil liberties such as free speech might pose a problem. My friend's mother became indignant. She said, 'Look at India, where I come from. You call that democracy? What is your vote worth? Corruption is spread throughout the government and bureaucracy. No, I prefer it here.' I asked her if she had any fear that one day the authorities might say, 'OK, you may go now.' She grew even more annoyed and said loudly, 'No! They would never. We live here quite well. We love it here.' And she and her family do. They have lived in Dubai for more than thirty years, their business has thrived and they have become quite wealthy, and own a freehold villa in one of the poshest neighborhoods in Dubai. The freedom that people have living in Dubai is largely economic, as workers and consumers. When my friend's mother says they live in Dubai quite well, she means that their business can operate without a great deal of bureaucratic interference, their living standards are high, and they do not have day to day worries that the secret police are watching (though they very well might be). Like my friend's mother, expatriates for the most part are uninterested in democracy so long as they are living well. The idea of living "quite well" means different things to expatriates of different class levels and nationalities.[35]

The attitude this woman expressed represents those similar to Yurchak's normal subjects in former USSR, individuals who know they can live a "normal" life (safe, self-manageable, enjoyable) so long as they stay out of politics.[36] Gooptu found a similar subjectivity among young workers in a mall in Kolkata, individuals who viewed politics as corrupt and driven by greed for power, a "sham" that does nothing to improve the lives of ordinary people.[37] Rather, they believed that young people should "keep their heads down" and be hard working, positing what they saw as an ethic of integrity against politics, the latter which they view as immoral. Gooptu refers to this as neoliberal subjectivity. However, being apolitical is not necessarily always driven by a neoliberal subjectivity. Koch shows that in Kazakhstan, citizens are apolitical (or "indifferent") as well as supportive of state-driven spectacles for a variety of different reasons.[38] It is also possible for people to eschew neoliberal ideals at times and be proponents of them at other times, such as when neoliberal ideals are seen to make the operations of everyday life run more smoothly. My interviewees in this chapter, many of whom have elected to live in Dubai over other places, inhabit a subjectivity that allows them to make a meaningful life in an "illiberal" society, particularly as they occupy a space in the socioeconomic hierarchy that makes it easier to benefit from the particular forms of order and regulations Dubai provides, which help cement the city's reputation for modernity.

Indeed, the modern, ordered, neoliberal city privileges the experiences of middle classes and elites. Meanwhile certain groups, such as some working-class inhabitants, may be relegated to the margins—both physically and metaphorically. What is a positive example of order and regulations for some is a form of exclusion for others. For instance, although not always stringently followed, local regulations prevent low-waged men from living together in villas or other "family"-designated neighborhoods, consigning them to specific areas of the city—and away from the upper-middle classes, who generally view these types of regulations positively.[39] In fact, one of the key aims of neoliberal urban policies is to assemble urban space as a field for market-led economic growth and privileged consumption while ensuring the order and control of the most marginalized groups, a topic further explored in chapter 5.[40] The cosmopolitan milieus and smooth regimes of modern municipal functioning favored by my interviewees exist within this larger system.

While my interlocutors found the quality of public services and order and regulations were better in Dubai than in other places, these modern amenities come with a price, both figuratively and literally. Some of the costs of exclusion have been noted above, but others complain about the literal costs. Take, for instance, road tolls. Some of those who can afford it are happy to pay these tolls. A Kuwaiti Twitter user said: "A simple comparison, you have to pay to use Dubai's roads but they are clean. Kuwait's roads are free but you have to spend money 24 hours on fixing your car because of our marvelous roads."[41] Those who contributed to my research for this chapter who chose to come to Dubai from other Gulf countries had disposable incomes that allowed them to benefit from services with higher up-front costs. For them, paying higher fees was a welcome exchange for smoother and faster interactions, perhaps interactions they considered to be more dignified. Nada, for example, recounted her first interaction with a UAE government office when she went for degree attestations. An employee asked her whether she wanted to pay for a fast-track process, which would get her paperwork completed on the spot. Otherwise, she could get them on the next day for free. "You wanna get something, you don't need to go about it in roundabout ways [*mafy daa'y tlif w tdoor*], there is no need for networking [*mafy wasta*]. There's a fee, you go pay for it and leave," she said, comparing these public services to business services. All my personal acquaintances complained about Dubai's high fees. But some of those I spoke to who have located themselves in Dubai, such as Nada, justify these fees and feel that the city has become better for them over time due to the kinds of service that accompany these fees.

Sara positively noted that enforcement of laws and policies in Dubai increasingly became more stringent and applied more fairly. She gave the example of her work environment: When she had first arrived in Dubai fifteen years ago, she said, her Western colleagues in particular had made fun of Arabs for being lazy and incompetent. She felt that this changed once the UAE introduced laws that criminalize racist language. She also described that it changed the attitudes of Emiratis:

> When I first came, I'm so sorry, I'll be honest. But you could see a bit, like the local [Emirati] attitude was ... [i]f they get a ticket fine, they get it cancelled. Or ... "I'm a local, I'm better than you. I don't stand in line." But you gradually saw it decreasing, decreasing, decreasing. ... And you saw when Sheikh Mohammed [bin Rashid] went to the municipality, he was very clear. ... When he went in the morning [and fired senior officials who were not at work]. ... And when he issued [his eight principles of governance] that no one is above the law. ... And that's why I'm so with the way Dubai does it. It disciplines people [*bit'aadib inas*].

Like Sara, Rami felt that the behaviors and attitudes of public employees changed from when he first arrived in Dubai twenty years ago in ways that felt more agreeably modern. Recalling the atmosphere at the government office where he went to complete his immigration paperwork after first arriving in Dubai, Rami described it as overcrowded, loud, and chaotic. "Until Sheikh Mohammad made a decision that these services should be easy, should be straightforward, they should have resting areas. Now when you go to the immigration areas, you have resting areas, you take a number, there's coffee and tea," he said. In the beginning, "even the people who worked there didn't work well. . . . There was a culture of, 'I'm a government employee, I don't need to [work].'" He believed that a "massive shift" took place as policymakers sought to promote Dubai as a modern, global city to the outside world.

For Rami, entering a government office where he feels there is order, and where he believes he can complain if need be, makes him feel more heard and respected. What Rami, along with some of my other interlocutors, essentially argue is that building a positive image for "Brand Dubai," even if based on neoliberal values that prioritize maximizing economic growth rather than concepts such as freedom, has resulted in meaningful, tangible benefits for the city and its inhabitants, including themselves.

Mayed, an Emirati in his twenties from one of the northern emirates, works in Abu Dhabi. He considers Dubai to be his favorite city, arguing that "the government of Dubai is different" [*hikoumat dubai ghair*], citing the example of his sister who works in Dubai Customs. In Dubai she was toiling [*gaa'da tinkirif*], he said, but being recognized and honored for her efforts, even voted employee of the month. "When you're in Dubai you don't feel like a first-degree citizen, you feel equal to everyone else," he said, referring to the perception that Dubai is a meritocracy, that a citizen has to work as hard as anyone else in Dubai, and that anyone who worked hard would be recognized and appreciated. Of course, the facts point to different realities for many, as the benefits of Dubai's project of order and regulations are certainly unequally distributed. Low-wage employees such as janitors, laborers, and waitpersons, and other manual workers and service providers work long hours and provide vital services but are rarely recognized (not least through higher pay), and most noncitizens do not feel equal to citizens. However, for privileged noncitizens from neighboring emirates and states, Dubai is the place whose version of modernity they prefer, despite not having political freedoms there they might gain elsewhere. In other words, the costs of Dubai's order, unequally distributed as they are, do not outweigh the benefits they attribute to this aspect of its development.

A PLACE OF ALTERITY: ANONYMITY, INDEPENDENCE, AND DIFFERENCE

Many women I interviewed who relocated to Dubai found that it afforded them a degree of anonymity and independence, and the ability to be different without being seen by their families and society as being in an inappropriate or immodest place. This allows these residents to have a "normal" life wherein what is normal for them can include things as mundane as jogging without worrying what people might say about them. The city thus becomes a space of alterity that paradoxically allows them a sense of normalcy. This can be seen in ways my interviewees, especially women but also some others, discuss the ways Dubai's spectacular development and attendant ethos of modernity combine to allow them to express or display difference from dominant cultural and social norms while making lives within the city.

One theme that recurred in my interviews was the relationship between anonymity and independence, and the ways Dubai's modernity makes these possible. Najla, a Saudi woman in her twenties, used to take a flight from Saudi Arabia to Dubai to go out with her boyfriend, Turki. Although they both lived in Saudi Arabia and she grew up in a liberal household, Najla had difficulties meeting Turki in public. Saudi Arabia has changed considerably in the past few years, but even less than a decade ago, their options were limited. So Najla and her boyfriend went to Dubai to date where they could watch movies and dine at restaurants with ease.

Dubai's neighbors came to the city for varying reasons, but many of these reasons were to get a degree of anonymity, independence, or freedom. This anonymity sometimes allowed them to transgress norms, but sometimes it also meant giving them a sense of normalcy; and of course, these could be related, as specific individuals and families can foster different norms than the wider national communities of which they are a part. In the chapter introduction, I wrote about Salama, who felt more comfortable jogging in Dubai than in Ajman. Her story is replicated among many other interviewees. Aisha, a woman from Umm Al Quwain (the smallest, and some might say the most "traditional" emirate), said her family did not like her going out in her own emirate—even if it was to the supermarket. Umm Al Quwain is very small and had no malls, and a woman going out anywhere (ranging from a coffee shop to a supermarket) stood out more than she did in other emirates. Aisha's family was fine with her going out in Dubai, however, as there were many Emirati women out in Dubai and the social norms of that place were different.

Social norms and attitudes change whenever people travel to other places. Saudi families who vacationed in Cairo during the summer engaged in activities they would otherwise not be able to do back home, such as socializing in mixed-gender settings and going to nightclubs— while still being cautious of the image they were representing to other Saudis there.[42] Another example is the many Emirati women traveling to Europe who do not wear the *sheila* and *'abaya* there even if they encounter other Emiratis on their trip. While some would consider it shameful *not* to be dressed that way at home, for others it was acceptable to change their forms of dress abroad even in the presence of their countrymen and countrywomen. Although they are generally more vigilant in places where a large number of *khaleejis* are present, cities like Cairo, London, and Dubai allow for different social norms to be practiced, marking them as spaces of alterity, or "otherness."

The spaces of alterity, however, are not ones where only transgressive acts take place in secret; these spaces also enable more mundane behavior done publicly. For instance, going jogging on the beach is not necessarily viewed as a transgressive act by Salama or her family. The reason they did not want her to be seen jogging in Ajman was because it connoted to them a rebellion against not their own social norms, but rather the social norms of some people in Ajman. In other words, jogging in Ajman would make Salama stand out and perhaps offend others. In their eyes, jogging in public was perfectly acceptable (or normal) in *certain* places—as opposed to drinking or going to a nightclub, for instance, which they would view as rebellious and shameful no matter where they took place. In that sense, going to Dubai to jog represented going to a space of alterity not to rebel but rather to engage in ordinary activities that had different social valences there.

The ways individuals from neighboring emirates and countries experience Dubai as a space of anonymity and independence is illuminated by what Tonkiss calls an "ethics of indifference," which my interviewees feel to be apparent in Dubai: "Cities in general are said to have an impersonality which involves a certain kind of freedom in the city, the lonely liberty of knowing that no one is looking. . . . It involves an ethics of indifference as a tacit relationship between urban subjects, the implicit exchange between strangers of what [writer E. B.] White called 'the gift of loneliness and the gift of privacy.'"[43]

Karp, furthermore, argues that "the completely anonymous situation is normally seen as providing a kind of 'freedom' which is inaccessible in less-anonymous settings. . . . [I]n the theoretically truly anonymous situation, we should not expect individuals to be constrained by others in the formulation and production of their acts."[44] In Dubai, this anonymity is sought by various people, but especially by women and individuals who may otherwise be considered different and nonconforming (to varying degrees) in their societies of origin. For women, freedom in the city is tied to them not being seen.[45] "A right to be anonymous, to be left alone, *not* to be looked at, seems minimal indeed. . . . There is no law to say that you should not be subject to hostile gazes. . . . [O]ur freedom relies . . . on the indifference of others."[46] Similarly, for some of those who come to Dubai to date, get away from societal pressure, or even just go jogging in comfort, part of the anonymity and freedom they experience is based on the indifference that a big city provides them. The fact that most of Dubai's inhabitants are from different parts of the world affords them more anonymity, and therefore certain registers of independence in terms of how they go about living their everyday lives within the spectacular city.

The indifference that the city provides is not afforded to all women in all spaces of the city equally, of course. Emirati women in Dubai who go to popular hangout spaces where Emiratis are easily encountered, such as Dubai Mall or City Walk, may experience Dubai as a small town rather than a big city in these scenarios. They may still bump into people who know them, even in spaces that do not have a large segment of Emiratis. Going to other emirates therefore provides *them* with more anonymity (although this is a less common flow than those coming to Dubai). Some Emiratis from Dubai who studied abroad in the West told me that they found their home city a very restrictive place in comparison. They could not dress the way they wanted, they had to worry about what people said, and they felt that they were tied to social and family obligations. In some instances, non-Emirati women who grew up in Dubai experience the city, or certain parts of it, as a small town as well. For instance, Divya, an Indian woman who grew up in old Dubai, avoids going there because she feels watched and judged by the Indian community, instead choosing to live and socialize in new Dubai. However, the small town can still be experienced as a big city because of the different options it provides. Emirati women from Dubai who may want anonymity or a degree of independence seek spaces that are often associated with Westerners to get away from their community, as Divya did (see chapter 3). While previous analysis discussed the ways the exclusion of working-class demographics from some spectacular spaces helped produce middle-class belonging, here the relative absence of socially conservative demographics (who may feel excluded from Dubai's version of urban modernity) allows for greater belonging.

Assaf found that youth in Abu Dhabi came to date in Dubai in secret because they knew fewer people in the emirate and because the variety of different spaces in the city, especially its spectacularly developed sections, allowed them some anonymity.[47] Similarly, in a public Instagram page (where one of the cocreators of the page is an Emirati woman), users send confessional letters to an account that then posts them anonymously. While countries and cities are anonymized as well, the largest number of people commenting are Emiratis, and it appears that the same goes for the letters. It is also often evident what locations the letter writers are referring to by the terms they use or the Arabic words they include in the English text. In one post, the Instagram user says:

> When I was married, I wanted to get an implant [for contraception] in my arm. I went to a clinic in the capital [Abu Dhabi] and they refused to give me the implant unless my husband signs a paper. This was only a requirement for locals [Emiratis] and no other nationality. I told them off and went to the city next door [Dubai] and they did it with no signature. I told my now ex-husband I was getting the implant but I would not let a man sign a paper on my behalf.[48]

Similarly, in a separate post, another user writes:

Tired of playing pretend. . . . I'm a happily divorced woman and I enjoy life to the fullest. I tend to pretend in the capital [Abu Dhabi] and live my actual life in the neighboring city [Dubai]. . . . Now with things locked down [COVID-19] and it's not so easy to go between the two, I feel a bit stir-crazy. I'm not used to pretending for so long.[49]

These letters indicate a more transgressive lifestyle and a resistance to social norms that limit control over interpersonal relationships and some policing of bodily autonomy. These types of transgressive acts can take place in Dubai because they are, there, apolitical. They may be controversial socially, but they are usually not controversial politically. Of course, these two can be interlinked, such as when some Emiratis become vocal about certain behaviors they consider immoral. Lori demonstrates this in her discussion of decency laws in Dubai. While drinking in public or public displays of affection are criminalized in the UAE, people are rarely arrested for these activities unless someone (usually an Emirati citizen) reports them. The police act on these complaints (but otherwise may disregard such behavior) as a way to balance the contestations and desires of different groups.[50] Yet in Yurchak's work on normal subjects, we find that normal subjectivity does not necessarily imply an absolute lack of transgressive acts.[51] It is possible at times that transgressions are relegated to certain spheres and done in certain manners that are not overtly getting in the way of someone living a safe, self-manageable, and enjoyable life.

For non-Emirati *khaleejis*, the city may hold more options in this regard than for Emiratis. Because it is close to their own countries and families in the Gulf and because of the cultural similarities, Dubai remained somewhat of a comfort zone for them rather than a space of isolation and solitude. Being away from family, but not too far away, was a major advantage for many. Laila said that her mother moved with them to Dubai when they were teenagers so that they could "lead a normal life," which to her entailed a degree of independence she didn't experience in Saudi Arabia. While her father remained in Saudi Arabia for work, Laila's mother wanted her children to become more independent. As soon as they arrived in Dubai, their mother pushed them to get their groceries and take taxis by themselves after having had a very protective life in Saudi Arabia, where a driver took them everywhere and where their mother would not let them go out on weekend nights. Laila said that her friends from Saudi Arabia and Jordan also moved to Dubai for similar reasons. In Jordan, people were more involved in her friends' personal lives, and she knew many women who left Amman to live their life without *tadakhkhulat* [interferences], "because they know here [in Dubai] everything goes and nobody judges you":

> One girl she came because she's a lesbian, and although Saudi is the hub for that, but there they're small communities where everyone knows everyone, so she came [here] to live her life.... Also I know an older woman, she came and started her own business, selling her own stuff. She wanted to live free from interference.... Another girl got divorced and staying in Amman isn't good [for a divorced woman], so she came here.

Likewise, some middle-class Indian women in Dubai found that the city offered them more freedom than they had in India, both because they felt safer in Dubai (and therefore had more independence in terms of where they could go and when), but also due to many of them not being around their extended families "who they felt often keep an eye on them, did not let them go out as much, and criticized their actions."[52]

Sometimes it was small things that made a difference. Lamya said that having space away from her family while still remaining in close proximity was a major reason for wanting to be in Dubai. She explained that being away from her extended family and society made her feel more at ease, ranging from what she wore, where she went, and what she did. She said, for instance, that even if mixed-gender gyms were to open in Saudi Arabia, she would feel awkward going there, both because of how society viewed it and because she is not comfortable "being in her own skin" around people related to her or her husband. As an adaptive agent, Lamya wants to live a *relatively* more (socially) liberal lifestyle but not in a necessarily transgressive way (going to mixed-gender gyms, for example, may be something that some people in her social circles frown upon but don't necessarily view as rebellious). For her, Dubai is an ideal place because she can fulfil her aspirations of having a more global, cosmopolitan lifestyle while simultaneously being in a *khaleeji* milieu. With over one hundred cousins, it also gives her and her husband increased independence, a "space to be themselves" away from societal pressures.

I see my friends or my cousins, they get sucked into these social events. . . . You know how, for us as *khaleejis*, you have to go to a wedding, you have to wear a different dress every time, you have to have this bag, and these shoes, and people will see. And you have to spend half of your day at the salon, getting your hair done and getting your makeup done, and you have to go to a really good place, and that really good place has a long queue, and the weekend is over. . . . And the next day you're tired and then you're back to work. . . . You spend your life performing social obligations [*twajbeen innass*] and it sucks the life out of you. [Also] in terms of appearances [*mathahir*] and clothes, and *kashkha* [being posh].

Even among people from countries that do not place strict legal restrictions on dress codes, alcohol, or gender mixing (such as Bahrain), being away from family and societal codes (rather than just legal ones) was a major reason given for moving to Dubai. For those who lived abroad and had become accustomed to the independence of living alone, it was difficult to go back home where they felt that parents and extended families monitored their moves. This was the case for Ghada, a Bahraini woman in her late twenties, as well as many other GCC citizens. Yet moving out while remaining in the same country (or city) was still a major taboo for Ghada (this is the case especially for unmarried women, but to an extent also for men). Coming to Dubai thus allowed women like her to remain in a familiar environment and in relatively close proximity to their families while obtaining a degree of independence.

Although most of the people I interviewed in this chapter who sought anonymity were women, men also related similar experiences of Dubai. On a flight from London to Dubai, a Kuwaiti man I briefly met told me he went to Dubai to do things he could not do in Kuwait (in his case this was specifically to go to bars, drink, or party). Although his family (including his wife) was not aware of his drinking, he was comfortable enough doing it in public in Dubai. Mayed, an Emirati man from Ajman, said that he preferred going out with his European ex-girlfriend in Dubai rather than in Ajman, where he worried that everyone would see him and talk about him. What is interesting, however, is that many people had already seen him in Dubai Mall with his ex-girlfriend and contacted his mother, asking her if he was married. Dubai is therefore not a completely anonymous place for him (and perhaps it is not for some *khaleejis* either). Yet its relative anonymity, and the view of it as a space of alterity, makes it some-what more comfortable as a place to negotiate social norms. While some people recognized him in Dubai, Mayed was still anonymous to many of Dubai Mall's patrons in a way he would never be in Ajman. In that sense, while publicly dating may be considered a transgressive act, he perceived it as more acceptable in Dubai (even if not entirely).

While the relative degree of social freedom in Dubai is viewed positively by most of my interviewees who chose to move to the city, there are cer-tainly others who view this aspect of the city's modernity negatively for the very same reason. The fact that some people come to Dubai specifically to party or drink represents to others that Dubai is a place that promotes and allows "morally corrupt behavior." Furthermore, many Emiratis of differ-ent ages and backgrounds say they enjoy going to Gulf countries like Kuwait or Bahrain because they see more citizens there, compared to the UAE. Their comments thus emphasize the reality that just as some *kha-leejis* like Dubai because they experience it as a global city, others would prefer it to be less "Western" or foreign. It is also not uncommon to hear Emiratis and other *khaleejis* saying they were impressed when they went to Oman or Bahrain and found that their taxi driver or other service employee was Omani or Bahraini, respectively. They express a longing for their countries to become more visibly national again (rather than for-eign), to have more encounters with those who they perceive to share a similar culture, values, and language. Therefore, as there are *khaleejis* who come to Dubai to be in a "global" city, and there are Emiratis who enjoy it, there are also those who lament these demographic and urban changes associated with Dubai's reputation for modern living.

There are many tensions to unpack in these desires. Most of those who find the idea of a citizen taxi driver laudable would not want themselves or their families to work in similar jobs that are low wage and deemed of low status. What they find charming is therefore marred with class divisions to which they heed no attention when service workers are noncitizens and are therefore viewed as having no right to better wages (because they can supposedly "vote with their feet" and leave). Their desires project an ideal-ized view of life among the citizenry, yet it reflects that even as some of them are yearning for the anonymity of the big city, they also long for a more communitarian environment at times.

Nevertheless, there are different types of freedom and anonymity that people seek, and even for more conservative members of society, the city can provide a comfortable space to engage in a sense of normalcy. For instance, in a Twitter post, a young Kuwaiti woman asks her followers: "Is it okay to go out for breakfast alone in Kuwait?"[53] She explains that she has done this in Dubai but she is not sure it will feel natural doing the same in Kuwait. The quest for anonymity and independence varies from those who want to go partying to those who simply want to have a solitary meal without feeling judged.

Some of these residents are actively pursuing a place where various kinds of social and cultural difference are more apparent and tolerated. Some of them pursue this for personal reasons (because of how they identify in some way that might be deemed unacceptable or transgressive); some see the presence of certain forms of difference itself as a modern value that should be pursued and thus choose Dubai for this reason. "I think Dubai, for many people today, allows for the kinds of things that some people [*khaleejis*] would only do in London," Hayat said, when I asked her about her reasons for moving to Dubai and why she thinks other people from the Gulf took a similar path. For Hayat, being in Dubai allowed her to live without feeling pressured to conform to societal expectations, as she does in Saudi Arabia:

> Maybe it's an imagined thing but [in Dubai] I didn't think I had to be Saudi in a particular way, like I could be myself . . . and I'm not defensive or apologetic about it. But [in Saudi Arabia] I think I'd have to contend with a lot of people who have expectations about me needing to represent myself and my family in a particular way. So, I didn't want that. And actually [that's] part of the reason I didn't go back even though I get offers all the time, for like really good jobs, [where] I would be making a lot more than I make or . . . [for] respectable positions. But I don't want to have to conform to something that doesn't feel like me, you know what I mean. So, I feel that Dubai has actually been very good for us. Really, it has . . . you know, we're in a neighborhood where it feels familiar to me, like, and you can hear the mosque . . . . [I haven't] felt that I've been mistreated because of the choices I've made in my life, you know.

As Tonkiss says, "The ability to go unnoticed in the streets of the city has particular resonance for women as well as for men whose bodies are marked in terms of racial, sexual, or cultural difference."[54] In Hayat's case, not conforming to the expectations of a Saudi woman in her society is what marks her as different there. As I noted earlier, the anonymity and freedom (or the ethics of indifference) that Dubai provides for *khaleeji* women or even some women from other emirates of the UAE is not experienced the same way by Emirati women from Dubai. Similarly, after having spent ten years in the UAE, Hayat does not feel anonymous in the way she did when she first came. However, she still feels that she does not have to exert herself in performing some aspects of "Saudiness," which she feels differ from her real identity.

The ethics of indifference allows some forms of diversity to exist, ones which the cosmopolitan-identifying classes of *khaleejis*, many of whom I interviewed in this chapter, seek. Lamya, for example, explained that she had learned to say hello in fifteen different languages because of the people she met, including her Chinese, Syrian, and Mexican neighbors. "I literally have neighbors from all around the world, and that's something that's beautiful," she said. She laughed about having found "the best Chinese hot pot place . . . or the best Syrian dish [*maa'luba*]." Lamya felt that diversity added to her as an individual by making her more tolerant and understanding of the world around her. She grew up hearing stereotypes about certain groups, but being exposed to others allowed her to challenge these generalizations. She said that she started learning about languages and histories that she never expected to learn about; for example, meeting her Chinese colleagues inspired her to read books about Chinese history. She was also happy to share her own culture with others in an effort to change stereotypes about the region. Likewise, in her work on middle-class Indians in Dubai, Vora found that her interlocutors "claimed to have become more open-minded since coming to Dubai, where they were exposed to other nationalities and cultures, and they had difficulty relating to the close-mindedness of friends and family" in their countries.[55] Some believe that this exposure allows them and others to overcome certain stereotypes. Rami, the Jordanian man who grew up in Kuwait, noted his Indian friend's experience in Kuwait compared with Dubai:

> For example, in Kuwait, when you see an Indian, there's a stereotype, that maximum he is someone who should be a driver. While [in Dubai] this

Indian could be someone who is CEO of Google coming to visit, or CEO of Microsoft. . . . [H]ere in Dubai, because the Indians, there's a driver, and there's a CEO, and there's a doctor and so on, so there isn't that perception. . . . You can't have it because you go to a bank and you see [them working there], so how can you have this perception? But in Kuwait, it's there. So it's happening to one of my friends, he was a GM [General Manager] of a company and still people don't believe it even when they see his residency. Even once the police [in Kuwait] stopped him and started laughing. He was like, "Look, an Indian is a general manager."

Stereotyping and the stigmatization of South Asians also takes place in Dubai, such as being paid less than Europeans and Arabs for the same jobs (salaries are based on what the worker would receive in their home country; the salary in Dubai is slightly higher).[56] Meanwhile, as Vora says, "Western expatriates . . . are provided with assistance at almost every level of the migration process, and many expenses—such as housing, moving costs, schooling, transportation allowances, healthcare, and visa fees—are included in their employment packages," which she says is not the same for many South Asians.[57] Still, Rami's quotation expresses that some Dubai residents who prefer it to other places believe that national difference from Emirati citizens does not equate as equally with degradations in social status as they might in other places because of Dubai's globalized white-collar sector.

Some parts of the city play into these racialized practices more than others. For instance, while one can find many South Asians in shopping malls and the new development projects discussed in earlier chapters, I have heard more than once of exclusions that take place in nightclubs. Kathiravelu quotes a young Indian model who said that bouncers at nightclubs turned her away, citing full capacity. Five minutes later when she arrived with her Lebanese friends, their response was different. "You have to be Lebanese, because most of the bouncers are Lebanese, or you have to be Iranian, or you have to be white-skinned. These are the criteria. There you obviously feel discriminated. It happens in most of the clubs . . . most."[58] At the same time, the large presence of South Asians and people's exposure to different nationalities can have its benefits. Writing about Keralite migrants' experiences in the Gulf, Osella and Osella mention that Saudi and Kuwait are more often singled out as difficult places to work in, while Dubai and Sharjah garner more favorable responses.[59] This exposure may allow inhabitants of different backgrounds better experiences without necessarily overcoming issues of racism and classism.

Zaleekha, quoted above, similarly felt that this diversity allowed her, as someone who did not appear to be *khaleeji*, to be treated better. Zaleekha felt that living alone in Dubai was more acceptable for her as a woman than in places such as Kuwait, Ajman, and AlAin. In those places, people often asked her if she lived with her family and were shocked to find out that she was living alone. "They're used to it here," she said about Dubai.

With short, dyed blond hair, green contact lenses, and eyebrow piercings, Zaleekha did not immediately appear to be *khaleeji*, something that she also felt was easier to live with in Dubai. She felt that she faced greater bias in other places. One example she recalled was when an Emirati man entered her clinic in AlAin and made a scene, waving his finger at her, asking, "Are you Iraqi?" Responding in the same tone, she said, "No, I'm Saudi." His demeanor instantly changed, as he apologized, assured her that he respected her and her work, and then complained about non-*khaleejis* whom he believed "ruined the country." Zaleekha believed that there were fewer people with these attitudes in Dubai; she said she had interviewed for jobs in Kuwait and Saudi Arabia but decided not to move to either place because of the way she saw doctors treat nurses, who were mostly Filipina or South Asian. Many of my upper-middle-class interlocutors see Dubai as a place that is more tolerant not just of them but also of others, which they express as an important personal value. How *others* experience the city, however, can be entirely different, as noted earlier.

Attitudes toward the value of diversity and the differences it brings can vary from one emirate to another, or from one Gulf country to another. The Ajam of Kuwait and Abu Dhabi, for instance, are often seen as more Arabized than those in Dubai.[60] Najat, an Ajami woman who grew up in Dubai but moved to Abu Dhabi, noted that the Ajamis in Abu Dhabi did not speak Ajami or practice some of the Ajami cultural practices. In her work about citizenship in the UAE, Lori compares the "more restrictive practices of Abu Dhabi on the one hand, and the more expansive incorporation practices of the remaining emirates on the other."[61] She explains that "Abu Dhabi's vision of the citizenry was more ethnically homogeneous than that of Dubai or the Northern Emirates."[62] Among my interviewees, a Baluch woman from Ajman said she grew up hiding her Baluchi family name but felt more comfortable acknowledging it in Dubai. Like others exhibiting this aspect of neoliberal subjectivity, she believed that Dubai was a meritocracy where anyone could advance if they worked hard enough. She gave examples of Emiratis of non-Arab backgrounds who were placed in high-government offices in Dubai, such as Minister of Cabinet Affairs Al Gergawi. Therefore, variations exist between various emirates and Gulf countries in the way difference and diversity are managed and viewed, both from official perspectives and among residents.

Yet for my interlocutors, *khaleejis* or upper-middle-class non-Westerners, Dubai was a place that felt accepting of *their* forms of difference. Because of that, they saw it as a modern, cosmopolitan place that accepts difference in general—even though it may not be experienced as such by others.

CONCLUSION

I explored the ways in which those who choose to come to Dubai from other Gulf states and emirates inhabit one aspect of Dubai's spectacular development—its modernity. For them, some of the most important aspects of this modernity entail what they perceive as the city's orderliness and regulations, as well as its diversity and centering of global cosmopolitan values as discussed in the previous chapter. This group comes to Dubai to live in a place that is, for them, *appropriately* modern. For them, the so-called balance of East and West is something they sought and found in Dubai through exerting adaptive agency in the form of relocation. This "balance" indicates a way of being in the world that is accommodating of both Western lifestyles and Arab/Muslim/non-Western cultural norms. It allows them a sense of normalcy by *not* marking them as minorities, with the degraded social status that can entail, as they fear would happen in the West. In Dubai, members of this group can fulfil their class aspirations for "modern" living without moving far away or necessarily transgressing (or resisting) the cultural norms and values they grew up with.

Often dismissed by critics as byproducts of Dubai's illiberal and neoliberal governance regimes, order and regulations are integral parts of what makes a "modern" society for many normal subjects who sought to live an ordered and safe life, one that catered to their particular interests as upper-middle-class inhabitants. For some of them, participating in the making of an ordered city through various acts of civic engagement and encounters with state institutions made them feel heard and gave them a sense of civic belonging, despite the absence of citizenship, as well as a feeling of having achieved progress. In such contexts, their development and enactment of neoliberal subjectivities speaks to their personal identification with and enmeshments in broader state projects of imposing orderliness through governance and regulation; yet it also highlights the ways their expectations of the state to provide specific services may influence some of its forms of development.

Finally, Dubai allows a segment of people who relocate to or visit it to have normal lives by granting them a degree of anonymity and independence and allowing certain forms of engagement with difference. For some, this could be as mundane as being able to pursue outdoor leisure activities in apparel of their choice. The city provides them normalcy in the sense that it is neither a restrictively "local" life nor an alienatingly "Western" one. As opposed to immigrating to the West, moving to Dubai does not indicate that they are breaking with their cultural norms or rebelling against them, but rather adaptively pursuing access to more "modern" ways of living in an Arab/Muslim/non-Western milieu that also features broader demographic, social, and cultural diversity. By exploring the experiences of these groups, we gain a better understanding of how Dubai sits in local and regional imaginings where the spectacle of Dubai often coexists with more ordinary imaginings of the city as a place to pursue mobility and modernity sans dramatic experiences of dislocation or rupture.

5 The Costs and Benefits of Safety in Sanitized Spaces

Faisal, an Emirati interlocutor, advised me *not* to interview people in one part of his neighborhood. "What would you want with them?" he asked me. "They're from Satwa." Satwa is a lower-income part of the city. Its inhabitants are often depicted by some media and my interviewees as being "lower class," and sometimes associated with crime and violence. Today Satwa has a demographic consisting mostly of South Asian "bachelors," Filipinas, and Africans, but before the financial crisis of 2008, its residents were Emiratis, Baluch, Iranians, and stateless people.[1] Even though many of them experienced a sense of vibrant community and belonging, their neighborhood was associated with poverty and criminality. Many residents lived in informal *chinko* houses, with corrugated zinc or steel roofs (see figure 16), or *shaabiya* houses (literally, folk houses; see figure 17).[2] But, as one interlocutor who was originally from Satwa told me, they were moved because their homes were "distorting the scenery" (*tashweeh man'thar*), or at least, the scenery the state hoped to create more of in its efforts to sanitize Dubai.

Satwa was located on prime real estate in what is now downtown Dubai. During the early 2000s, the government undertook the early stages of a development plan, hoping to move Satwa's residents—both

Figure 16. The only *chinko* left in Satwa (and the only *chinko* I saw in all of Dubai).

Emirati and non-Emirati—to other parts of the city. Although in the wake of the 2008 financial crisis the rebuilding of most of Satwa has not yet materialized, most of the old residents were moved out before plans were halted. The government gave them the option of moving to new, ready-made housing in other parts of the city or receiving monetary compensation. Some of those who received compensation moved to other emirates because it was cheaper, although it is not clear how often this happened. Others remained in Dubai. Both Emiratis and non-Emiratis were compensated, including those who lived in *chinko*s. Today, there are very few of the old residents still living in Satwa, even in the houses that the government did not request to be vacated. In most houses where owners have left, the rooms are rented out to mostly low-income South Asian men.[3] This is the case not only in Satwa but in many, if not almost all, the neighborhoods with *shaabiya* housing in Dubai. Their Emirati owners have left to inhabit villas in other, more upscale neighborhoods of the city.

Above, I quoted an interlocutor who said that they were moved out of Satwa because their neighborhood constituted a "distortion of scenery."

Figure 17. Shaabiya houses.

This points to the state program of creating the spectacular city through "sanitation" or "hygienization," terms that aptly describe the processes that took place in these neighborhoods. As scholars have shown, this is part of a global trend. In their work on Brazil, for instance, Garmany and Richmond define hygienization, as follows:

(1) It is a process whereby low-income people are forced from specific urban areas, not necessarily for ground rent maximisation or investment opportunities, but primarily to impose/restore hygienic urban landscapes; (2) the state, and more specifically state violence, play central roles; (3) low-income residents facing displacement are frequently depicted as trespassers, perceived as out of place, and therefore pathologized and considered delinquent; (4) it tends to repress and induce urban informality, by smothering it in one space, and then—rather than address the drivers of social inequality—ensuring it reemerges elsewhere; and (5) it is often justified according to modernist discourses that emphasise the greater urban good.[4]

This is similar to the process that unfolded in Satwa but also different in some telling ways. The reason that inhabitants were removed from Satwa and relocated to other neighborhoods *was* for investment opportunities (although the financial crisis slowed this process down). However, there is certainly an interest among higher-ups in Dubai, as well as other emirates, to impose "hygienic urban landscapes," evident in the ways they impose fines on those who hang their laundry on balconies or who drive dirty cars: "Dubai does not allow residents to distort the image of the city by hanging clothes, install dish antennas, or place junk in their balconies and those not paying attention to warnings could face penalties as high as Dh1,500, according to a Dubai Municipality official."[5] Meanwhile, an article in *Gulf News* reports that "Dubai Municipality has warned residents not to leave their cars unwashed for a long time as this type of uncivilised behaviour can tarnish the aesthetic appearance of the city."[6] These processes of hygienization are justified through modernist discourse about the greater urban good, but the consequences of sanitization or hygienization leave some residents with conflicting feelings.[7] As we will see, I spoke with a number of Emirati residents who had left *shaabiyas*—whether through government initiatives or on their own accord—and, though they had all experienced upward mobility during efforts to sanitize Dubai, they described a sense of loss too.

This chapter shows how middle-class inhabitants navigate a certain aspect of their city's spectacle—one also often associated with Dubai's perceived inauthenticity: the highly regulated, controlled, and sanitized urban environment, which has in some cases been layered over preexisting communities during their own lifetimes. How they negotiate such change is most potently demonstrated by those who grew up in Satwa, as well as other *shaabiyas* such as Al-Quoz and Shaabiyat alshurta, as the sanitized city has in particular replaced their earlier communities and experiences.

After providing background on these neighborhoods and the development changes planned for them, this chapter highlights how a particular form of spectacle making, namely sanitization or hygienization, has led to a loss of community and decreased informality for some of the city's inhabitants. Next, it investigates how these individuals, even amid ongoing feelings of loss, depict *certain* aspects of a highly controlled, regulated, and sanitized urban environment positively, particularly the versions of safety it offers them. As I discuss safety, I expand on how my interlocutors *beyond* Satwa and the *shaabiyas* also talk about it, and who benefits—and who does not—from the kinds of safety that have attended the redevelopment of older neighborhoods into more spectacular spaces.

In previous chapters, I argued that middle- and upper-middle-class citizens and residents inhabit various aspects of Dubai's spectacle through exerting adaptive agency. In this chapter, we find that some members of this demographic appear less adaptive to some aspects of the city's changes given the deep sense of loss these changes caused them. Still, even then, we cannot understand this nonhomogeneous group as supporters/resistors or merely oppressed. Those who express a deep sense of loss also express an admiration for some aspects of the city's tight regulations enacted in the name of sanitization, viewing safety and order as a positive example of Dubai's modernity, which they tend to view as an inevitable (and in many instances, desirable) direction of development.

A place like Satwa, then, might be understood as a site of arrested spectacular development: a place where top-down development has stopped and started but not been completed, and a place that therefore evokes especially intense memories and feelings about the city's development trajectory and what constitutes progress for Dubai. By focusing on how residents in and out of Satwa and other *shaabiya* neighborhoods understood the changes to their city, it is possible to zero in on how attitudes about state regulation and control are shaped and mediated by experiences of personal safety, which I argue often exists in unresolved tension with ideals of community that residents can simultaneously possess.

To study these dynamics, it was necessary for me to spend time in these neighborhoods located at the precipices of change. While Shaabiyat alshurta was razed in 2017, I was able to spend time in Satwa and Al-Quoz, to get a sense of place and contemporary patterns of socializing there. The individuals I came across were Emiratis and non-Emiratis (perhaps Baluchs, Minawis, or Iranians—who are part of an Emirati milieu). Sometimes a friend joined me on my walks through these neighborhoods, and on several occasions, I approached older residents walking or relaxing outside their houses and spoke with them for fifteen to thirty minutes. But I also sought out residents who had grown up in all three areas, and the bulk of this chapter's analysis is based on in-depth interviews with these former occupants, most of whom were in their thirties and forties, and who now live in middle-class neighborhoods. I found them mostly through the snowball technique, and in some cases by reaching out to people on social media.

What became an overwhelming theme in my interviews was my inter-locutors' interest in discussing the sense of community that existed in old Dubai. These were nostalgic accounts, perhaps in part because people who remembered their old neighborhood fondly may have been the ones more interested in talking with me about them. In the end, only two of my interviewees spoke negatively about their old neighborhood (Satwa in both cases), and one of them was very reluctant to speak with me before he eventually agreed. Most people described their days in Satwa (and the other *shaabiyas*) as the "good old days," using language similar to that of other, older Emiratis I interviewed who reminisced about their lives in Dubai three or four decades ago. While the communal lifestyle of the "good old days" that middle- and upper-middle-class residents referred to existed in most parts of Dubai until the 1980s or early 1990s, in Satwa, in particular, it existed well into the new millennium. Therefore, Satwa offered an especially fertile site of memory and analysis of Dubai's changes.

While I was not initially expecting this, discussions of this neighbor-hood in the "good old days" and the bonds of community that existed there repeatedly brought up another theme—that of safety, with many of my interlocutors from Satwa arguing that the city is safer today (this is in contrast to other older Emirati interlocutors, who considered the "good old days" to be the safer days since everyone knew one another and there were fewer "foreigners"). Those who grew up in Satwa told me stories about knife fights, drugs, and violence, even though I was expecting them *not* to confirm the neighborhood's associations with danger. But at the same time, they often wanted me to understand that the more important thing about Satwa for them was its strong community, characterized by bonds between neighbors that they said did not exist elsewhere. My inter-locutors' constant contrasting of the costs and benefits of strong commu-nity in the "good old days" and increased forms of sanitization and safety today provides insights into how these inhabitants weigh the costs and benefits of spectacular development more broadly.

In general, all my interviewees talked about safety as one of the biggest advantages of the city's development trajectory. Emiratis and non-Emiratis alike contrasted Dubai with Europe, the US, India, and other Middle Eastern cities (including in the Gulf), arguing that the safety in Dubai was unparalleled elsewhere. Women spoke constantly about how comfortable they were being out in the city alone at night, and families said that it was a good place to raise children. Similarly, government newspapers boast about Dubai being one of the safest cities in the world, a major selling point for people to move there. As I explored in previous chapters, however, the quest for safety results in the exclusion of some people (often the most marginalized groups in society) from certain spaces to make others feel comfortable. Sanitation, as it is practiced here, removes certain "undesirable" people and signs of "disorder" or informality, and this can be vividly seen in the patterns of urban redevelopment that have affected neighborhoods such as Satwa.[8]

The making of the safe, sanitized, and orderly city has resulted in changes in the lifestyles of many of those hailing from Satwa and other low-income neighborhoods. As one of them put it, they have become more VIP. Meanwhile, peers who they remember as troublemakers, even those they described as gang leaders, now work in government jobs and live in new housing developments with their families. Assessing these changes, they tend to appear neither supportive of nor resistant to the top-down developmental project; rather, they weigh its costs and benefits while navigating a deeply felt sense of loss toward their older lifestyles. Still, even as they dearly miss the informality and community feel of their old neighborhoods, we find that they also view the increased form of state control and order positively as a form of care or protection.[9]

EXPERIENCES AND MEMORIES OF COMMUNITY LIFE IN AND BEYOND SATWA

Amin is an Iranian man who speaks perfect Emirati with a hint of an Iranian accent. We met through Raj, his Indian friend who grew up with him in Satwa. Raj was the first person from Satwa whom I interviewed, and it is through him that I developed an interest in the topics of this chapter. Raj, who now lives and works in new Dubai, offered to introduce me to Amin (one of his childhood friends). Even though they were both non-Emiratis, Satwa's previous inhabitants grew up in an Emirati milieu, albeit in a relatively lower-income one. The backgrounds of Satwa's inhabitants were a mix of Emiratis, as well as those without citizenship, Iranians, Minawis (from the Iranian town of Minab), and Baluch.[10] All of Amin's family, except for himself, are now Emirati. His mother had married an Emirati man and she and his half-siblings became UAE citizens.

The environment that people like Amin grew up in, however, was often viewed negatively by mainstream Emirati society. At times, it was also depicted disapprovingly by some people who grew up in Satwa, because he is Minawi. Although not all Minawis have Emirati citizenship, many of them generally speak the Emirati dialect (and are much closer to Emirati cultures than other noncitizens). However, "Minawis," unlike the term *Ajamis* (Emiratis who originally come from Southern Iran), was used not only as an ethnic description (of Emiratis who originally came from Iran) but to imply that someone was "lower class." "Minawis" was often used to denote people considered dangerous, poor, and lacking in morals and manners.

In terms of demographics, Satwa and other lower-income neighborhoods in Dubai were quite diverse and can be described as cosmopolitan in the sense that they brought together people of different backgrounds who possessed knowledge about how to navigate different cultures and experiences.[11] Satwa and some of the other *shaabiya*s were very cosmopolitan not only because of the mix of people in them, but particularly because the different groups there intermingled in part due to the built environment. Everyone I met from Satwa spoke several languages, the three or four main ones being Arabic, Urdu, English, and either Minawi, Ajami, or Baluchi (or a collection of those languages). While for many others I spoke to, being exposed to people of different nationalities took place in schools or at work, those hailing from Satwa were not just *exposed* to others but developed close friendships with them. These were friends whose houses they visited on a regular basis, whose languages they spoke and food they ate.

This, however, did not mean an absence of cross-cultural conflict. Raj told me that friends like Amin "protected" him (an Indian) from being teased and allowed him to become part of the accepted group. Similarly, an Emirati Indian man who grew up in Satwa said he was mocked by his neighbors and schoolmates for being half Indian, arguing that the South Asians in the community (the bodega workers, barbers, etc.) bore the brunt of the abuse that happened there. For Amin, a Minawi, his ethnic identity was also often stereotyped by others within and beyond Satwa as meaning "lower class."

Describing the nature of conflicts in Satwa was a common theme among those recalling the neighborhood's past. While they spoke about social issues and the presence of knife fights, drugs, rape, and other forms of violence, some of my interlocutors from Satwa argued that their neighborhood developed an unfair reputation for being dangerous even though similar problems took place in other *shaabiya*s that later became associated with lower-income status (notably, these were places where most Emiratis lived during the 1970s and 1980s). Middle-class and elite communities such as Jumeirah also have issues of drug misuse/abuse and violence, they pointed out; however, these communities and their inhabitants are afforded more privacy and perhaps protection if caught misbehaving due to their higher social capital. This privacy might explain why narratives of violence or drug use among middle- and upper-middle-classes do not circulate in the same manner as they do about inhabitants of Satwa. In short, no other neighborhood carried the same stigma that Satwa did, and inhabitants of different neighborhoods who received the former "Satwajis" claimed that they were negatively impacted by the latter's presence.

Here it is important to note that it was not necessarily economic class that sparked such comments. Indeed, inhabitants of more modest neighborhoods viewed Satwa similarly as did other Emiratis. Neither was it always necessarily ethnic background since other neighborhoods had diverse ethnic compositions. Crime was not absent from these areas either. My interlocutors from other *shaabiya*s spoke about acquaintances who went to prison, friends who got involved in dangerous fights or who passed away from overdoses. Yet places like Satwa are more infamous, and given the lack of data, it is difficult to determine whether this was actually because they had higher rates of crime. When people from Satwa were moved to other areas of the city, such as Al-Quoz, Al-Warqa, and Oud Almateena, parts of these neighborhoods also began carrying some stigma (although none to the extent that Satwa did). For example, an article on knife crime in Dubai says:

> Police insist there is no systemised gang fighting in Dubai and say that such attacks should be treated as isolated occurrences. . . . Many residents disagree. Eisa Ebrahim, a 22-year-old Emirati salesman who has lived in Al Quoz for six years, said there were fights "almost daily" in his area of Sha'abiyat Hamadan and that "some get really bloody." . . . Eisa Asafi, a 26-year-old Iranian hospital administrator who has lived in Al Quoz all his life, said the problem became noticeably worse when residents of condemned buildings in Satwa moved to the area about five years ago. "Before, we hardly saw any fights but since people from Satwa moved here, the fights started happening," he said.[12]

I should clarify here that while Satwa is sometimes *associated* with crime and danger, it is also not necessarily considered *dangerous*, not today nor in the past. Satwa had (and has) a market area that people of different socioeconomic classes use to buy textiles, go to tailors, print books for low prices, repair mobile phones, and so on. According to my interlocutors in this chapter, it is the residential areas that were more prone to crime, and people who were shopping or going to tailors normally did not go to the residential parts of Satwa. I bring up these distinctions to highlight that while Satwa has a reputation for being less safe, it is not necessarily considered a "no-go" place (at least in the market areas), and many people (including elite women) did go there in the past, and still do today. Although Satwa has changed in terms of its demographics, some of the old houses, streets, and alleys still remain. Almost all my interviewees have already left it, however. Meanwhile, other *shaabiya*s have already been completely physically changed, such as Shaabiyat alshurta, which I will discuss later.

When I asked my interlocutors who grew up in Satwa what they missed most about it, the answers came flooding in. Amin remembered the neighborhood kids sitting together in the *freej* in Satwa. They had a tray and stood in front of their houses selling chips and *bajila* (chickpeas). Raj said that during Ramadan, Satwa became "like a festival" and that everyone grilled meat in front of their house and sold it, with a skewer going for a dirham (less than fifty cents). Mohammed, an Emirati man in his forties who grew up in Satwa, said that his neighbors were like family. When they saw him, his elder neighbors asked him to get them groceries or to run errands for them, indicating that they did not have the same formalities that neighbors in other parts of the city often did. Mohammad felt a sense of community there that he did not find elsewhere. When one of his neighbors did not attend the *asr* prayer at the mosque, the *freej* members stood at the neighbor's door calling for him. Not hearing a response even though his car was parked in the drive-way, they broke down the door and found him in diabetic shock. There was no one else at home and he might have otherwise died, but he lived thanks to their intervention. Breaking down a neighbor's door because they missed one prayer was inconceivable in many other neighborhoods of Dubai at that time, and even more so today. Similar depictions of strong community bonds—bonds they associate positively with care and protection—are relayed by interviewees who grew up in some of the *shaabiyas*.

While my interlocutors have become socioeconomically upwardly mobile and experienced lifestyle changes in the past decade or so, they spoke fondly about their days in Satwa as the best days of their lives, even as these memories sometimes included stories of crime (which I was sur-prised that many of them were very willing to tell me about, perhaps indi-cating their sense of pride at how "tough" people from Satwa are). One of the people that Amin reminisced about, for instance, was a man who used to steal cars and change their license plates. Amin said that the man liked to play *shirta haramy* (hide and seek) with the police, but that he kept a small blade in his lower lip in case the police ever caught him, so that if he was ever caught, he could hurt himself and claim that it was the police who hurt him. There was another notorious man—he was just a scrawny little guy, Amin said, and you would never suspect anything just by look-ing at him. But he was (in)famous, and people from different emirates searched for him to buy drugs. Mohammed, on the other hand, said that drugs, violence, and other social ills did take place—but that they were not accepted. He recounted a time when a young neighbor was seen bringing a prostitute home and the whole neighborhood intervened to stop him. Those who continued to engage in "immoral behavior" were shunned, he said, and at times even made to leave the neighborhood.

When I asked Mohammed what made him feel nostalgic about his older life given the many stories of crime, he stressed that I should be aware of the more important thing about Satwa, namely its community spirit. There was a real community there, a neighborhood connection that made them feel that they were one family. Compared to most neighborhoods that have little social interaction among neighbors (aside from sending food in Ramadan or rare visits between friends), Satwa was considered a place where the whole neighborhood was connected, *ala galb wahed*—"as one heart," as Amin put it. Many of my interviewees even expressed a strong desire to return to their old neighborhood. "There was the good and the bad in Satwa," Amin said, when I asked him the same question I asked Mohammed: What made him nostalgic for his older life when he spoke about so much crime? Amin claimed that he knew people who went to their old houses in Satwa and cried as they reminisced—him being one of these people.

On the other hand, two of my interviewees spoke about their relief at leaving Satwa, which Khalil, an Emirati man in his thirties, labeled as a hotbed for crime (*marta' alijram*). Whenever I asked Khalil if he missed Satwa or wanted to return, he laughed at what he considered a ridiculous question, saying that he lived in fear growing up there. Khalil argued that the community life that people longed for existed everywhere in Dubai in the past anyway. I mention Khalil's response here because, although his views represent a minority among those I spoke to, he may or may not be a minority in general. As I mentioned previously, I only interviewed people who wanted to speak about Satwa or associate themselves with it, and I therefore have a larger repertoire of stories from people who are nostalgic for their old lives than I do of people who experienced life in Satwa negatively.

For the majority of people I spoke to, the community life in Satwa was something they dearly missed. My interlocutors in Satwa recounted practices of neighborly informality (even if it was just placing chairs outside their homes in Satwa to socialize in the street) that no longer existed. While they could physically do some of these things they did before, their community had been displaced. Even for those who ended up in similar neighborhoods, the place was no longer the same, they stressed. These feelings were also evident among those who chose to move earlier on. Those who had the opportunity to move from *shaabiya*s often moved to higher-income neighborhoods long before the government mandated it, even if they regretted moving away from their neighbors. They also expressed a sense of loss.

The things people told me they missed were often similar: if they were in the hospital today, only their immediate family and a few close friends would visit them. In Satwa, however, all the neighbors would come. Their stories reiterate the same narratives that older Emiratis told about their childhood memories. The days when neighbors visited one another daily without making appointments were perhaps common three or four decades ago, but for those from Satwa, these strong community bonds existed until the early 2000s. In Shaabiyat alshurta, a neighborhood near Satwa, they remained until recently, when the last part of the *shaabiya* was razed in 2017. I later discuss the possible reasons for why this community life existed in certain areas of the city, but for now I highlight how my interlocutors described it and, in particular, the fond memories they have of it—some of which are very recent ones.

Manal, an Emirati woman in her early thirties, was one of those people who grew up in Shaabiyat alshurta and lived there until 2017, when it was demolished to build the City Walk. Shaabiyat alshurta was *not* considered to be like Satwa in terms of "danger" and crime, but it was similar in terms of it being a more modest neighborhood with a mixed ethnic demographic (Emiratis, Baluch, Yemenis, Omanis, etc.). Everyone living in that neighborhood had a family member working for the police (or perhaps retired from the police force) and lived rent free on police-owned land (hence the neighborhood's name—*Shaabiyt al-shurta* means "the police quarter"). Like those who had lived in Satwa, people in other *shaabiya*s also talked about strong community bonds. When I asked her about her life in the *shaabiya*, from which she had only recently moved a few months ago, Manal said:

I grew up with our neighbors, they were Yemenis. They were very simple, their life was very simple. I was used to eating from their food. . . . During Eid, we would give away some of our clothes, we would give some to our neighbors . . . [b]ecause we know their circumstances. It was normal, they would ask us, "So, do you have any extra clothes?" They would never take it in a sensitive way. . . . Sometimes in Eid, when people visit my mother, my mom knows who needs and she would give them money. . . . It was normal. They would not take things personally at all. . . . I used to go for the IELTS exams. And [a] father [in the neighborhood] will take [his] daughter there. So he would pass by and take the rest of the girls from the neighborhood too.

It was like that, they all used to think of each other. . . . So they were sad, when they had to leave . . . . Until today, when I come to my [new] house, I mutter to myself. I think, *what is this*? It was easier in the *shaabiya*. It was easier. Our neighbors, for example, haven't cooked. They will knock on our doors and ask, "Do you have lunch?" Sometimes my mom hasn't cooked, I would knock on my neighbor's door and ask them, "What's for lunch today?" [or] you would send the housemaid to pick up food from them. It was very normal. . . . It's like you went to your brother's house. . . . Our neighbor, she would just come into our storage room [at home], she would get salt, she would get vegetables, she would put it in her bag and go. . . . My father would tell her, I got extra tomatoes, get for yourself. She would come into the kitchen and get rice and go. It was natural. It was easy.

What makes this kind of community exist in some Emirati neighborhoods but not others? In his research on Shaabiyat alshurta and Shaabiyat aldifaa', Alawadi portrays similar scenes of community and connectedness as the ones Manal describes. The scenes he depicts are uncommon in most Emirati neighborhoods today, where (almost) the only activity in the street is that of cars being driven, perhaps a person here or there walking to the mosque.[13] On the other hand, the *shaabiya* was lively, with children playing in the streets, adults socializing outside their homes, and people walking to their destinations. Alawadi and Elsheshtawy ascribe this community spirit to the length of time inhabitants have lived in the neighborhood as well as the built architecture of the space, with Satwa being a "human-scale" place.[14] However, in addition to the built architecture, it is also the socioeconomic status of residents that created the community spirit my interviewees describe.

Indeed, socioeconomic class plays a large role in what is considered "appropriate" behavior and how that has changed over time. People entering one another's houses without phoning is uncommon in neighborhoods where protocol requires calling ahead. Going to a neighbor's house for food, as Manal described, is similarly unusual in middle- or upper-class Emirati neighborhoods today, where families typically have ample food for themselves. Socioeconomic class plays a role not only in attitudes toward etiquette but also in terms of changing people's needs. For instance, my older upper-middle-class interlocutors recalled how neighbors used to offer rides to one another and the fun they had congregating together in one car. This changed once they reached higher standards of living and every individual in the household owned a personal car (as did the social norms regarding gender segregation, since teenage boys and girls who are not relatives gathering in one car is no longer acceptable among most Emiratis). The need for sharing also no longer existed due to changes in material status. My interlocutors looked back at many memories nostalgically, yet many also valued improvements in their consumer power and material standards of living.

For women, some of this nostalgia might seem surprising if one considers that some social and cultural norms regarding gender may have been more conservative in older neighborhoods. The sight of women walking to the grocery store or congregating outside their own houses is also uncommon in middle- and upper-class Emirati neighborhoods—although that was something women did in some *shaabiya*s. During my fieldwork, there were very few times that I found Emirati women in Dubai sitting outside their houses on the ground, with their tea, coffee, and afternoon snacks. In all three cases, they were in relatively lower-income neighborhoods, and particularly in *shaabiya* housing.[15] Meanwhile, middle- or upper-class Emirati neighborhoods valued privacy to the extent that they grew high trees and built high fences so that neighbors or those in cars driving by would not be able to look in. My observations are consistent with those of other researchers, who spoke with similarly privileged women in Abu Dhabi who explained that they could not open the door of their house without being well-dressed.[16] Historically, working-class women in the Gulf were more present in the public sphere, while middle-class women were associated with domesticity.[17] As people's socioeconomic status increased, "prestige" and restrictive ideas about female modesty changed people's daily interactions. For instance, while Emirati women could be seen wearing (modest) indoor clothes (these were usually long, colorful dresses and colorful hair covers) as they sat outside their houses a few decades ago, they now wear the *'abaya* (the "outdoor" national dress) in public and are rarely seen socializing in the neighborhood (but rather in places like malls or coffee shops, as we have seen in previous chapters). Middle- and upper-class respectability therefore also play a role in delineating what is considered an appropriate community space or social interactions.[18]

Manal, Amin, and others who had to move out of their neighborhoods noticed changes in their social lives after they moved. They said that neighbors did not know one another anymore, that life was no longer social. Their narratives are similar to those of older Emiratis who experienced social changes in the 1980s and 1990s. In her work on pre-oil Kuwait, Al-Nakib said that the loss of community bonds between neighbors was the result of the growth in state services that replaced the need for community support. The state provided health care and education as well as other public and security services that the community previously delivered. Increased state welfare and higher standards of living meant that "neighborhood responsibilities" decreased. "These benefits and services made Kuwaitis externally dependent on the state. But this was not true of the less affluent townspeople," she said.[19] Furthermore, an encroaching state and private sector is seen as a main contributor to people's loss of their right to the city.[20] In the case of my inhabitants in Satwa, we similarly find that the state's efforts at hygienization have resulted in community displacement. The effects of community displacement have been discussed in various settings.[21] Some inhabitants express not only a sense of loss but a sense of grief and sorrow at being evicted from their neighborhood due to urban renewal.[22]

In this section, I showed how many of Dubai's inhabitants continue to value and remain nostalgic about the informal and community life of their old neighborhoods. In this way, it might be said that the people I spoke to in this chapter appear less adaptable to the spectacular city and the modes of community and belonging that they find there. At the same time, they express pockets of approval—albeit ambivalent approval, for sure—about personal benefits that have accrued to them due to Dubai's developmental trajectory, particularly material upward mobility and safety. It is to these themes, socioeconomic status and safety, that I will now turn to.

TRADING INFORMALITY FOR UPWARD MOBILITY

When I asked Amin if there was anything positive about moving out of Satwa and about his new lifestyle, he told me that perhaps the only positive thing to come out of it was "becoming VIP," although that was not something he particularly cared about. Although they had higher standards of living—large houses, better cars, and higher-paying jobs—Amin and most of my other interlocutors from Satwa argued that they would go back to their old lives if they could. Those whose experiences informed this chapter therefore seem to have a harder time adapting to the spectacular city's development trajectory compared to those featured in other chapters, especially in terms of the ways they discussed its impact on neighborhoods and community. Still, the upward socioeconomic mobility many of them experienced had come to shape many aspects of their everyday lives, and nostalgia for the past was often mixed with expectations that better material conditions were possible and desirable.

Only two of my interlocutors, although upwardly mobile, may still be classified as low income. One of them is Khaleefa, a Comoros Island passport holder, who remains in Satwa. His Emirati friends have already left the neighborhood, and he socializes with them in the new parts of the city but to limited degrees. Spending time in shopping malls; eating at restaurants in City Walk; and even some holiday trips abroad were things that he was able to do with his friends, although sporadically. He went out on weekends, he said, but weekdays were spent in Satwa. Because all his older neighbors had moved out and he now lives near South Asian "bachelors," Khaleefa rarely socializes in the *freej* anymore. He only does so occasionally, when his friends pass by or if his brothers visit and want to sit outside their house on the bench.

Similarly, in Al-Quoz, also a central neighborhood in Dubai inhabited by low-income residents (as well as wealthier ones), I found a group of older Emirati women wearing their colorful "indoor" clothes and sitting on the pavement outside their house, having tea and chatting. Even though the demographic of that specific neighborhood had changed and many blue-collar South Asian men shared houses in that area, these Emirati women continued using the neighborhood as a community space. After speaking to them on two occasions it became clear that, like the inhabitants of Satwa, they had lived there for decades and felt a sense of connection with their old-time neighbors. Like Khaleefa, the younger people said they visited spaces like the Dubai Mall, City Walk, La Mer, and other new developments. But to what extent these were spaces of socializing is unclear. Perhaps they were places they frequented on occasions but not with the regularity that Emiratis with more financial means did. It is also possible that the younger women worked in better-compensated positions than their parents did and could afford a lifestyle their own parents could not. Thus, the sanitized and glitzy city was not necessarily outside their purview and, at least for the younger women there, seemed to contain places they enjoyed (if on occasion). At the same time, commercialized areas of new Dubai do not seem to hold the same importance as they did for my other interlocutors in the previous chapters. This does not mean they are necessarily unimportant to them socially, but rather they may view older neighborhoods as allowing for categorically different or more intimate forms of bonding with others.

Because they have become upwardly mobile (even if a few of them had limited financial means), because they all had their own cars, and because shopping malls and new developments have become such a large part of other people's lifestyles (including their friends'), it seemed that privatized spaces became *more* a part of these interviewees' lives today than they were in the past. For example, Al-Ghurair Center, the oldest shopping mall in Dubai, which many of my interlocutors in other chapters remembered as an important weekend hangout spot, was not necessarily viewed in the same way by my interviewees who grew up in Satwa and other low-income neighborhoods. Although all of them had been there on occasion and had memories, for instance, of being there in Eid, a few of them referred to it as having been a place for the wealthy. Manal said that growing up, her family did not shop in malls but in more affordable areas:

> We knew [a classmate] is "wow" [in this case, rich] because the driver used to pick her up. People didn't wear brands, no one used to wear brands at that time. The biggest "wow, wow" was when a girl wore shoes from Bershka [a high street shop]. I used to save my money so that I could get the shoes from Bershka and be "wow" and wear them to school. I used to make my dad get used to buying things for me from the mall. He didn't buy things from the mall, he used to buy from *souq naif, sanadig* [from markets with relatively cheap prices]. Later when I went to high school I used to say "no, I want it from the mall." . . . I used to tell him, "*lazim*, the school said so [we have to buy from there]."

At the time that Manal was in school, wearing expensive brands was not the norm, even among students from wealthier backgrounds. Bershka was popular among teenage girls from different income levels. Shopping in *souqs*, however, was relatively uncommon (although not nonexistent) among middle classes and in many ways looked down upon. While Manal wanted to get her clothes from the mall, and therefore change the patterns of consumption that were common among her family, she still felt very connected to the *shaabiya*.

On the other hand, when Manal was about to get engaged, her older sister, who dreamed of relocating, advised her not to let her boyfriend approach her family until they moved into their new house so that he would not see where they lived. Manal joked that her sister often said, *"inshallah yhidmoun ishaabiya"* (inshallah they raze the *shaabiya*). It is unclear to what extent her sister's perceptions were commonly shared among people who lived nearby. Most of my interlocutors in this chapter, like Manal, referred to their neighborhoods lovingly and with pride. However, some of my interviewees from Satwa mentioned knowing people from their neighborhood who try to hide the reality of where they grew up.

Manal, who lived in Shaabiyat alshurta before it was razed to build the City Walk, now visited the City Walk on an almost weekly basis after she had moved out of the neighborhood. Our mutual friend, Sandra, lived there, and we all met at her apartment. Manal wistfully remembered her days in the *shaabiya* and, like others, said they were the best days of her life. Like my other interlocutors in chapters 2 and 3, however, the spectacular city was also part of her everyday socializing and interactions. She was interested in visiting the new coffee shops and developments that opened, going to nice restaurants, and seeing and being seen in them. Manal's sense of loss may be slightly ameliorated by several factors that are not unrelated to her new patterns of leisure and socializing: Emiratis are provided with free higher-end housing by the government, homes which are larger and more "modern" than the ones they formerly lived in. Although they had to move away from their central neighborhood, many other high-income Emirati neighborhoods are in the suburbs or outskirts of the city, and living further from the center, although less convenient, provides space, privacy, and other amenities not relegated to low-income groups.

The scenario is more dire, and the tradeoffs different, for residents who are *not* Emirati or those who are not provided with alternative options. Inhabitants of Shaabiyat alshurta did not own the land or their houses— they were owned by the police while inhabitants lived there (rent free).

When the *shaabiya* was razed, Emiratis and, according to an interview, non-Emiratis who were *still* working in the police were provided alternative free housing. However, according to Alawadi, Emiratis could also choose a compensation of $1.5 million, while non-Emiratis in contrast were provided with $81,700, which was enough to rent a three-bedroom apartment for the next three years in Sharjah or Ajman.[23] Manal said that her Yemeni neighbors were provided the same housing as other Emiratis and moved to the same neighborhood as they did (perhaps because they worked with the police force for a very long time). However, it appears that other non-Emiratis did not receive such benefits and thus would not have experienced the same kinds of processes of material upward mobility.

Manal's trajectory may be similar to that of Emiratis who moved from Satwa to other neighborhoods, got relatively well-paying jobs, and lead a more "typical" middle-class lifestyle. Even as she experiences a sense of loss, she also exhibits adaptive agency toward the city's neoliberal changes. This is not entirely different from other, older interlocutors who did *not* grow up in Satwa but in "simpler" times elsewhere in Dubai. While they consider the old days as the best days of their lives and say they wish they could go back in time, they also make comments stating that people must "develop" and "evolve," that they must go forward and not backward. To them, the new developments in the city, although resulting in a loss of community, are emblems of a modernity that they believe is (and should be) inevitable.

Khaleefa and Abdulrazzaq, the ones who still lived in Satwa, initially said they wanted to remain there. But further conversation provoked more ambivalent responses. Khaleefa said that although Satwa's location was excellent and his memories there were dear to him, his neighbors had all left, rendering it somewhat pointless to remain there. Like others, Khaleefa associated the presence of low-wage South Asian men with crime and "immoral behavior" (he gave the example of seeing some people walking in the streets drunk on weekends or strangers peeking into his house) and claimed that these were on the rise with their presence. Based on these changes, Khaleefa said he would move if he was offered newer housing elsewhere. Abdulrazzaq, meanwhile, argued that a best-case scenario would be if Satwa's inhabitants were provided with funds to renovate their houses and remain in their neighborhood. In fact, Abdulrazzaq said he was happy to see tourists coming to his *freej* and taking pictures of his house because it showed that people were interested in Satwa—an indication that he believed showed that it was worth preserving. Rather than tearing it down and building something new, he hoped the area would be regenerated. But at the end of our conversation, however, he said he would move if he was offered a villa elsewhere. These answers are likely to be different if Khaleefa's and Abdulrazzaq's neighbors were not South Asian "bachelors" but their childhood friends and if the *freej* held the same kinds of community bonds for them that it once did.

Similarly, the group of women who congregated outside a house in the *freej* also said they wanted to move, but only if the circumstances allowed them to be with one another. One of them said that she wished a sheikh would pass by, see how they are living, and provide them with new houses. Although they did not want to be separated, she said that they desired newer housing, even if in a different part of the city, so long as they remained neighbors. In that sense, they sought some aspects of a middle-class life common in newly developed neighborhoods as long as they retained other aspects of their lifestyle. However, it is possible that precisely by moving into these middle-class neighborhoods or becoming upwardly mobile, they would come to rely more on the state rather than their community for social support and order, and in doing so lose the connections and bonds they wish to maintain. This is affirmed in an interview with Haitham, an Emirati man in his early forties who was only a teenager when his family moved to Mirdif (a more well-off neighborhood). When I asked him how he would compare the neighborhoods he lived in, he recalled how surprised he was at the differences in the behavior of people in his new neighborhood. Not only was community life different, he said, but also the attitudes of people in the new place:

> When I first moved to Mirdif I felt myself developed [*mi'tawir*]. I felt that I moved to a higher class [laughing]. . . . Suddenly I felt civilized [*mit'hathir*] and developed [*mi'tawir*]. And I found a new group of people in Mirdif, it made me feel that I was really with lower-class people [*shelaitiya*] before [laughs jokingly]. . . . First of all, of course, it was strange for me to see most houses there had drivers. We didn't have a driver. Second thing is that most of them had Filipino maids at their houses, and I saw them speaking English with them. We mostly have Indians, and a maid stays with us for ten

years. . . . Of course, playing in the *freej* is uncommon in Mirdif. . . . And if I [want to visit a friend] . . . . When I would ring the doorbell, I used to see the intercom. And they [the parents] would call to me [from the intercom] and say, "Come stand in front of the intercom, I want to see your face." And they would ask, "Who are you? And what do you want? Whose son are you? Who's your father? Who's your mother? What *freej* did you live in?" And all of that through the intercom [laughs]. . . . Then, an interrogation with [their son] as well. Of course, these things, in [my old neighborhood]—who you are, where did you come from, from which neighborhood, [they never asked]. The only thing you would hear from parents [if the doorbell rang], is "Who is this? Go see who's at the door and don't be late." . . . [In the new neighborhood], you notice someone from inside [the house] looking at you through the windows. They might keep doing this for one or two months.

The behavior that Haitham described appeared cold and uninviting compared to the open doors he had been accustomed to. The increased policing that the parents in Mirdif practice (such as the "interrogation" through the intercom) is a function of people in the neighborhood not knowing one another. Of course, Satwa's inhabitants had practiced their own policing as well. All of them said that "outsiders" who entered Satwa would be stopped and questioned, at times even beaten up by the younger residents for entering the *freej*; but because everyone knew one another in Satwa, there was no reason to have the sort of impersonal policing that parents in Mirdif practiced.

This does not mean that middle-class ways of policing are not violent, albeit not necessarily physically. For instance, the UAE based newspaper *The National*, in an article that was deleted a few hours after it was published online, reported about food courier delivery drivers who had to endure delivery in the UAE's summer heat without the availability of resting spaces. When they tried to take short respites on people's lawns, individuals sometimes turned on their sprinklers on them. They also said that security guards asked them to move when they took breaks in public settings, including in the parks. This highlights how middle-class forms of policing can be extremely harmful, racist, and classist, as I will discuss more below.

The move from the old neighborhood to the modernity of new neighborhoods brought not only more formality in many social customs but also more formal modes of regulation of social interactions and uses of space, which would emanate not only from private sources (such as the above video intercom system) but also from expanded forms of policing and surveillance in everyday life. Like they do in terms of upward mobility and the trade-offs it requires, middle-class residents weigh these benefits, as well as the costs of such changes, in ways that reflect their personal histories and positionalities as well as where they hope to see themselves— and their city—in the future.

ORDER AND SAFETY IN AND BEYOND SATWA

Hamed, a Yemeni man, grew up in an Emirati milieu in Satwa. He dressed, spoke, and felt that he was Emirati, and not only his friends but some of his relatives were UAE citizens. Hamed dropped out of school when he was about eight years old, when his father left his family. His mother lacked a formal education, so she cooked and did other forms of informal labor to make a living. They lived in a *chinko* in Satwa until Hamed's older brother started working and built their house. Although he did not continue his education (which was free for non-Emiratis at that time), Hamed may be considered somewhat upwardly mobile—although he has limited financial means. At about $1900 a month, his job is relatively well paid for someone who did not complete elementary school (by UAE standards, where there is no minimum wage), probably due to his Emirati cultural and social capital. Hamed is still able to afford some travel with his Emirati friends on holidays (to certain locations), to eat with them at restaurants in malls on weekends, and to occasionally socialize in other upscale spaces of the city.

Explaining the strong community bonds that neighbors had, Hamed recalled a period when everyone in his house was unemployed. For three years, he said, his neighbors sent every meal—breakfast, lunch, and dinner—to his house. Satwa's community fulfilled some of the roles that the state does (or does not) today. While the social support that Hamed described can still be found between family members and perhaps very close friends, it rarely exists at a community (neighborhood) level. Aside from family, Emiratis rely on the state for social services and support. While individuals had access to social services in the past, these institutions have become more prominent today. "Dubai has come of age," one person told me, describing the state's consolidation of its power through stronger institutions.

A crucial ingredient in this consolidation is institutions that provide services specifically related to safety, which in practice means heightened capacities for centralized surveillance and policing. When the state provides more services to residents, including policing, inhabitants naturally tend to become more reliant on the state for safety.[24] Those who grew up in less-ordered environments view their (sheltered) children as spoiled and leading relatively dull lives compared to their own. Haitham, an Emirati man in his forties whom I quoted earlier, felt that his children were pampered (*murafaheen*) and that getting into fights or even spending time in the neighborhood's streets would be completely out of character for them (compared to his childhood):

> In the past we would do things. For example, if the bus leaves and doesn't pick us up, we would come home walking. Even though it wasn't close, and we had to cross main streets . . . and it was dangerous, but it wasn't something that stopped us. I was like my kid's age, or younger. But I can't imagine my kid doing this, or that he would know how to go, and where, or that he'll even try.

Haitham felt that this privileged life did not allow his children to "think outside the box" as he did. He said that his children, upon meeting other kids in a *majlis*, would ask one another which school they attend and which grade, followed immediately by questions about the games they play, emphasizing their more "domestic" upbringing. He was not the only one to argue that children today are not street smart like they were in the past. "Before, if you called police you were a coward. Now, it's a different mentality," Haitham said. "Now if a fight is captured, the police will find everyone involved, whether they were the ones in the fight or those video recording it. There's CCTV, security, plainclothes officers, and it's difficult to get away with things like before," he continued.

Shireena, a Filipina Pakistani woman who grew up in Satwa, reiterated this when I asked her if knife fights between young people, which interviewees had discussed, had declined now, saying: "I don't know if [knife fights] happen less now. I think it's just that cops are there in two seconds. I mean, before you could find so many car parks. And you'd find guys fighting [there]. How do you do that now with your cameras and CIDs [plainclothes officers]. You can't get away with that stuff." These responses indicate that through the loss of community (and therefore of community policing), people begin to rely more on the state and state policing. This reliance on the state creates the space for adaptive agency, one which is less likely to disrupt the status quo. My interlocutors had more opportunities to "grow out" of their old ways and become adaptive agents because they were provided with state social support and opportunities on the one hand, and more surveillance and possible punishments on the other. As the state provides services that citizens rely on, they become less dependent on their own communities for these forms of support and more so on the state, and therefore less likely to rock the boat, which can be enhanced by concerns about state policing of their own actions and reactions.

The tendency to contrast how some people behaved in the past to how they may behave today is represented in other examples. When I expressed to Mohammed that I was trying have a better understanding of crime rates (rather than just the stories) in Satwa, he told me it was unlikely that I would find useful statistics because they just did not exist—people did not report them in the past. When he was stabbed as a teenager, Mohammed said, he told the police he did not know who the perpetrators were even though he did. He and others often told me that Satwa was difficult to control, something they feel has entirely changed today. They argued that it was common for people in Satwa to take "justice" into their own hands in the past.

Other forms of policing, perhaps among older people, were more diplomatic. Mohammed recalled the way his neighbors interacted with people who squatted in empty houses and appeared drunk in the neighborhood on various occasions. The neighbors, he said, made a deal with the squatters: they would bring them food every day in exchange for them keeping their drinking activities indoors. Strong community bonds along with weaker institutions allowed individuals to police their neighborhoods in this way. Over time, however, heavier policing and bigger social service programs that accompanied Dubai's development trajectory and were shaped by it meant that the state exerted stronger control.

My interlocutors described these changes positively as examples of Dubai becoming a modern society, thus reflecting both the impact of past fears of violence as well as their class aspirations. Khalil, who described Dubai as having come of age, explained that new laws and regulations were being developed and enforced, that "you can't call people names, you can't pass comments on girls," and that people are becoming more concerned about getting their documents in order and not getting deported (as some of them were stateless or non-Emiratis who had to apply for citizenship or visas). His comment reiterates an important point: as policymakers were in the process of creating the safe, sanitized, and orderly city that it is today, it filled the gaps in its interstices, including by providing citizenship, legal documentation (or in a less positive scenario, deporting some people), education, housing, and employment as well as stronger policing in the name of order.

For my interviewees, their sense of loss and nostalgia for more informal forms of community life existed alongside positive associations with the higher degrees of order and control brought by expansions of surveillance technologies.

Much of the academic literature critiques states such as Singapore for their high degrees of surveillance.[25] Clammer argues that such measures include an insidious internal security apparatus; social policies established in ways that monitor the population; surveillance-heavy policing; and "a punitive system of fines, punishments and mechanisms of public humiliation."[26] Fines apply to smaller misdemeanors such as not flushing the toilet or chewing gum.[27] Some academics also argue that this produces "if not an authoritarian personality, at least a bureaucratic one— inflexible, rule-bound and subservient to authority."[28] Setting aside these essentialized representations of Singapore and its people, this vein of literature raises concerns about the impacts of increased state control over the everyday lives of populations.[29]

Attitudes toward surveillance can also be positive, however. Some people regard the state's increasing presence in their daily lives as a form of protection.[30] Others may themselves engage in lateral forms of surveillance, which is surveillance among their peers, seeking increased forms of order that they can control.[31] Meanwhile, some are more positive about surveillance by the state than surveillance by private entities.[32] Huey argues that homeless people viewed CCTV also in ambivalent ways, with some homeless people specifically choosing to stay in places that have

CCTV to feel safe and others finding that it made no difference to their safety.[33] While individuals may seek more forms of state control and order, academics argue that these quests easily reproduce a society where its members are driven by fear (such as fear of legal repercussions or public shaming, although the latter can also be common with older, community-based forms of informal policing).[34] People seek order and "safety" even when they know it can be invasive, and this appears to be the case for many citizens and long-term residents of Dubai who as adaptive agents find benefits in increased police presence and surveillance, which they have personally experienced as bringing greater levels of personal protection.

Shireena, an upwardly mobile middle-class Filipina Pakistani woman who grew up in Satwa, talked about how different the city in general is today for women compared to the way it was when she was growing up. The effect of policing was felt not only inside Satwa but also outside of it:

> I definitely feel it's more calm now. I remember being groped in the past. Many times. And it was in a public place. Like once I was in a book fair. And someone kept touching me every time. . . . Now there is this fear [of being caught]. I remember I was at Carrefour and I was looking for food. And I remember . . . someone tried to touch me. And I started yelling, yelling, and I said call the security. Back then they didn't, I don't think they had rules. Now it's very serious. . . . Even when it comes to family disputes, like there are options now. There are ways of sorting things out. Women have rights, back then was different. Women weren't seen out as much. . . . I literally remember my mom was wearing a lipstick in Ramadan and the taxi driver was like, "How come you're wearing lipstick? It's Ramadan." Like, you're a taxi driver, it's not your business. . . . The cultural mentality was different. It's like people felt . . . women were something you could control.

Shireena felt that the influx of Western women in daring outfits in the streets, malls, and beaches changed the city—that society adapted to their presence in the public sphere. But aside from the influx of people, she, like other people I interviewed, said that as laws and policing had become stronger and more efficient, people could no longer get away with doing things they once could. Shireena did not grow up in a privileged environment, based on racial/class factors, but she has become upwardly mobile. Her views of safety are shared by my other middle-class and upper-middle-class women.[35]

The exclusion of the most marginalized through the making of the "safe" city is a reality in many parts of the world. Nevertheless, the support for order and state control is not necessarily only held by the elite. Low-income inhabitants also have class aspirations that make them view policing similarly as other middle-class inhabitants, even if this policing may disadvantage them in other ways. Of course, this is not to deny the practical considerations for safety that these individuals have and which also result in them seeking more policing.

Similarly, rather than claiming that safety is available only to elites and the middle class, what appears is that it is *certain* forms of safety that Dubai effectively provides to larger segments of society (such as safety to walk in the street without fear of being robbed), but other forms of safety and security that it does not (such as safety from an exploitative and abusive workplace, which affects the working classes more than privileged groups). A fitting example is an initiative that began in 1993 and ran until 2001 in Dubai under the directives of Sheikh Mohammed bin Rashid Al Maktoum (Crown Prince of Dubai at that time). The initiative sought to reduce street harassment by arresting perpetrators and posting their photographs in newspapers. In the newspaper archives I accessed, harassers' names were not provided, but their faces were completely shown and never blurred.[36] The topic of harassers' photos in newspapers is interesting because most of them appeared to be Emirati men—whom most would argue constitute the most privileged and therefore likely to be protected group in Emirati society. As the names of these individuals were not provided, I cannot claim they were all Emiratis, but according to some of my interviewees, the photos were of citizens. Furthermore, the fact that people were photographed wearing the "national dress" indicates that this initiative did not seek to sanitize Emirati identity or distance it from negative behavior.

According to Nayla, a Palestinian woman who grew up in Dubai, this initiative "made a huge difference [and] harassment stopped almost immediately. No nationalities or families [were] exempt from naming and shaming in the paper." While it is highly unlikely that no one was exempt, in the specific case of harassment it was not necessarily members of marginalized racial groups whose faces appeared in the papers. Similarly, it was generally the opinion among my interlocutors that the expanded policing that has accompanied Dubai's spectacular development has been applied to most groups of society.

Of course, a highly ordered and policed society can lead to a culture of surveillance among citizens, one that may also lead to distrust and further marginalization of groups already disadvantaged. Ibrahim gives examples of naming and shaming practices that ordinary Singaporeans engage in using cameras and online posting to show that citizen monitoring is produced through a society that focuses on discipline and policing.[37] The "fear society" that results can target those engaging in even mundane activities if society deems them inappropriate at a given time. There is also a real concern that marginalized groups anywhere can elicit harsher reactions as well as tougher legal repercussions than privileged members of society for similar actions. Yet some of these forms of citizen policing do not seem to be entirely different from those that are described in liberal contexts as necessary to produce a wholesome urbanity. One example is iconic urban theorist Jane Jacobs's idea of "eyes on the street," which posits that neighborhoods stay safe through a variety of factors, including through members of society policing their communities.[38] Yet white residents calling the police on Black neighbors or passersby can be examples of the problems associated with the "eyes on the street," so this critique should not be limited to illiberal contexts such as Dubai.

Despite the major issues associated with the making of safe and sanitized cities through increased policing and surveillance, urban dwellers in Dubai have ambivalent—or even positive—attitudes toward surveillance because it makes them feel safer (whether they are or not is another issue). Some people find the policing and shaming of harassers in newspapers discussed above to be an effective way to protect women from different backgrounds, including those in non-elite spaces. Like others who recounted experiences of catcalling and harassment, Nayla somewhat apologetically told me that most of the catcalls came from Emirati men. Raj, an Indian man who grew up in Satwa, spoke about women from his family (as well as young boys) not feeling comfortable going out alone because of the harassment they endured, often from Emirati men. Shireena reiterated something similar. These individuals feel that this type of policing has protected them from more privileged members of society. For example, Shireena said:

> There were guys all the time riding cars saying "Come here. You're pretty come here, this or that." And [we] would come because we don't know, we're young. And then when we're in the car, we're like "no, screw you." So, you always have to watch out. . . . If we [went] to beach center, it's a very quiet place. So my mom would say "you and your sister should always go in the bathroom together." Because there were some men who would wear 'abayas and go into the bathroom. There are instances of girls getting harassed in changing rooms. That happened more back then.

How common such occurrences were is unclear, but women, in general, noted a difference in the way they experience the city today compared with the ways they did in the past. They remembered, for example, how driving in the street (and particularly long distances, such as from Dubai to Abu Dhabi) used to be a hassle as harassers followed them in their cars. Some also discussed reduced instances of domestic violence. Shireen said:

> As a woman, I feel good now. I feel that if I go to the police and complain about sexual harassment, that they will take you seriously. I don't think I had that option fifteen years ago. . . . I feel like there's more security for a woman now. I feel like if I had a problem, I can have my say. I don't feel like the option was there before. Because I have had experiences. I've seen my parents fight. I've seen my mom call the cops. They didn't do anything. And now it's changed. Before if the cops would come, the cops didn't do anything back then. The cops used to come and say: "Oh, this is a family matter. We can't do anything about it." Now they'll say [take] this guy to fricking prison.

This comment illustrates how *some* women feel safer in these highly ordered and policed cities, including in homes in their new neighborhoods.[39]

However, international scholarship on different parts of the world has shown that low-income individuals and ethnic minorities are less likely to benefit from policing for several reasons, as they are the groups most criminalized, their complaints are not taken seriously, and they face harsher punishments, among many other reasons.[40] What I present here is not a debate about whether or not these initiatives are effective, but rather an exploration of how they are regarded by some segments of society, specifically Dubai residents who are not the working poor, whose experiences of safety (such as safety from abusive employers at home or harmful work conditions) are not being addressed in this chapter. Also, while women of different backgrounds have benefited from policing efforts described here, not all women have, and different forms of hierarchies and privilege are clear reasons for this disparity.

In summary, Dubai's spectacular development trajectory has made some forms of safety accessible to a *larger* segment of society—such as safety for inhabitants to walk in the street without fear of being robbed or catcalled. Meanwhile, *other* forms of safety (such as from abusive employers or dangerous working conditions) are sidelined, as they often affect the working classes more than elites. My upwardly mobile interlocutors' support for the more surveilled city—despite them getting into trouble with the law when they were younger—signifies their adaptive agency, their class aspirations, and their desires to be part of a "modern" society, where *certain* types of safety exist at greater levels now, not exclusively to the benefit of privileged groups, but *more* likely for their benefit.

SAFETY AND ITS DISCONTENTS BEYOND SATWA

[My driver] doesn't look like a rich guy. He's dressed, he looks like a working-class, blue-collar. He looks like that. His attire is like that. He looks Indian. His mannerism is like that. The police stopped him at the [Jumeirah Beach Residence (JBR)] beach, asked him what he's doing there, asked him to show his Emirates ID. They told him he's not allowed there. So the security [safety] that I so cherish, which is my number two reason for living in Dubai, I wonder if the price we're paying for that security is not a bit too high. . . . There's a lot of segregation. . . . I am always thinking, am I a hypocrite? I enjoy the security that this segregation provides.

Samira, an upper-class Indian woman in her forties, prided herself on her ethical value system and progressive outlook. She was socially conscious and cared about equality, convictions that she realized somewhat clashed with her appreciation for Dubai's safety—a safety that was at times made possible through the exclusion of certain segments of society, often low-income South Asian men.[41] I could relate to how Samira felt.

What her driver experienced at JBR was clearly racist and classist, but people like Samira and I chose our spaces of socializing (consciously or subconsciously) along class lines, one reason being their perceived safety. We rarely socialized in the low-income spaces of the city. To what extent were we complicit in a system of exclusion?

In her reflection about her ethnography of Indian middle-class residents of old Dubai, Vora says that "the mostly male spaces of the *souk* [in old Dubai] were taking a daily toll" on her.[42] In comparison, she felt more comfortable in shopping malls, which she described as more feminine spaces that provided "not only middle-class comfort but also gendered safety."[43] As a visibly brown woman (Vora is an American of Indian descent), Vora assumed she would feel most at home in old Dubai. And in some ways, she did. Old Dubai was the first place in which Vora felt she could forget the color of her skin, something she was constantly reminded of in the US.[44] Yet as a woman and a US citizen, Vora felt more at ease in parts of new Dubai such as its shopping malls. This was not a complete and uncontested comfort: Vora says that "the shopping malls and hotels in New Dubai also produced anxieties around wealth, leading to what I always felt were false performances of fully belonging in those spaces."[45] The safety and comfort being created in Dubai sometimes excludes and includes people in clear ways—and sometimes in ways that are more ambiguous.

As I showed previously, the making of a "safe" space results in marginalizing certain groups (often low-income South Asian or African men) who are deemed a threat to safety. Some of my interlocutors eagerly endorsed these exclusions. Hannah, a half Arab, half South Asian woman, for example, said that there are verses in the Quran about God elevating some people over others in rank, citing this as an example that class divisions are therefore "acceptable" in society. Others were more diplomatic, but nevertheless expressed that they felt that low-income South Asian men stared at them. Some endorsed racist or classist tropes, while others argued that certain policies create this environment of "staring." For example, the latter group explained that "bachelors" look at women because they come to the Gulf countries without their families (i.e., wives, whom they are not financially able to sponsor), and because they end up living in neighborhoods that are male dominated (sometimes exclusively male).

Men from various backgrounds are guilty of staring, and some (or many) women similarly express discomfort in these spaces as well.

Others believed it was not always someone's identity but "inappropriate" behavior that dictates who gets excluded or not. Adnan, a Lebanese man in his thirties, said that he saw South Asian men being asked to leave the public beach at times, but it was because they were not following the rules. In one particular case, they wore their underwear rather than swimming suits. The question, of course, is to what extent are these standards applied equally for all members of society? For instance, a white man dressed inappropriately might be stopped and requested to leave. Would he be regarded as suspicious for loitering around the beach? Not likely.

Randa, a Lebanese woman in her late thirties, told me that she saw a security guard stopping a South Asian man at the beach and asking him to leave. She was glad, she said, because he was taking photos of women in their swimsuits. It is these contentions that make it difficult to navigate how to approach topics of gender, class, and race in the city as related to safety—particularly a city where the majority of the population is men, and where questions about what an inclusive space can look like given that demographic are especially difficult to answer. On the one hand, in a quote in an article from the *New York Times*, we find a Moroccan woman at Dubai's public beach frustrated at the authorities for not doing enough to stop men from invading her personal space and making her feel uncomfortable.[46] On the other hand, intentions to create a space for these women results in segregating and further marginalizing certain groups more than others, as we have seen in previous analysis of spaces of consumption such as malls that are built in ways that either directly or indirectly exclude lower-income groups. Here, it is useful to note how transforming norms of surveillance and policing in the name of safety for the middle and upper classes provide the mechanism for such segregation.[47]

In her work on American Muslims who moved to the UAE, Sanchez shows that "Muslim migration flows are not one-way journeys from Muslim-majority countries to the so-called West" and that "contrary to popular thought ... migration out of the EU and United States into Middle Eastern countries is informed by migrants' desires for safety and security." Sanchez argues that people initially assumed the safety American Muslims sought was out of fear of racism they had experienced in the US, but in reality, they sought safety in its more general sense. Many of her interlocutors said they left the US because of fears of violence, drugs, or even their children being kidnapped, unrelated to their religious identity.[48] Comparing Dubai with the West, Sara said: "You know, even Europe, Europe is not safe . . . Europe is awful." Sara often brought up issues of safety and seemed passionate about it, so I asked her to expand on the topic as we sat together at a coffee shop for an interview. "My husband and I, we don't lock the door [to the house]. We always lose keys. . . . So now for example, my door is unlocked," she said.

Sara also felt safer in Dubai than in other Middle Eastern countries. She had previously lived in Iraq, Lebanon, and Jordan, and although she had grown up in a privileged household, her parents had expected her to be independent at a young age. She said that she'd had to take taxis in Jordan since she was ten years old:

> Can you imagine the experiences that I was in, they were low class. . . . Like, for example, they would adjust their mirror, their rear-view mirror . . . they would put it low . . . that's why you don't wear shorts or skirts in a taxi. That's why you cover up. And also, the comments they make. . . . Once in Lebanon I was waiting for a shared taxi and felt someone's breath on my neck. There was a guy who was trying to kiss me.

Sara said that the taxi drivers in Jordan and Lebanon often tried to trick her by shutting the meter so she would have to pay more. This was why for her, "Dubai is heaven," due to its high degree of regulations. While Sara frequently described harassers in Jordan and Lebanon as "low-class people," she felt safe in Dubai's low-income spaces. Unlike some of my female interviewees in chapter 3 who did not feel at ease in male-dominated, low-income neighborhoods such as Souq Naif and Satwa, Sara said being stared out didn't bother her; in Dubai, she walked everywhere and was certain no one would harass her. She contrasted this sense of safety to her experience of Jordan: "In Jordan, I avoid—because of the people, because they're very low-class . . . I'm sorry, I'm sounding very classist. . . . [But I can't] walk wherever I want the way I do in Dubai. I can't do that in Jordan." She explained that in Jordan, she often had to think about what she was wearing and what time she was going out, and that taking public transportation had been out of the question because "it's hot and the people are rude and just not respectful." When I asked how she felt about taking public transportation in Dubai, she said it was different because

> Dubai has laws and policies. And the regulators whose eyes are everywhere, and people fear the law. They respect the law, no one is above the law ... [in] Jordan, if I [were] on a bus, I would be with the same type of people [as in Dubai]. I would be there with the same economic classes. ... [But] in Dubai, I would actually take my kids. ... Even if it's crowded here [in public transportation], it's still good. I went to Burj Khalifa [by metro] for New Year's. ... The estimated number of people was 1 million. And ... I went by the metro. You don't understand how it was. It wasn't just with the masses. I was with *umam* [literally "nations"]. ... All the nationalities, and my sister and I were by ourselves. ... We stood with all the people. We came back at 3:00 or 4:00 a.m. [on] the metro. ... It was a beautiful experience. It was amazing, very organized ... we were stuck to each other. But everyone was so respectful. Everyone was polite, we would let each other [pass]. ... And other than that, the organizers were there, the police was there, everywhere. ... There were families ... there were groups of men. ... There were women who covered their hair. There were many women in miniskirts. There were all types of people, but no one bothers anyone.

When Sara said that people fear the law, she was invoking a conceptual difference between safety and security in the UAE. As Sanchez explains, for American Muslims who moved to the UAE in the 1990s, the UAE presented them with comparative safety, but *security* was a different matter.[49] Noncitizens are always at risk of being forced to leave the country if their visas aren't renewed or even of being deported if they lose their job. As a result, Sanchez says, American immigrants felt safe in the UAE but not secure. Sara believed that this lack of security increased people's fear of the law and that this fear led to increased safety.

Both the law and power dynamics play a role here. While Sara was a privileged member of society in both Jordan and Lebanon, she found it was difficult to argue with service workers in Jordan because they were "locals." Having a Jordanian waiter made it difficult to "ask for their manager," she explained. Although a taxi driver in Jordan does not have the economic capital that Sara does, his status as an Arab citizen gives him more power than a low-income South Asian or Southeast Asian man in the Middle East would. In Dubai, where neither Sara nor the taxi driver are citizens, the racial and class factors together put Sara in a position of power over a taxi driver. Thus, as an upper-middle-class woman, Sara benefits in particular ways from the making of the "safe" and orderly city.

Ultimately, many middle-class inhabitants of Dubai found that state control and sanitization made Dubai a safe and comfortable place for them. Those from Satwa shared similar beliefs to an extent, noting this positively as an example of the city's modernity. Yet, in comparison with some of their peers, for Satwa's previous inhabitants this positive aspect was coupled with other realities, such as the loss of community they had grown up with.

CONCLUSION

As various groups of inhabitants have faced community ruptures in the course of Dubai's spectacular development, as seen in Satwa, this process has been combined with increasing state promises of sanitization and safety in public spaces, as well as access to other related forms of privilege such as home privacy. Upwardly mobile inhabitants from Satwa and other *shaabiyas* miss the old days when life was informal and less ordered, when they had a sense of community and ownership over their neighborhood. This chapter thus highlights relationships to the spectacular city that are much more strained than in previous chapters, given the deep sense of loss these inhabitants experience. Indeed, not everyone can adapt themselves to the spectacular city, given their context and backgrounds, and what they feel they have lost in the process. Yet these inhabitants have also responded to these changes through the embrace of forms of surveillance and policing that promote their comfort and unfettered access to the city's spaces while lessening their vulnerability to street-level crimes, which can be seen as a form of adaptation. This conceptualization of safety renders heightened regimes of surveillance and enforcement to be utterly normal parts of, and even preconditions for, living a modern, upwardly mobile life in which anxieties about development are mediated by combined feelings of nostalgia and progress. I demonstrated that forms of ambivalence toward the spectacular city rooted in memory and nostalgia are being actively mediated by residents' desires for safety and sanitization. This also elucidates what types of safety the spectacular city provides, as well as the forms of security it simultaneously withholds.

Conclusion

As I wrote this book, my mind often went back to my earlier research that I had written before beginning my doctoral studies. I found that my perception had changed on many things. This made me wonder how different this book would look not only if I had written it at a different point in time, but if I was someone else—particularly someone who did not grow up in Dubai having the same privileges I did. I pondered this question many times: How can one write about (myriad) lived experiences, when doing so inevitably prioritizes (and marginalizes) some experiences over others? This question was a common thread that connected my current and earlier work. I will briefly shift to my previous research, only to highlight my thought process as I was conducting the research that led to this work.

A few years ago, I wrote about the topic of "national dress" in the Gulf and constructions of authenticity. I argued that Gulf states use national dress to construct an idea of a homogeneous citizenry and to promote national cohesion, but that this inevitably results in various forms of exclusion. At that time, my interest was in highlighting how ethnic diversity among the citizenry was being homogenized through national narratives that imposed a "Bedouin" form of dress that sidelined Ajami, Indian, and African influences on *khaleeji* cultures. Other forms of exclusion are also created through these national symbols. For instance, for some (particularly low-income) noncitizens, the Gulf national dress can be seen and experienced as a symbol of social hierarchy.

These perceptions and (systemic) exclusions are important to interrogate. Yet I had also neglected to explore another important aspect: how familiar this dress was to me. I wrote about the *dishdasha* (or *kandora*) as a reinvented tradition, but not about the warm personal connections I have toward it. In reality, the first thing that comes to mind when I think of the white robe is not cultural homogenization but of my father who wears it. The *dishdasha* was always a part of my life growing up. Not only is the way it looks familiar, but even the way it *sounds*. I can tell when my father comes home from work because of the sound his *dishdasha* makes when he walks.

The academic literature about Gulf national dress that I had read and was influenced by, although very insightful, did not relay that experience. Despite its nuances and valuable contributions, it *could not* relay these personal experiences because it was not written by Gulf citizens or those who had personal connections with these forms of dress. This highlights, as I briefly noted in my Introduction, the contentions of being a privileged but also underrepresented minority. I was extremely privileged in various ways in my own country, but in the international academic literature (and media and other mainstream representations), Emiratis were not the ones writing about their own societies. The questions this raised were ones I had to constantly negotiate as I wrote this book.

The *dishdasha* may be in some ways a top-down construction of "authentic" and exclusive homogeneity, but to me it is also a reminder of home and familiarity. Yet I recognize that for others it is the exact opposite, and that it serves purposes of creating and enforcing social distinctions. Despite this, my previous research feels incomplete without including my personal connections to it. Affect has the potential to reframe current scholarly narratives about the Gulf. The more complicated aspect of this is finding out how to balance my own lived experiences as a privileged woman with more critical inquiry that recognizes that others' lived experiences are entirely different from my own, and that various social hierarchies frame these experiences.

Coming back to my current research about urban spaces in Dubai, discourses of authenticity and belonging and exclusion, I grapple with similar questions. My work explores the adaptive work that citizens and residents engage in to inhabit the spectacular city—its shopping malls, new developments, chain restaurants, and fancy coffee shops. These are neoliberal spaces that can and should face critique: they are not accessible to all (and sometimes many) segments of society; they often put small businesses at great competitive disadvantage; and they are built to generate profit rather than to create community, among many other issues. Inhabitants do not have an official say in the making of their cities in this development model.

Yet for many middle-class (as well as wealthier and less wealthy) inhabitants, both citizens and noncitizens, these are everyday spaces. These are spaces where they have childhood and teenage memories. These are places where they go to bump into other members of their community. They are also where social contestations and cultural negotiations happen, where people who have different ideas about appropriate social and cultural norms— for instance, around gender comportment and modesty—encounter one another and observe (and later sometimes critique) their respective interactions. They are significant social and cultural spaces. The argument about these spaces' exclusionary nature is indeed important. But those who use them to intermingle have created a reality not only about spectacle and extravagance but rather (or also) of everyday socializing.

What inspired me to write about some of these questions is an article by Nandini Kochar, who illustrated the complexity of writing about any place.[1] Kochar, a female photographer who worked on a project about low-income noncitizen men in the UAE, wanted to highlight the experiences of a demographic neglected by mainstream official narratives. While Kochar said she made incredible human connections through her work, she also stated her discomfort at being subject to the male gaze and some instances of sexual harassment during her work with the men (although it is important to note, as she did, that these instances were not specific to a certain class or nationality of men). She wrote of her complicated feelings regarding photographing them, saying "I felt pathetic for attempting to tell dignifying stories of their lives while they relished in a moment of my indignation."

Kochar photographed and wrote about the low-income spaces of the city that some depict as the truly "authentic" spaces. She moves, however, beyond the binaries of good/bad, authentic/fake, and belonging/exclusion. Her article resonated with me because it reflected my own struggles when thinking about the complex realities of any place and how to navigate contradictory feelings about them. Kochar thought of her photography as an act of solidarity and a form of activism, but her experiences and positionality show the complexity of navigating intersectional forms of privilege and vulnerability. Her story raises questions of how to understand, interact with, and write about different places—whether they are the old, low-income, and "authentic" places or the new and glitzy ones.

My argument is not that all these places are the same because they are all exclusionary in their own ways. The low-income noncitizens whom Kochar describes are living in precarious conditions, while those with whom I conducted my ethnography live more privileged lives. Well-off inhabitants benefit from and reproduce exclusions in ways that low-income inhabitants cannot. Rather, my point is that there is a need for more research on the Gulf that navigates these complexities instead of maintaining the aforementioned binaries. Middle-class inhabitants are important to study too, in part because they can play such an important role in defining what becomes normative in a place.

Alongside a critical inquiry, these lived experiences provide valuable insights. Reprising the example of the *dishdasha*, it can be at once a symbol of social hierarchy and a top-down homogenization drive, and yet also provoke feelings of comfort or familiarity for some—sometimes through its exclusionary nature, but sometimes also despite it. The same contradictions can be said for the city at large. Acknowledging these complexities may allow us to critique exclusions while providing more nuanced understandings of spectacular cities and moving beyond moralizing narratives about them.

I hoped to do this in my book, where I showed how in the middle of Dubai's "glitziest" shopping mall, South Asian teenagers practice their dance moves and old Emirati men have their daily chat at a coffee shop. I demonstrated that these scenes are at odds with scholars', journalists', and even some residents' routine descriptions of Dubai's neoliberal developments as sterile, alienating, and hostile to personal expression and community bonds. Such narratives depict inhabitants of politically "illiberal" cities either as helplessly watching as elite-driven spectacles unfold around them or engaging in (at the very least, subtle) acts of resistance toward the spectacle. Close observation of how Dubai's inhabitants make use of their city's spectacular spaces as they go about their daily lives, however, indicates more complex social processes at play.

This book presented a view of "new Dubai" that centers the work residents do to adapt to the city's rapid changes. Through this work, Dubai's spectacular places are transformed into personally and communally important cultural sites: they house memories; provide a place to gather, connect with one another, and "see and be seen"; and serve as public spaces where residents observe and negotiate social norms. The spectacular city becomes a site of not only loss and marginalization but also belonging and community. Residents do not respond to neoliberal development with oppressed passivity, wholehearted support, or active resistance, but with an array of individual and communal strategies that aim to make its developments fit their everyday social needs. In their relationships to Dubai, many of my interlocutors are adaptive agents who are neither resistors nor zealous supporters of the city's development trajectory but rather individuals seeking to live a normal life. Inhabiting the spectacle often requires engaging in an adaptive agency, one that is characterized by daily habits of adapting one's own lifestyle to fit given structures while adapting these same structures to daily personal needs.

I showed that it is a common scholarly and popular pursuit to seek, implicitly or explicitly, to uncover the "real" city that lies beneath the veneer of the spectacles of Dubai, which advances a problematic binary that contrasts supposedly "authentic," "local" spaces with "alienating," "tourist" ones. The notion that Dubai's spectacular developments are objectively foreign, alienating, and oppressive is part of what I call the *discourse of authenticity* that pervades public and scholarly discussions of the city. This discourse voices sincere concerns about neoliberalism, exclusionary urbanism, and rapid changes. Yet, it also elides many residents' complex feelings of not only loss but also gain in relation to the new developments, fetishizes "authentic" low-income spaces, and creates a false binary of fake/authentic. *Everyday Life in the Spectacular City* shows that, in contrast to this discourse's assumptions, many of Dubai's inhabitants form meaningful relationships with these "inauthentic" spaces, which they use to meet needs of socializing, expression, and navigating social mores. In doing so, middle-class inhabitants construct layered and intersectional practices of *ambivalent belonging* through which they position themselves and others.

Inhabitants' activity in forming meaningful connections with and within spectacular spaces grounded the book's conceptual contribution to understanding how contemporary subjects living in illiberal societies actively respond to their societies' neoliberal spectacles. If we are guided by dominant discourses of authenticity, alienation, and disempowerment, these connections come as a surprise: How can we understand demonstrated patterns, revealed through my research, of residents' making them into resonant spaces of meaning and belonging? The scholarly discourse of authenticity conceptualizes certain ways residents might relate to spectacular developments such as those in Dubai: by resisting the neoliberal agenda the developments represent, helplessly watching as the spectacle unfolds, or accepting it without question. In this view, any kind of belonging that inhabitants might form in relation to these developments represents either false consciousness or the dominant form of agency this paradigm recognizes: resistance. I argue that my interlocutors' adaptive work, through which they create new paradigms of authenticity and belonging, constitutes a form of agency that this discourse elides. Therefore, adaptive agency offers a tool for understanding not only the actions of middle-class residents of contemporary Dubai but also a more globalized phenomenon.

Notes

1. While considered neoliberal, these cities are also often understood as politically "illiberal."

2. A *majlis* is traditionally a semipublic room detached from the main house, open to men in one's neighborhood.

3. Furthermore, there are developments in Dubai that may appear to be mundane and everyday but are referred to in the literature as glitzy spaces or as nonplaces (and implied to be spectacular). For instance, Acuto refers to the Dubai metro as a "comfort-proof enclave"—even though a metro is normally regarded as a mundane and everyday space for working and middle classes. Similarly, a Starbucks may usually be referred to as a nonplace or a sanitized space, as well as a "superficial" place. These are all characteristics of the spectacle, and therefore I refer to them all as "spectacles" here.

4. Michele Acuto, "High-Rise Dubai Urban Entrepreneurialism and the Technology of Symbolic Power," *Cities* 27 (2010): 272–284; Khaled Alawadi, "Whatever Happened to Dubai's Public Spaces?," *International Journal of Middle Eastern Studies* 50 (2018): 562–567; Farah Al-Nakib, *Kuwait Transformed: A History of Oil and Urban Life* (Stanford, CA: Stanford University Press, 2010) and "This Is Not What I Thought: The Pitfalls and Potentials of Kuwait's Segregated Nocturnal Landscape" (presentation, After Dark: Nocturnal Landscapes and Public Spaces in the Arabian Peninsula, Harvard University, Cambridge,

MA, 2017); Omar AlShehabi, "Removing Roots" [*Iqtilaa' aljuthoor*], "Right to the City" [*Alhaq fee almadina*], and "AlMuharraq and the Changing City of the Arab Gulf" [*Almuharraq wal madina almutahawilla*], Gulf Centre for Development Policies (2019); Mike Davis, "Sand, Fear and Money in Dubai," in *Evil Paradises: Dreamworlds of Neoliberalism*, ed. Mike Davis and Daniel Bertrand Monk (New York: New Press, 2007); Yasser Elsheshtawy, *Temporary Cities: Resisting Transience in Arabia* (London: Routledge, 2019); Ahmed Kanna, "Class Struggle and De-exceptionalizing the Gulf," in *Beyond Exception: New Interpretations of the Arabian Peninsula*, ed. Ahmed Kanna, Amélie Le Renard, and Neha Vora (Ithaca, NY: Cornell University Press, 2020), 100–122.

5. Elsheshtawy, *Temporary Cities*, 37. Emphasis added.

6. Elsheshtawy, 6.

7. Saba Mahmood, *Politics of Piety: The Islamic Revival and the Feminist Subject* (Princeton, NJ: Princeton University Press, 2004).

8. Here I build on Alexei Yurchak's *Everything Was Forever, Until It Was No More: The Last Soviet Generation* (Princeton, NJ: Princeton University Press, 2005). He coined the concept of "normal subjects" who were neither supporters nor resistors of the USSR, but individuals who wanted to live a safe, self-sufficient, manageable life within the political structures they were living under.

9. Jim Krane, *Dubai: City of Gold* (New York: St. Martin's Press, 2009).

10. M. Pacione, "City Profile Dubai," *Cities* 22, no. 3 (2005): 255–265.

11. Yasser Elsheshtawy, *Planning Middle Eastern Cities: An Urban Kaleidoscope* (London: Routledge, 2004); Pacione, "City Profile Dubai."

12. Elsheshtawy, *Planning Middle Eastern Cities*.

13. Elsheshtawy, *Planning Middle Eastern Cities*; Todd Reisz, *Showpiece City: How Architecture Made Dubai* (Stanford, CA: Stanford University Press, 2020).

14. Reisz, 178.

15. Reisz, 146.

16. Reisz, 138.

17. Reisz, 159.

18. Reisz, 148.

19. Reisz, 149.

20. Reisz, 201.

21. Elseshtawy, *Planning Middle Eastern Cities*.

22. Todd Reisz, "Future Flyovers: Dubai in 1971," *Architectural Design* 85, no. 1 (2015): 100–105.

23. Elseshtawy, *Planning Middle Eastern Cities*, 195.

24. Pacione, "City Profile Dubai."

25. Ziauddin Sardar, "After the Sheikhs: The Coming Collapse of the Gulf Monarchies, by Christopher Davidson," *The Independent*, January 18, 2013.

26. Natalie Koch, *The Geopolitics of Spectacle: Space, Synecdoche, and the New Capitals of Asia* (Ithaca, NY: Cornell University Press, 2018), 22.

27. Natalie Koch, "Urban 'Utopias': The Disney Stigma and Discourses of 'False Modernity,'" *Environment and Planning A: Society and Space* 44 (2012): 2445–2462.

28. Koch, "Urban 'Utopias.'"

29. Ryan Centner, "On Not Being Dubai: Infrastructures of Urban Cultural Policy in Istanbul and Beirut," *International Journal of Cultural Policy* 26, no. 6 (2020): 722–739.

30. Guy Debord, *Comments on "The Society of the Spectacle,"* trans. Malcom Imrie (New York: Verso, 1988), 2.

31. Koch, *The Geopolitics of Spectacle.*

32. Anne-Marie Broudehoux, "Delirious Beijing: Euphoria and Despair in the Olympic Metropolis," in *Evil Paradises: Dreamworlds of Neoliberalism,* ed. Make Davis and Daniel Bertrand Monk (New York: New Press, 2007): 87–101, and "Spectacular Beijing: The Conspicuous Construction of an Olympic Metropolis," *Journal of Urban Affairs* 29, no. 4 (2007): 383–399; Harry H. Hiller, "Mega-Events, Urban Boosterism and Growth Strategies: An Analysis of the Objectives and Legitimations of the Cape Town 2004 Olympic Bid," *International Journal of Urban and Regional Research* 24, no. 2 (2000): 439–458; Koch, *The Geopolitics of Spectacle*; Hyun Bang Shin, "Unequal Cities of Spectacle and Mega-Events in China," *City* 16, no. 6 (2012): 728–744.

33. Anne-Marie Broudehoux, "Images of Power: Architectures of the Integrated Spectacle at the Beijing Olympics," *Journal of Architectural Education* 63, no. 2 (2010): 54; Hiller, "Mega-Events, Urban Boosterism"; Shin "Unequal Cities of Spectacle."

34. Broudehoux, "Images of Power," 54; Hiller, "Mega-Events, Urban Boosterism"; Shin, "Unequal Cities of Spectacle."

35. David Harvey, *A Brief History of Neoliberalism* (Oxford: Oxford University Press, 2007).

36. Koch, *The Geopolitics of Spectacle,* 14.

37. Koch, 16.

38. Natalie Koch and Neha Vora, "Laboratories of Liberalism: American Higher Education in the Arabian Peninsula and the Discursive Production of Authoritarianism," *Minerva* 57 (2019): 555; Koch, *The Geopolitics of Spectacle,* and "Post-Triumphalist Geopolitics: Liberal Selves, Authoritarian Others," *ACME* 18, no. 4 (2019): 909–924.

39. Elsheshtawy, *Temporary Cities,* 1–2. Emphasis added.

40. AlShehabi, "AlMuharraq and the Changing City of the Arab Gulf"; Khaldoun Al-Naqeeb, *Society and State in the Gulf and Arab Peninsula: A Different Perspective* (London: Routledge, 1990), 91.

41. Lila Abu-Lughod, "The Romance of Resistance: Tracing Transformations of Power through Bedouin Women," *American Ethnologist* 17, no. 1 (1990): 53.

42. Elsheshtawy, *Temporary Cities*, 2.

43. Mahmood, *Politics of Piety*, 8.

44. Acuto, "High-Rise Dubai Urban Entrepreneurialism"; Alawadi, "Whatever Happened to Dubai's Public Spaces?"; Al-Nakib, *Kuwait Transformed* and "'This Is Not What I Thought'"; AlShehabi, "Removing Roots," "Right to the City," and "AlMuharraq and the Changing City of the Arab Gulf"; Davis, "Sand, Fear and Money in Dubai"; Elsheshtawy, *Temporary Cities*; Kanna, "Class Struggle and De-exceptionalizing the Gulf."

45. Alexei Yurchak, "The Cynical Reason of Late Socialism: Power, Pretense, and the Anekdot," *Public Culture* 9, no. 2 (1997): 161–188; "Soviet Hegemony of Form: Everything Was Forever, Until It Was No More," *Comparative Studies in Society and History* 45, no. 3 (2003): 480–510; and *Everything Was Forever, Until It Was No More: The Last Soviet Generation* (Princeton, NJ: Princeton University Press, 2005).

46. Yurchak, "Soviet Hegemony of Form," 482–484.

47. Yurchak, "The Cynical Reason of Late Socialism," 164.

48. Mahmood, *Politics of Piety*, 5.

49. Koch, "Urban 'Utopias,'" 2447.

50. Koch, *The Geopolitics of Spectacle*.

51. Koch, "Urban 'Utopias,'" 2456.

52. Koch, *The Geopolitics of Spectacle*.

53. Koch, 105.

54. Koch, *The Geopolitics of Spectacle*.

55. Michael Marrus, *The Holocaust in History* (Toronto: Key Porter, 2000), 91.

56. Yurchak, "The Cynical Reason of Late Socialism."

57. "Dubai Police Combat Menace of Begging, Arrest 416 since the Beginning of Ramadan," *Gulf Today*, May 22, 2020, https://www.gulftoday.ae/news /2020/05/22/dubai-police-arrest-416-beggars-since-the-beginning-of-ramadan.

58. Idil Akinci, "Culture in the 'Politics of Identity': Conceptions of National Identity and Citizenship among Second-Generation Non-Gulf Arab Migrants in Dubai," *Journal of Ethnic and Migration Studies* 46, no. 11 (2019): 2309–2325; Ali Sayed, *Dubai: Gilded Cage* (New Haven, CT: Yale University Press, 2010); Laure Assaf, "'Abu Dhabi Is My Sweet Home': Arab Youths, Interstitial Spaces, and the Building of a Cosmopolitan Locality," *City* 24, no. 5–6 (2020): 830–841; Natalie Koch, "Is Nationalism Just for Nationals? Civic Nationalism for Noncitizens and Celebrating National Day in Qatar and the UAE," *Political Geography* 54 (2015): 43–53; Shaundel Nicole Sanchez, "Migrating to the Middle East in Search of Safety," *Anthropology News*, August 14, 2019, https://www.anthropology-news .org/articles/migrating-to-the-middle-east-in-search-of-safety/; Nada Soudy,

"Home and Belonging: A Comparative Study of 1.5 and Second-Generation Egyptian 'Expatriates' in Qatar and 'Immigrants' in the U.S.," *Journal of Ethnic and Migration Studies* 43, no. 9 (2017): 1544–1561; Neha Vora, *Impossible Citizens: Dubai's Indian Diaspora* (Durham, NC: Duke University Press, 2013); Koch and Vora, "Laboratories of Liberalism."

59. Marco Antonsich, "Searching for Belonging—An Analytical Framework," *Geography Compass* 2, no. 6 (2010): 647–648.

60. Koch and Vora, "Laboratories of Liberalism," 541.

61. Nira Yuval-Davis, "Belonging and the Politics of Belonging," *Patterns of Prejudice* 40, no. 3 (2006): 197–214.

62. Ulf Hedetoft and Mette Hjort, *The Post-National Self: Belonging and Identity* (Minneapolis: University of Minnesota Press, 2002).

63. Arshad Isakjee, "Dissonant Belongings: The Evolving Spatial Identities of Young Muslim Men in the UK," *Environment and Planning A: Society and Space* 48, no. 7 (2016): 1339.

64. I have anonymised most of the social media posts I refer to in this thesis. Most of them are from public accounts but *not* from public figures, and some of them make their accounts private on and off. I did this to maintain their privacy (particularly in a society where many people know one another, and where some people's older social media posts might embarrass them today). I published one of my chapters with the largest degree of references to social media posts (chapter 2) in *Arab Studies Journal*. I discussed this issue of anonymity with the editors (and shared with them the original tweets and URL links). They have checked the validity of the tweets and agreed to publish the article while anonymizing the social media users I reference. Most of the references to social media posts in this thesis, therefore, have been already published and verified in this published article (AlMutawa 2020 in the Bibliography).

65. For more work on the experiences of low-income inhabitants in the Gulf, please refer to Andrew Gardner, *City of Strangers: Gulf Migration and the Indian Community in Bahrain*, (Ithaca, NY: Cornell University Press, 2010); Lavaanya Kathiravelu, *Migrant Dubai: Low Wage Workers and the Construction of a Global City* (London: Palgrave Macmillan, 2016); Elsheshtawy, *Temporary Cities*; Pardis Mahdavi, *Gridlock: Labor, Migration, and Human Trafficking in Dubai* (Stanford, CA: Stanford University Press, 2011); and Rhacel Salazar Parrenas, *Unfree: Migrant Domestic Work in Arab States* (Stanford, CA: Stanford University Press, 2021). For work on middle-class noncitizens, please refer to Vora, *Impossible Citizens*; and for elite noncitizens, please refer to Amélie Le Renard, *Western Privilege: Work, Intimacy, and Postcolonial Hierarchies in Dubai*, trans. Jane Kuntz (Stanford, CA: Stanford University Press, 2021); and Katie Walsh, " 'It Got Very Debauched, Very Dubai!' Heterosexual Intimacy amongst Single British Expatriates," *Social and Cultural Geography* 8, no. 4 (2007): 507–533. For work on Indian middle classes and working classes, please

refer to Andrea Wright, *Between Dreams and Ghosts: Indian Migration and Middle Eastern Oil* (Stanford, CA: Stanford University Press, 2021); and Sayed Ali, *Dubai: Gilded Cage* (New Haven, CT: Yale University Press, 2010) on citizens and noncitizens in Dubai.

66. *Khaleeji* or *khaliji* refers to citizens of the Gulf Cooperation Council states.

67. Elizabeth Buckner, "The Other Gap: Examining Low-Income Emiratis' Educational Achievement" (working paper 15, Al Qasimi Foundation, Ras Al-Khaimah, UAE, 2018). Also, according to a director at a charity organization, an Emirati *family* with less than $4,000 per month may be considered low-income and be eligible for social support. Aside from Buckner's research, it was difficult to find any research on low-income citizens in the UAE.

68. Isakjee, "Dissonant Belongings," 1339.

69. Khaled Alawadi, "Urban Redevelopment Trauma: The Story of a Dubai Neighbourhood," *Built Environment* 40, no. 3 (2014): 357–375.

70. Laure Assaf, "Le Shopping Mall Comme Moment Urbain" [The Shopping Mall as an Urban Moment], *Ateliers D'Anthropologie* 44 (2017); Kathiravelu, *Migrant Dubai*; Vora, *Impossible Citizens*, and "Anthropology and the Educational Encounter," in *Beyond Exception: New Interpretations of the Arabian Peninsula*, ed. Ahmed Kanna, Amélie Le Renard, and Neha Vora (Ithaca, NY: Cornell University Press, 2020), 80–99.

71. Anjana Kumar, "All You Need to Know: How to Sponsor Your Family in the UAE," *Gulf News*, November 5, 2019, https://gulfnews.com/uae/all-you-need-to-know-how-to-sponsor-your-family-in-the-uae-1.1572935794448.

72. Margaret Crawford, "Contesting the Public Realm: Struggles over Public Space in Los Angeles," *Journal of Architectural Education* 49, no. 1 (1995): 4–9; Nancy Frazer, "Rethinking the Public Sphere: A Contribution to the Critique of Actually Existing Democracy," *Social Text*, no. 25–26 (1990): 56–80; Peter Jackson, "Domesticating the Street: The Contested Spaces of the High Street and the Mall," in *Images of the Street*, ed. Nicholas Fyfe (New York: Routledge, 1998), 176–191; Loretta Lees, "Urban Renaissance and the Street: Spaces of Control and Contestation," in *Images of the Street*, ed. Nicholas Fyfe (New York: Routledge, 1998), 236–253; Sylke Nissen, "Urban Transformation: From Public and Private Space to Spaces of Hybrid Character," *Czech Sociological Review* 44, no. 6 (2008): 1129–1449.

73. Acuto, "High-Rise Dubai Urban Entrepreneurialism," 281.

74. Miriam Cooke, *Tribal Modern: Branding New Nations in the Arab Gulf* (Oakland: University of California Press, 2014); Ahmed Kanna, *Dubai: The City as Corporation* (Minneapolis: University of Minnesota Press, 2010); Anh Nga Longva, *Walls Built on Sand: Migration, Exclusion, and Society in Kuwait* (Boulder, CO: Westview Press, 1997).

75. Jane Jacobs, *The Death and Life of Great American Cities* (New York: Vintage Books, 1961). Most Emirati women wear the *'abaya* (a long, black cloak) and most Emirati men wear the *kandora*, a long, white dress (*kandora* in Emirati dialect or *thoub* and *dishdasha* in Saudi and Kuwaiti dialects, respectively). For more on how national dress is used to distinguish citizens from noncitizens, please refer to Akinci, "Culture in the 'Politics of Identity'"; Rana Khalid AlMutawa, "National Dress in the UAE: Constructions of Authenticity," *New Middle Eastern Studies* 6 (2016): 1–13; and Sulayman Khalaf, "National Dress and the Construction of Emirati Cultural Identity," *Journal of Human Sciences* 11 (2005): 230–267.

76. Akinci, "Culture in the 'Politics of Identity.'"

77. Amélie Le Renard, "How Western Residents in Riyadh and Dubai Produce and Challenge Exceptionalism," in *Beyond Exception: New Interpretations of the Arabian Peninsula*, ed. Ahmed Kanna, Amélie Le Renard, and Neha Vora, 55–79 (Ithaca, NY: Cornell University Press, 2020). Le Renard, a French academic whose research largely focuses on Saudi women, noted a discrepancy between the way other academics reacted to her research on Saudi women as opposed to her research on Westerners in the Gulf, saying she received more pushback from academic reviewers when she wrote about the latter. Peer reviewers found this work more controversial than when she was "interpreted as a white Arabic-speaking expert on 'Saudi women'" (51). Although she felt that she was analyzing her ethnographic material with the same methods she used when conducting ethnographies with Saudi women, academics found her work on Westerners in the Gulf somewhat offensive and having a "denouncing tone" (51). Vora and Kanna note similar pushback from Western academics when they presented their work about "expats" and white privilege and complicity in the Gulf at an international conference. I present these as examples of who is "allowed" to speak about whom, who gets questioned about their positionality, and who is seen as a fair object of study (e.g., Saudi women, Emiratis) and who is not.

78. Talal Al-Rashoud (@tsalrashoud), "As Gulf academics . . .," Twitter, December 13, 2020, 5:00 p.m., https://twitter.com/tsalrashoud/status /1338166849721290754.

CHAPTER 1. (IN)AUTHENTICITY IN BRAND DUBAI

1. Yasser Elsheshtawy, "Mapping Nightscapes: Scenes from Dubai and Abu Dhabi" (presentation, After Dark: Nocturnal Landscapes and Public Spaces in the Arabian Peninsula, Harvard University, Cambridge, MA, 2017.)

2. Michele Acuto, "High-Rise Dubai Urban Entrepreneurialism and the Technology of Symbolic Power," *Cities* 27 (2010): 282–283.

3. Acuto, 282.

4. Natalie Koch and Neha Vora, "Laboratories of Liberalism: American Higher Education in the Arabian Peninsula and the Discursive Production of Authoritarianism," *Minerva* 57 (2019): 546.

5. Ahmed Kanna, *Dubai: The City as Corporation* (Minneapolis: University of Minnesota Press, 2010).

6. Idil Akinci, "Dressing the Nation? Symbolizing Emirati National Identity and Boundaries through National Dress," *Ethnic and Racial Studies* 43, no. 10 (2020): 1776–1794; Rana Khalid AlMutawa, "National Dress in the UAE: Constructions of Authenticity," *New Middle Eastern Studies* 6 (2016): 1–13; Kanna, *Dubai: The City as Corporation*; Sulayman Khalaf, "National Dress and the Construction of Emirati Cultural Identity," *Journal of Human Sciences* 11 (2005): 230–267; James Onley, "Transnational Merchant Families in the Nineteenth- and Twentieth-Century Gulf," in *The Gulf Family: Kinship and Politics*, ed. Alanoud Alsharekh (London: Al Saqi Books and London Middle East Institute SOAS, 2007), 37–56; Neha Vora, *Impossible Citizens: Dubai's Indian Diaspora* (Durham, NC: Duke University Press, 2013).

7. Akinci, "Dressing the Nation?"; AlMutawa, "National Dress in the UAE"; Miriam Cooke, *Tribal Modern: Branding New Nations in the Arab Gulf* (Oakland: University of California Press, 2014); Kanna, *Dubai: The City as Corporation*; Khalaf, "National Dress"; Anh Nga Longva, *Walls Built on Sand: Migration, Exclusion, and Society in Kuwait* (Boulder, CO: Westview Press, 1997); Onley, "Transnational Merchant Families"; Vora, *Impossible Citizens*.

8. Natalie Koch, "Urban 'Utopias': The Disney Stigma and Discourses of 'False Modernity,'" *Environment and Planning A* 44 (2012): 2445–2462; Koch and Vora, "Laboratories of Liberalism"; Benjamin Smith, "'The Sheikh of Araby Rides a Cadillac': Popular Geoeconomic Imaginations, Positional Anxiety and Nouveau Riche Territories," *Environment and Planning D: Society and Space* 34, no. 3 (2016): 564–580.

9. I build on Florida's description of the "creative class"—engineers, doctors, and others working in the knowledge-based economy. Richard Florida, *The Rise of the Creative Class . . . and How It's Transforming Work, Leisure, Community and Everyday Life* (New York: Basic Books, 2002).

10. William Roseberry, "The Rise of Yuppie Coffees and the Reimagination of Class in the United States," *American Anthropologist* 98 no. 4 (1996): 762–775; and David Ley, *The New Middle Class and the Remaking of the Central City* (Oxford: Oxford University Press, 1996). Roseberry describes the spread of "yuppie coffees" in the 1980s and 1990s, arguing that certain sections of the US middle class tried to distinguish themselves from others by using products that invoked more "exotic," "traditional," and "authentic" places and people, with the coffee beans' places of origin and flavors being described in detail to invoke this authenticity. In some North American cities, gentrification happened through a

postwar counterculture, which included groups like artists and bohemians who gathered in places such as New York's Greenwich Village. Ley uses the term "cultural middle class" to refer to the people of the "counterculture" and the gentrifiers of poorer neighborhoods, who varied from students, social workers, teachers, and shopkeepers to journalists, lawyers, and architects. Through their counterculture, this cultural middle class differentiated themselves from others in the middle class whom they saw as "suburban" and "boring." There is a similar demographic of "bourgeois bohemians" who wanted to have a comfortable life but "don't want to live like their parents do—especially not in the suburbs—and don't mind a little dirt on the streets as long as they feel safe."

11. Khaled Alawadi, "Place Attachment as a Motivation for Community Preservation: The Demise of an Old, Bustling, Dubai Community," *Urban Studies* 54, no. 13 (2017): 2973–2997; Farah Al-Nakib, "'This Is Not What I Thought': The Pitfalls and Potentials of Kuwait's Segregated Nocturnal Landscape" (presentation, After Dark: Nocturnal Landscapes and Public Spaces in the Arabian Peninsula, Harvard University, Cambridge, MA, 2017); Barbara Brown and Douglas Perkins, "Disruptions in Place Attachment," in *Place Attachment*, ed. Irwin Altman and Setha M. Low (New York: Plenum Press, 1992): 279–304; Katherine Brickell, Melissa Fernández Arrigoitia, and Alexander Vasudevan, *Geographies of Forced Eviction: Dispossession, Violence, Resistance* (London: Palgrave Macmillan, 2017); Yasser Elsheshtawy, *Temporary Cities: Resisting Transience in Arabia* (London: Routledge, 2019); Marc Fried, "Grieving for a Lost Home," in *The Urban Condition: People and Policy in the Metropolis*, ed. Leonard J. Duhl (New York: Simon & Schuster, 1963): 151–171; Goksenin Inalhan and Edward Finch, "Place Attachment and Sense of Belonging," *Facilities* 22, no. 5–6 (2004): 120–128; Douglas Porteous and Sandra Smith, *Domicide: The Global Destruction of Home* (Montreal: McGill-Queen's University Press, 2001).

12. Fried, "Grieving for a Lost Home."

13. Elsheshtawy, *Temporary Cities*.

14. Elsheshtawy, *Temporary Cities*; Kanna, *Dubai: The City as Corporation*.

15. Elsheshtawy, *Temporary Cities*; Michael Herb, *The Wages of Oil: Parliaments and Economic Development in Kuwait and the UAE* (Ithaca, NY: Cornell University Press, 2014); Kanna, *Dubai: The City as Corporation*.

16. Elsheshtawy, *Temporary Cities*, 222. Emphasis added.

17. *Shalwar kameez* is a traditional dress worn by South Asians, although it has classed and gendered implications here. Most of my interlocutors referred to it when they were speaking about men, although women also wear it. For most of my interlocutors (Arabs and South Asians), the *shalwar kameez* denotes that someone is working class.

18. Roger Brubaker, *Ethnicity without Groups* (Cambridge, MA: Harvard University Press, 2004).

19. Brubaker, *Ethnicity without Groups*.

20. Alawadi, "Place Attachment as a Motivation"; Farah Al-Nakib, *Kuwait Transformed: A History of Oil and Urban Life* (Stanford, CA: Stanford University Press, 2016); Omar AlShehabi, "Removing Roots" [*Iqtilaa' aljuthoor*], "Right to the City" [*Alhaq fee almadina*], and "AlMuharraq and the Changing City of the Arab Gulf" [*Almuharraq wal madina almutahawilla*], Gulf Centre for Development Policies (2019); Elsheshtawy, *Temporary Cities*; Kanna, *Dubai: The City as Corporation*; Vora, *Impossible Citizens*.

21. Alawadi, "Place Attachment as a Motivation"; AlShehabi, "Removing Roots" and "Right to the City"; Elsheshtawy, *Temporary Cities*.

22. Quoted from the Brand Dubai website: "Brand Dubai is the creative arm of the Government of Dubai Media Office. We come up with and execute projects and initiatives for our fast growing and culturally diverse city. Everything we do reflects all our forward-thinking nation has achieved." https://branddubai.ae/en/about-brand-dubai.

23. Gillian Duncan, "Coronavirus: Seven-Year-Old Reunited with Mother after Writing to RAK Ruler," *The National*, May 13, 2020, https://www.thenationalnews.com/uae/health/coronavirus-seven-year-old-reunited-with-mother-after-writing-to-rak-ruler-1.1018912; Sarwat Nasir, "Heart-Warming Moment German Mum Is Reunited with Daughter in Abu Dhabi after a Month," *The National*, April 7, 2020, https://www.thenationalnews.com/uae/transport/heart-warming-moment-german-mum-is-reunited-with-daughter-in-abu-dhabi-after-a-month-1.1003000; Daniel Sanderson, "Pregnant American Teacher Flown Home to UAE after Government Help," *The National*, March 30, 2020, https://www.thenationalnews.com/uae/health/pregnant-american-teacher-flown-home-to-uae-after-government-help-1.999425.

24. Ali Sayed, *Dubai: Gilded Cage* (New Haven, CT: Yale University Press, 2010); Ahmed Kanna and Najib B. Hourani, "'A Group of Like-Minded Lads in Heaven': Everydayness and the Production of Dubai Space," *Journal of Urban Affairs* 36, no. 2 (2014): 605–620; Vora, *Impossible Citizens*.

25. Sayed, *Dubai: Gilded Cage*; Kanna and Hourani, "'A Group of Like-Minded Lads in Heaven'"; Lavaanya Kathiravelu, *Migrant Dubai: Low Wage Workers and the Construction of a Global City* (Basingstoke: Palgrave Macmillan, 2016); Vora, *Impossible Citizens*.

26. Vora, *Impossible Citizens*.

27. David Harvey, *A Brief History of Neoliberalism* (Oxford: Oxford University Press, 2007).

28. Randall Amster, "Patterns of Exclusion: Sanitizing Space, Criminalizing Homelessness," *Social Justice* 30, no. 1 (2003): 195–221; Marco Castrignanò Maurizio and Pia De Rubertis, "The Homeless and Public Space: Urban Policy and Exclusion in Bologna," *Papers in Political Economy* 51 (2014), https://journals.openedition.org/interventioneconomiques/2441; Elsheshtawy, *Temporary Cities*.

29. John Paul Brammer, "I'm from a Mexican Family. Stop Expecting Me to Eat 'Authentic' Food," *Washington Post*, May 15, 2019.

30. David Grazian, *Blue Chicago: The Search for Authenticity in Urban Blues Clubs* (Chicago: University of Chicago Press, 2003), 13.

31. Alawadi, "Place Attachment as a Motivation"; Al-Nakib, *Kuwait Transformed*; Elsheshtawy, *Temporary Cities*, and "Urban Enclaves and Transient Cosmopolitanism," *City* 24, no. 5–6 (2020): 805–817.

32. Elsheshtawy, "Urban Enclaves and Transient Cosmopolitanism," 814.

33. Elsheshtawy, *Planning Middle Eastern Cities: An Urban Kaleidoscope* (London: Routledge, 2004), 195.

34. Alawadi, "Place Attachment as a Motivation"; Al-Nakib, *Kuwait Transformed*; AlShehabi, "Removing Roots," "Right to the City," and "AlMuharraq and the Changing City of the Arab Gulf"; Elsheshtawy, *Temporary Cities*, and "Urban Enclaves and Transient Cosmopolitanism"; Ahmed Kanna, "Class Struggle and De-exceptionalizing the Gulf," in *Beyond Exception: New Interpretations of the Arabian Peninsula*, ed. Ahmed Kanna, Amélie Le Renard, and Neha Vora (Ithaca, NY: Cornell University Press, 2020), 100–122.

35. Natalie Koch, *The Geopolitics of Spectacle: Space, Synecdoche, and the New Capitals of Asia* (Ithaca, NY: Cornell University Press, 2018), 17.

36. Calvert Jones, *Bedouins into Bourgeois: Remaking Citizens for Globalization* (Cambridge: Cambridge University Press, 2017).

37. Koch and Vora, "Laboratories of Liberalism." Also see Natalie Koch, "We Entrepreneurial Academics: Governing Globalized Higher Education in 'Illiberal' States," *Territory, Politics, Governance* 4, no. 4 (2016): 438–452; and Neha Vora, *Teach for Arabia: American Universities, Liberalism, and Transnational Qatar* (Stanford, CA: Stanford University Press, 2018).

38. Omar AlShehabi (omaralshehabi), "A faculty member . . .," Twitter, December 10, 2019, 2:48 p.m., https://twitter.com/omaralshehabi/status/1204412467238989824.

39. Omar AlShehabi (omaralshehabi), "How does it make sense . . .," Twitter, December 10, 2019, 3:23 p.m., https://twitter.com/omaralshehabi/status/1204421374539948032.

40. Abbas Lawati, "Gulf Cities Have a Long Way to Go before Leading the Arab World," *Al-Monitor*, October 13, 2014, https://www.al-monitor.com/pulse/ar/originals/2013/10/gulf-dubai-abu-dhabi-doha-arab.html.

41. Yasser Elsheshtawy, "We Need to Talk about the Modernism Fetish in the Gulf," *Dubaization*, December 26, 2017, http://dubaization.com/post/168964409563/we-need-to-talk-about-the-modernism-fetish-in-the-Gulf.

42. Elsheshtawy, "We Need to Talk."

43. Michael Kubo, "Building Identities: Transnational Exchange and the Authorship of Modern Gulf Heritage" (presentation, "Re-engaging with the Gulf Modernist City," Gulf Research Meeting, Cambridge, UK, 2019).

44. Marc Augé, *Non-places: Introduction to an Anthropology of Supermodernity* (London: Verso, 1995).

45. Omar AlShehabi (omaralshehabi), "The region is not a tabula rasa. There is a rich tradition that focuses on resistance, liberation, anti-colonialism, anti-imperialism, etc. How could 'decolonising' in the manner it is discussed now (mainly in the west) detract or enhance this tradition? This should be the focus," Twitter, December 10, 2019, 3:23 p.m., https://twitter.com/omaralshehabi/status /1204421380126720000.

46. Koch and Vora, "Laboratories of Liberalism," 557.

47. Koch, "We Entrepreneurial Academics"; Koch and Vora, "Laboratories of Liberalism"; Vora, *Teach for Arabia*.

48. Vora, *Teach for Arabia*.

49. Vora, 9.

50. Jones, *Bedouins into Bourgeois*, 130.

51. This is the case at Zayed University and Higher Colleges of Technology but less so at UAE University.

52. Those who have *marsoom* are individuals who are due to be given Emirati passports and/or citizenship (citizenship confers full citizenship, a UAE passport does not) but who have not yet received it.

53. Pierre Bourdieu, *Distinction*, trans. Richard Nice (Cambridge, MA: Harvard University Press, 1984). For an example of this in a Middle East context, see Christa Salamandra, *A New Old Damascus: Authenticity and Distinction in Urban Syria* (Bloomington: Indiana University Press, 2005).

54. Koch, "Urban 'Utopias.'"

55. Acuto, "High-Rise Dubai Urban Entrepreneurialism," 282. For examples of artists who do the same, please refer to Elizabeth Derderian, "Authenticating an Emirati Art World: Claims of Tabula Rasa and Cultural Appropriation in the UAE," *Journal of Arabian Studies* 7, no. 1 (2017): 12–27.

56. Simon Jenkins, "As They Did Ozymandias, the Dunes Will Reclaim the Soaring Folly of Dubai," *The Guardian*, March 20, 2009, https://www.theguardian .com/commentisfree/2009/mar/20/dubai-decline-middle-east.

57. Smith, "'The Sheikh of Araby Rides a Cadillac,'" 565.

58. Smith, 577.

59. Smith, 577.

60. Natalie Koch, "Post-Triumphalist Geopolitics: Liberal Selves, Authoritarian Others," *ACME* 18, no. 4 (2019): 914.

61. Natalie Koch, "Orientalizing Authoritarianism: Narrating US Exceptionalism in Popular Reactions to the Trump Election and Presidency," *Political Geography* 58 (2017): 145–147; and Koch, "Post-Triumphalist Geopolitics."

62. Ryan Centner, "On Not Being Dubai: Infrastructures of Urban Cultural Policy in Istanbul and Beirut," *International Journal of Cultural Policy* 26, no. 6 (2020): 722–739.

63. Elsheshtawy, *Temporary Cities*, vii–viii. Emphasis added.

64. Grazian, *Blue Chicago*.

65. Grazian, 21.

66. Sharon Zukin, *Naked City: The Death and Life of Authentic Urban Places* (Oxford: Oxford University Press, 2009), 11.

67. Zukin, 28.

68. Terressa Benz, "Urban Mascots and Poverty Fetishism: Authenticity in the Postindustrial City," *Sociological Perspectives* 59, no. 2 (2016): 467–478.

CHAPTER 2. NEGOTIATING BELONGING IN DUBAI'S GLITZY, NEOLIBERAL SPACES

1. Reem Al-Kamali, "Bin Souqat Mall," *Al-Bayan*, September 18, 2019, https://www.albayan.ae/opinions/white-ink/2019-09-18-1.3651603.

2. Michel de Certeau, *The Practice of Everyday Life*, trans. Steven Rendall (Berkeley: University of California Press, 1984).

3. Michael Sorkin, *Variations on a Theme Park: The New American City and the End of Public Space* (New York: Hill & Wang, 1992), 159.

4. Anke Reichenbach and Najla Ibrahim, "Pulling at Our Heartstrings: Emirati-Themed Leisure Venues as Places of Belonging," *Urban Anthropology* 48, no. 1–2 (2019): 129–181; Henri Lefebvre, *Writings on Cities*, trans. Eleonore Kofman and Elizabeth Lebas (Oxford: Blackwell, 1996).

5. Sorkin, *Variations on a Theme Park*; Omar AlShehabi, "Removing Roots" [*Iqtilaa' aljuthoor*], "Right to the City" [*Alhaq fee almadina*], and "AlMuharraq and the Changing City of the Arab Gulf" [*Almuharraq wal madina almutahawilla*], Gulf Centre for Development Policies (2019); Yasser Elsheshtawy, *Temporary Cities: Resisting Transience in Arabia* (London: Routledge, 2019); Ahmed Kanna, *Dubai: The City as Corporation* (Minneapolis: University of Minnesota Press, 2010).

6. Farah Al-Nakib, "'This Is Not What I Thought': The Pitfalls and Potentials of Kuwait's Segregated Nocturnal Landscape" (presentation, After Dark: Nocturnal Landscapes and Public Spaces in the Arabian Peninsula, Harvard University, Cambridge, MA, 2017).

7. Mike Davis, "Sand, Fear and Money in Dubai," in *Evil Paradises: Dreamworlds of Neoliberalism*, ed. Mike Davis and Daniel Bertrand Monk (New York: New Press, 2007); Sorkin, *Variations on a Theme Park*.

8. Khaled Alawadi, "Lifescapes beyond Bigness: The UAE's Exhibition at the Venice Architecture Biennale 2018" (lecture, NYUAD, Abu Dhabi, April 11, 2018).

9. Nira Yuval-Davis, "Intersectionality, Citizenship and Contemporary Politics of Belonging," *Critical Review of International Social and Political Philosophy* 10, no. 4 (2007): 561–574.

10. Elsheshtawy, *Temporary Cities*, 41.

11. Lila Abu-Lughod, "The Romance of Resistance: Tracing Transformations of Power through Bedouin Women," *American Ethnologist* 17, no. 1 (1990): 47.

12. Walter Benjamin, *The Arcades Project*, trans. Howard Eliland and Kevin McLaughlin (Cambridge, MA: Harvard University Press, 1999).

13. Anke Reichenbach, "A Ladies' Paradise? Reflection on the Shopping Mall as a Place for Female Flânerie" (presentation, Varieties of Emirati Womanhood, NYUAD, Abu Dhabi, 2018).

14. Amélie Le Renard, "Shopping Mall Practices by Young Saudi Women: Sociability and Consumerism in Riyadh" [Pratiques du shopping mall par les jeunes Saoudiennes: Sociabilité et consumérisme à Riyad], in *Mondes et places du marché en Méditerranée: Formes sociales et spatiales de l'échange*, ed. Franck Mermier and Michel Peraldi (Paris: Editions Karthala, 2011), 188–190.

15. Nazgol Bagheri, "The Emancipated Flâneuse in Tehran's Shopping Malls," in *Walking in Cities: Quotidian Mobility as Urban Theory, Method and Practice*, ed. Timothy Shortell and Evrick Brow (Philadelphia, PA: Temple University Press, 2015), 83–100.

16. Reichenbach, "A Ladies' Paradise?"

17. Marc Augé, *Non-places: Introduction to an Anthropology of Supermodernity* (London: Verso, 1995).

18. A *meelas* is a detached building next to the main house found in many Gulf countries, mostly used by males to socialize and discuss different topics, ranging from business to social issues, although there are some women who attend the (women's) *meelas* as well. The *meelas* existed in the pre-oil era and is still used today.

19. Lefebvre, *Writings on Cities*.

20. Twitter user, "Some guys . . .," Twitter, December 19, 2012, 3:13 p.m.

21. Hussein Musharbek (@hmusharbek), "I passed by Deira City Centre . . .," Twitter, December 27, 2011, 4:28 p.m., https://mobile.twitter.com/hmusharbek /status/151700998056976384.

22. Twitter user, "In regard to the men in Starbucks Mercato, as soon as you enter everyone looks at you, don't tell me I entered your milas," Twitter, July 3, 2012, 4:32 p.m.

23. Twitter user, "A girl enters Home Bakery," Twitter, June 24, 2019, 10:24 a.m. (tweet no longer available), https://twitter.com/63_eq/status /1143087413222420480.

24. Sneha Krishnan, "Style-ish Girls and Local Boys: Young Women and Fashion in Chennai," in *Styling South Asian Youth Cultures: Fashion, Media and Society*, ed. Lipi Begum, Rohit K. Dasgupta, and Reina Lewis, 49–64 (London: I. B. Tauris, 2018). Krishnan refers to a similar phenomenon in India, particularly in regard to the attitudes of upper-middle-class women who are part of a more global cosmopolitan habitus toward lower-middle-class individuals'

socializing and courtship patterns. She says that these upper-middle-class women "typically did not stand around at bus stops, or even go to malls, to engage in sight *adikkarathu*—gazing—more often than not having access to social spaces where they could meet, interact with, and 'date' within western idioms of this term, young men of their own age and social class. Some of these women described sight and style to me, as 'juvenile' and not clued into global discourses of erotics and romance."

In the case of my interlocutors who criticize courtship and other socializing habits in malls as being "backward," these practices of distinction reflect a cultural class distinction more than an economic one. Performances of social distinction take place at various dimensions. They take place among non-mallgoers who criticize different mall attendees, but they also take place among mallgoers who engage in "inappropriate" behavior at the mall. Similarly, some of those who engage in "inappropriate" behavior themselves engage in practices of distinction, seeking, for example, to be found only in certain exclusive coffee shops at the mall.

25. Elshestawy, *Temporary Cities*, 27. Emphasis added.

26. Twitter user, "Mirdif City Centre = A neighbourhood full of Emiratis <3 <3," Twitter, October 13, 2012, 5:46 p.m.

27. Kanna, *Dubai: The City as Corporation*.

28. Assaf, "Le Shopping Mall Comme Moment Urbain."

29. In almost all these examples, women are central to these discussions, highlighting how women (everywhere) are more scrutinized in public spaces than men.

30. Twitter user, "No, I don't think so [in response to a comment about women in Saudi Arabia dressing more modestly than in neighboring countries]. In 20 years it would be normal to see many without abayas, go to any mall here and see the colors of the abayas, 5 years ago they weren't wearing colored abayas," Twitter, November 19, 2015, 9:25 p.m.

31. Twitter user, "The situation in Dubai Mall . . .," Twitter, February 1, 2020, 3:24 p.m.

32. "Sheikh Mohammed Orders Stunt Drivers to Clean Dubai Streets," *Khaleej Times*, February 24, 2017, https://www.khaleejtimes.com/news/crime /stunt-drivers-to-clean-dubai-streets-for-reckless-driving-at-city-walk.

33. L. L. Wynn, *Pyramids and Nightclubs: A Travel Ethnography of Arab and Western Imaginations of Egypt, from King Tut and a Colony of Atlantis to Rumors of Sex Orgies, Urban Legends about a Marauding Prince, and Blonde Belly Dancers* (Austin: University of Texas Press, 2007).

34. Twitter user, "Secretly dating in the cafe that used to be in debenhams! . . . in deira city centre where i spent most of my teen age days! Memories," Twitter, March 26, 2011, 2:43 p.m.

35. Twitter user, "It's the first time I like Mercato . . .," Twitter, August 19, 2010, 10:15 a.m.

36. Twitter user, "Brother Muhammad Al Suwaidi's stand was not insignificant and should not be ignored. A warning bell has rung regarding a dangerous matter in a society that is considered conservative, and which took place under the eyes of both individuals and institutions. In the name of trends there is a desire for our youth to deviate and ally with the devil. We don't want God's wrath and don't want to disobey him. We want official institutions to take a stand," Twitter, March 9, 2020, 6:23 p.m.

37. Assaf, "Le Shopping Mall Comme Moment Urbain."

38. Twitter user, "The sunset prayer is sounding and our youth are drinking their coffee in Starbucks Mercato. Let the prayer be patient, they are busy. God be with you," Twitter, July 12, 2012, 4:48 p.m.

39. Twitter user, "You [a woman] sit in Starbucks . . .," Twitter, August 8, 2013, 7:44 p.m.

40. Twitter user, "I saw Rafeea Al Hajesi in Mercato, the clothes that she's wearing!!!!!!!!!!!!!!," Twitter, March 6, 2017, 5:44 p.m; "It's over [overly revealing], I swear when I saw her from behind I thought she's English based on these clothes," Twitter, March 6, 2017, 5:46 p.m.

41. Twitter user, "I swear it's ridiculous, an old woman from a Gulf country, [wearing] abaya and niqab [and smoking] shisha!!!!! In *souq* Jumeirah. If you have no shame do as you please," Twitter, November 13, 2012, 3:20 p.m.

42. Assaf, "Le Shopping Mall Comme Moment Urbain."

43. Anouk de Koning, *Global Dreams: Class, Gender, and Public Space in Cosmopolitan Cairo* (Cairo: AUC Press, 2009); Mark Allen Peterson, *Connected in Cairo: Growing Up Cosmopolitan in the Modern Middle East* (Bloomington: Indiana University Press, 2011).

44. Teresa Platz Robinson, *Café Culture in Pune: Being Young and Middle Class in Urban India* (New Delhi: Oxford University Press, 2014).

45. Twitter user, "This is from my childhood memories, I had bought it from Deira City Centre when I was young in year 1996 and I still keep it. At that time Deira City Centre was like Dubai Mall today. Beautiful days, my father used to take us to Magic Planet and into the play cage and next to the cage was a an Arkid Sonic game that drives a police car, I always used to play in," Twitter, May 8, 2018, 10:13 a.m., https://twitter.com/uaexlr/status/993780849077379073.

46. Al-Nakib, "'This Is Not What I Thought.'"

47. Twitter user, "Walking around Deira City Center . . .," Twitter, July 8, 2017, 5:30 p.m., https://twitter.com/NassaKB/status/883725061961768963.

48. de Certeau, *The Practice of Everyday Life*; Marta Wieczorek, "Introduction: Anthropological Debates on Place-Making," *Urban Anthropology* 48, no. 1–2 (2019): 6.

49. Abdalla Al Neaimi (@AbdllahAlneaimi): "In Deira City Centre . . .," Twitter, May 5, 2019, 7:48 p.m., https://twitter.com/AbdllahAlneaimi/status/1125110042108280833.

CHAPTER 3. GLOBALIZATION AND DIVERSITY AT A COSMOPOLITAN CROSSROADS

1. Old Dubai is quite clean but less sanitized than new Dubai; "dirty" here may convey that reality rather than necessarily a lack of cleanliness.

2. Neha Vora, *Impossible Citizens: Dubai's Indian Diaspora* (Durham, NC: Duke University Press, 2013).

3. Hélène Thiollet and Laure Assaf, "Cosmopolitanism in Exclusionary Contexts," *Population, Space and Place* 27, no. 1 (2020).

4. Amin Moghadam, "The Staging of Cultural Diversity in Dubai: The Case of Dubai Art Fair," *Identities: Global Studies in Culture and Power* 28, no. 6 (2021): 717–733.

5. Sayed Ali, *Dubai: Gilded Cage* (New Haven, CT: Yale University Press, 2010); Yasser Elsheshtawy, *Temporary Cities: Resisting Transience in Arabia* (London: Routledge, 2019); Andrew Gardner, *City of Strangers: Gulf Migration and the Indian Community in Bahrain* (Ithaca, NY: Cornell University Press, 2010); Ahmed Kanna, *Dubai: The City as Corporation* (Minneapolis: University of Minnesota Press, 2010); Ahmed Kanna and Najib B. Hourani, "'A Group of Like-Minded Lads in Heaven': Everydayness and the Production of Dubai Space," *Journal of Urban Affairs* 36, no. 2 (2014): 605–620; Lavaanya Kathiravelu, *Migrant Dubai: Low Wage Workers and the Construction of a Global City* (London: Palgrave Macmillan, 2016).

6. Asef Bayat, *Life as Politics: How Ordinary People Change the Middle East* (Stanford, CA: Stanford University Press, 2013), 186–187. Emphasis added.

7. Omar AlShehabi, "Right to the City" [*Alhaq fee almadina*], Gulf Centre for Development Policies (2019).

8. Kathiravelu, *Migrant Dubai*.

9. Jon Binnie, Julian Holloway, Steve Millington, and Craig Young, *Cosmopolitan Urbanism* (London: Routledge, 2006), 8.

10. Binnie et al., *Cosmopolitan Urbanism*; Pnina Werbner, "Global Pathways: Working Class Cosmopolitans and the Creation of Transnational Ethnic Worlds," *Social Anthropology* 7, no. 1 (1999): 17–35.

11. James Onley, "Transnational Merchant Families in the Nineteenth- and Twentieth-Century Gulf," in *The Gulf Family: Kinship and Politics*, ed. Alanoud Alsharekh (London: Al Saqi Books and London Middle East Institute SOAS, 2007), 37–56; Vora, *Impossible Citizens*; Rana AlMutawa, "Monolithic Representations and Orientalist Credence in the UAE," *Identity & Culture in the 21st Century Gulf* (Autumn 2016): 23–25, https://www.academia.edu/30056784 /Monolithic_Representations_and_Orientalist_Credence_in_the_UAE; Arang Keshavarzian, "From Port Cities to Cities with Ports: Towards a Multiscalar History of Persian Gulf Urbanism in the Twentieth Century," in *Gateways to the*

World: Port Cities in the Persian Gulf, ed. Mehran Kamrava (Oxford: Oxford University Press, 2016), 19–41.

12. Yasser Elsheshtawy, "Urban Enclaves and Transient Cosmopolitanism," *City* 24, no. 5–6 (2020): 805–817.

13. "Number of Population," Dubai Statistics Centre, modified 2020, https://www.dsc.gov.ae/Report/DSC_SYB_2020_01_03.pdf.

14. Binnie et al., *Cosmopolitan Urbanism*, 25; Mike Raco, "Remaking Place and Securitising Space: Urban Regeneration and the Strategies, Tactics and Policies of Policing in the UK," *Urban Studies* 40 (2003): 1869–1887.

15. Not all spaces in "new Dubai" are the same. The spectacular and glitzy shopping malls allow for more forms of difference compared with the restaurants at DIFC; more diversity not only in terms of nationality and ethnicity but also in terms of class, as I showed in the previous chapter.

16. Nira Yuval-Davis, "Intersectionality, Citizenship and Contemporary Politics of Belonging," *Critical Review of International Social and Political Philosophy* 10, no. 4 (2007): 561–574.

17. Notable exceptions include Laure Assaf, "'Abu Dhabi Is My Sweet Home': Arab Youths, Interstitial Spaces, and the Building of a Cosmopolitan Locality," *City* 24, no. 5–6 (2020): 830–841; Idil Akinci, "Culture in the 'Politics of Identity': Conceptions of National Identity and Citizenship among Second-Generation Non-Gulf Arab Migrants in Dubai," *Journal of Ethnic and Migration Studies* 46, no. 11 (2019): 2309–2325.

18. Vora, *Impossible Citizens*.

19. Vora.

20. Kanna, *Dubai: The City as Corporation*, 135.

21. Akinci, "Culture in the 'Politics of Identity'"; Rana Khalid AlMutawa, "National Dress in the UAE: Constructions of Authenticity," *New Middle Eastern Studies* 6 (2016): 1–13; Kanna, *Dubai: The City as Corporation*; Sulayman Khalaf, "National Dress and the Construction of Emirati Cultural Identity," *Journal of Human Sciences* 11 (2005): 230–267.

22. Whether it was really Russian women who "changed" the beach scene is not something I can comment on.

23. While Russians may be regarded as part of the East by Europeans and US Americans, for my non-Western interlocutors they are regarded as Western in their appearance, culture, and behavior.

24. Despite this, of course, these places are characterized by their exclusivity, particularly in that it is their segregation from the majority of society that gives them their appeal.

25. Jane Bristol-Rhys, *Emirati Women: Generations of Change* (Oxford: Hurst, 2010).

26. Elizabeth Wilson, *The Sphinx in the City* (Berkeley: University of California Press, 1992).

27. Fran Tonkiss, *Space, the City and Social Theory: Social Relations and Urban Forms* (Cambridge: Polity Press, 2005).

28. Gavin Brown, "Cosmopolitan Camouflage: (Post-)Gay Space in Spitalfields, East London," in *Cosmopolitan Urbanism*, ed. Jon Binnie, Julian Holloway, Steve Millington, and Craig Young (London: Routledge, 2006), 141.

29. Deborah Philips, "Parallel Lives? Challenging Discourses of British Muslim Self-Segregation," *Environment and Planning D: Society and Space* 24, no. 1 (2006): 35.

30. Sneha Krishnan, "Style-ish Girls and Local Boys: Young Women and Fashion in Chennai," in *Styling South Asian Youth Cultures: Fashion, Media and Society*, ed. Lipi Begum, Rohit K. Dasgupta, and Reina Lewis (London: I. B. Tauris, 2018), 49–64. The word "local" does not have the same meanings in the UAE (rather, "local" means "citizen"), but the meaning behind "local" among Krishnan's interlocutors is similar to the way some "cosmopolitan" or "modern" Emiratis speak about "old-fashioned" or "traditional" Emiratis.

31. Elsheshtawy, *Temporary Cities*.

32. Kanna, *Dubai: The City as Corporation*.

33. Paul Dresch, "Debates on Marriage and Nationality in the United Arab Emirates," in *Monarchies and Nations: Globalisation and Identity in the Arab States of the Gulf*, ed. Paul Dresch and James P. Piscatori (London: I. B. Tauris, 2013); Kanna, *Dubai: The City as Corporation*; Sulayman Khalaf, "The Evolution of the Gulf City Type, Oil, and Globalization," in *Globalization and the Gulf*, ed. John W. Fox, Nada Mourtada-Sabbah, and Mohammed Al Mutawa (London: Routledge, 2006), 244–265; Anh Nga Longva, "Neither Autocracy nor Democracy but Ethnocracy: Citizens, Expatriates and the Socio-political System in Kuwait," in *Monarchies and Nations: Globalisation and Identity in the Arab States of the Gulf*, ed. Paul Dresch and James Piscatori (London: I. B. Tauris, 2013).

CHAPTER 4. AN APPROPRIATELY MODERN CITY

1. This is a term Osella and Osella used to describe Indians who moved to the Gulf, favoring it over India or the West because they viewed it as appropriately modern. Caroline Osella and Filipo Osella, "Nuancing the Migrant Experience: Perspectives from Kerala, South India," in *Transnational South Asians: The Making of a Neo-Diaspora*, ed. Susan Koshy and R. Radhakrishnan (Oxford: Oxford University Press, 2008), 146–178.

2. Natalie Koch, "Urban 'Utopias': The Disney Stigma and Discourses of 'False Modernity,'" *Environment and Planning A* 44 (2012): 2445–2462; and

The Geopolitics of Spectacle: Space, Synecdoche, and the New Capitals of Asia (Ithaca, NY: Cornell University Press, 2018).

3. Neha Vora, *Impossible Citizens: Dubai's Indian Diaspora* (Durham, NC: Duke University Press, 2013), 76; Ahmed Kanna and Najib B. Hourani, "A Group of Like-Minded Lads in Heaven: Everydayness and the Production of Dubai Space," *Journal of Urban Affairs* 36, no. 2 (2014): 616.

4. Sayed Ali, *Dubai: Gilded Cage* (New Haven, CT: Yale University Press, 2010).

5. Vora, *Impossible Citizens*; Ali, *Dubai: Gilded Cage*.

6. "Revealed: The Nationalities Investing the Most in Dubai's Real Estate," *Arabian Business*, November 15, 2020, https://www.arabianbusiness.com /real-estate/454595-revealed-the-nationalities-investing-the-most-in-dubais-real-estate.

7. Cleofe Maceda, "15.8 million People Visited Dubai in 2017," *Gulf News*, February 7, 2018, https://gulfnews.com/business/tourism/158-million-people-visited-dubai-in-2017-1.2169807.

8. Osella and Osella, "Nuancing the Migrant Experience."

9. Studying abroad in the West may be viewed positively, but *moving* to live abroad is not, as it connotes rejecting a place, and leaving one's family, one's culture, etc., behind.

10. Noncitizens cannot buy land or property in all areas of Dubai.

11. Lavaanya Kathiravelu, *Migrant Dubai: Low Wage Workers and the Construction of a Global City* (London: Palgrave Macmillan, 2016); Pnina Werbner, "Global Pathways: Working Class Cosmopolitans and the Creation of Transnational Ethnic Worlds," *Social Anthropology* 7, no. 1 (1999): 17–35.

12. Kathiravelu, *Migrant Dubai*, 144.

13. Amélie Le Renard, "How Western Residents in Riyadh and Dubai Produce and Challenge Exceptionalism," in *Beyond Exception: New Interpretations of the Arabian Peninsula*, ed. Ahmed Kanna, Amélie Le Renard, and Neha Vora (Ithaca, NY: Cornell University Press, 2020), 76.

14. Tina Mangieri, "Refashioning South-South Spaces: Cloth, Clothing and Kenyan Cultures of Economies" (PhD diss., University of North Carolina at Chapel Hill Graduate School, 2007).

15. Mangieri, 207.

16. Manja Stephan-Emmrich, "Playing Cosmopolitan: Muslim Self-Fashioning, Migration, and Belonging in the Tajik Dubai Business Sector," *Central Asian Affairs* 4, no. 3 (2017): 270.

17. Stephan-Emmrich, 272.

18. Stephan-Emmrich, 278. Emphasis added.

19. Amin Moghadam, "De l'Iran imaginé aux nouveaux foyers de l'Iran: Pratiques et espaces transnationaux des Iraniens à Dubai" [From imagined Iran to

new homes of Iran: Transnational practices and spaces of Iranians in Dubaï], *Arabian Humanities* 2 (2013).

20. Hassan Fattah, "Young Iranians Follow Dreams to Dubai," *New York Times*, December 4, 2005, https://www.nytimes.com/2005/12/04/world/middleeast/young-iranians-follow-dreams-to-dubai.html.

21. Saba Mahmood, *Politics of Piety: The Islamic Revival and the Feminist Subject* (Princeton, NJ: Princeton University Press, 2004).

22. Kanna and Hourani, "A Group of Like-Minded Lads in Heaven."

23. Calvert Jones, *Bedouins into Bourgeois: Remaking Citizens for Globalization* (Cambridge: Cambridge University Press, 2017).

24. Vora, *Impossible Citizens*, 43.

25. Vora, 43.

26. Jassim Al Awadi and Geoffrey Martin, "Where the Bus At? Public Transportation Challenges in Kuwait," *LSE Middle East*, January 21, 2020, https://blogs.lse.ac.uk/mec/2020/01/21/where-the-bus-at-public-transportation-challenges-in-kuwait.

27. Vora, *Impossible Citizens*, 129.

28. Ali, *Dubai: Gilded Cage*; Vora, *Impossible Citizens*, 43.

29. Noora Lori, *Offshore Citizens: Permanent Temporary Status in the Gulf* (Cambridge: Cambridge University Press, 2019).

30. Kathiravelu, *Migrant Dubai*.

31. Jones, *Bedouins into Bourgeois*.

32. During a pivotal closed session on December 8, 2009, the then-prime minister Sheikh Nasser Mohammad al-Sabah was questioned directly about allegations of fraud and was forced to resign.

33. "Kuwait: Population by Nationality Group 2018," Gulf Labour Markets, Migration, and Population Programme, https://gulfmigration.grc.net/kuwait-population-by-nationality-group-2018.

34. Ali, *Dubai: Gilded Cage*, 114–115.

35. Alexei Yurchak, "The Cynical Reason of Late Socialism: Power, Pretense, and the Anekdot," *Public Culture* 9, no. 2 (1997): 164.

36. Nandini Gooptu, "Neoliberal Subjectivity, Enterprise Culture and New Workplaces: Organised Retail and Shopping Malls in India," *Economic and Political Weekly* 44, no. 22 (2009): 45–54.

37. Koch, "Urban 'Utopias.'"

38. Kathiravelu, *Migrant Dubai*, 262.

39. Jamie Peck, Nik Theodore, and Neil Brenner, "Neoliberalism Resurgent? Market Rule after the Great Recession," *South Atlantic Quarterly* 111, no. 2 (2009): 265–288.

40. Hamad M Alrashed (@alrashed_7md), "A simple comparison . . .," Twitter, June 4, 2012, 10:11 p.m., https://twitter.com/alrashed_7md/status/209754237972905985.

41. Vora, *Impossible Citizens*, 129.

42. L. L. Wynn, *Pyramids and Nightclubs: A Travel Ethnography of Arab and Western Imaginations of Egypt, from King Tut and a Colony of Atlantis to Rumors of Sex Orgies, Urban Legends about a Marauding Prince, and Blonde Belly Dancers* (Austin: University of Texas Press, 2007).

43. Fran Tonkiss, *Space, the City and Social Theory: Social Relations and Urban Forms* (Cambridge: Polity Press, 2005), 22.

44. David A. Karp, "Hiding in Pornographic Bookstores: A Reconsideration of the Nature of Urban Anonymity," *Urban Life and Culture* 1, no. 4 (1973): 4281.

45. Elizabeth Wilson, *The Sphinx in the City* (Berkeley: University of California Press, 1992).

46. Tonkiss, *Space, the City and Social Theory*, 24.

47. Laure Assaf, "'Abu Dhabi Is My Sweet Home': Arab Youths, Interstitial Spaces, and the Building of a Cosmopolitan Locality," *City* 24, no. 5–6 (2020): 830–841.

48. The Letters Project, Instagram, August 7, 2020.

49. The Letters Project, Instagram (post now removed from the page).

50. Lori, *Offshore Citizens*.

51. Yurchak, "The Cynical Reason of Late Socialism," and *Everything Was Forever, Until It Was No More: The Last Soviet Generation* (Princeton, NJ: Princeton University Press, 2005).

52. Vora, *Impossible Citizens*, 140.

53. Twitter user, "Is it okay to go out for breakfast alone in Kuwait? I would do it in Dubai but in Kuwait people are nosy. Is it normal?" Twitter, August 31, 2013, 8:11 a.m., https://twitter.com/Maisalmutawa/status/373704463472947200.

54. Tonkiss, *Space, the City and Social Theory*, 23.

55. Vora, *Impossible Citizens*, 139.

56. Vora, *Impossible Citizens*.

57. Vora, 77–78.

58. Kathiravelu, *Migrant Dubai*, 169.

59. Osella and Osella, "Nuancing the Migrant Experience."

60. Ajam in the Gulf are citizens who originally came from (often Southern) Iran and migrated to the Gulf pre-oil. Unlike naturalized citizens who are usually Arabs from other non-Gulf countries, Ajam have "first degree" citizenship but are still not considered as "pure" as citizens of an Arabian Peninsula/Bedouin background (but "purer" than naturalized citizens of other Arab backgrounds).

61. Lori, *Offshore Citizens*, 50.

62. Lori, 51.

CHAPTER 5. THE COSTS AND BENEFITS OF SAFETY IN SANITIZED SPACES

1. In the Gulf, "bachelor" is a term used to refer to low-income men who cannot afford to sponsor their families. Many are married and have children—and are therefore not really bachelors.

2. For more details about *shaabiya* housing, please refer to Yasser Elsheshtawy, *Temporary Cities: Resisting Transience in Arabia* (London: Routledge, 2019). In his description of *shaabiyas*, he says they were

> introduced by the founder of the UAE, Sheikh Zayed, in the late 1960s, with the stated purpose of housing a largely Bedouin population by resettling them in urbanized areas thus tying them to the land. . . . While providing shelter they were seen by many as cheap, lacking basic infrastructure and in many ways also disposable. The UAE was a budding country at the time and benefits of oil wealth had not yet completely materialized, but it was clearly understood that this would be forthcoming and that residents would move out of this modest accommodation into more spacious settings.

3. This is the case for the areas of Satwa I went to, but there are also Filipino areas in Satwa. Khaled Alawadi, "Urban Redevelopment Trauma: The Story of a Dubai Neighbourhood," *Built Environment* 40, no. 3 (2014): 357–375.

4. Jeff Garmany and Matthew A. Richmond, "Hygienisation, Gentrification, and Urban Displacement in Brazil," *Antipode* 52, no. 1 (2019): 139.

5. Parag Deulgaonkar and Mohamad El Sidafy, "Dh1,500 Fine for Hanging Clothes in Balcony," *Emirates 24/7*, July 21, 2011, https://www.emirates247.com/news/dh1-500-fine-for-hanging-clothes-in-balcony-2011-07-21-1.408894.

6. Mariam Al Serkal, "Dubai Clamps Down on Dirty Cars with Dh500 Fine," *Gulf News*, September 30, 2018, https://gulfnews.com/uae/transport/dubai-clamps-down-on-dirty-cars-with-dh500-fine-1.2284212.

7. Garmany and Richmond, "Hygienisation, Gentrification."

8. Elsheshtawy, *Temporary Cities*.

9. Although some of them were engaged in subversive acts when they were younger, this does not necessarily mean that their actions were intended as a challenge to the status quo (and engaging in the difficult task of trying to understand their subjectivities at *that* point in time—as opposed to today—is beyond the scope of this thesis).

10. For more information about noncitizen Emiratis (those who are linguistically, culturally, and socially like other Emiratis but who are stateless), and to whom the UAE government gave Comoros Island citizenship through an agreement with the Comoros Islands, please refer to Noora Lori, *Offshore Citizens: Permanent Temporary Status in the Gulf* (Cambridge: Cambridge University Press, 2019).

11. Pnina Werbner, "Global Pathways: Working Class Cosmopolitans and the Creation of Transnational Ethnic Worlds," *Social Anthropology* 7, no. 1 (1999): 17–35.

12. Wafa Issa, "Gang Violence Rises in Some Dubai Neighbourhoods," *The National*, May 13, 2012. https://www.thenationalnews.com/uae/gang-violence-rises-in-some-dubai-neighbourhoods-1.394773.

13. Khaled Alawadi, "Place Attachment as a Motivation for Community Preservation: The Demise of an Old, Bustling, Dubai Community," *Urban Studies* 54, no. 13 (2017): 2973–2997.

14. Alawadi, "Place Attachment as a Motivation"; Elsheshtawy, *Temporary Cities*.

15. It is also possible that some of these women are not Emiratis but, like the inhabitants of Satwa and Shaabiyat alshurta, grew up in an Emirati milieu. They might be *bidoon* (or currently Comoros Island citizens), Baluch, Iranians, Zanzibaris, Minawis, etcetera. The group of women I sat with said they were Emirati, but I am unsure of the citizenship status of others I spoke with. Nevertheless, the non-Emiratis that I refer to here grew up similar to Emiratis and share similar cultures and lifestyles as other low-income Emiratis.

16. Jane Bristol-Rhys, *Emirati Women: Generations of Change* (Oxford: Hurst, 2010).

17. Mervat Hatem, "In the Shadow of the State: Changing Definitions of Arab Women's 'Developmental' Citizenship Rights," *Journal of Middle East Women's Studies* 1, no. (2005): 20–45.

18. Some may argue that the presence of "strangers" and "outsiders" in a city that experienced rapid population growth changes the social dynamics of the *freej*. This is true, but the women and men I saw congregating in the *freej* (a few of whom I saw in Satwa and Al-Quoz while I was conducting this fieldwork) remained there even when many of their neighbors left their homes and rented them out to low-income South Asian men. Therefore, it is not only urban and population changes but also socioeconomic class that dictates how people inhabit the *freej* and interact in it.

19. Farah Al-Nakib, *Kuwait Transformed: A History of Oil and Urban Life* (Stanford, CA: Stanford University Press, 2016), 190.

20. Al-Nakib, *Kuwait Transformed*; Elsheshtawy, *Temporary Cities*.

21. Alawadi, "Place Attachment as a Motivation"; Al-Nakib, *Kuwait Transformed*; Barbara Brown and Douglas Perkins, "Disruptions in Place Attachment," in *Place Attachment*, ed. Irwin Altman and Setham Low (New York: Plenum Press, 1992), 279–304; Katherine Brickell, Melissa Fernández Arrigoitia, and Alexander Vasudevan, *Geographies of Forced Eviction: Dispossession, Violence, Resistance* (London: Palgrave Macmillan, 2017); Elsheshtawy, *Temporary Cities*; Marc Fried, "Grieving for a Lost Home," in *The Urban Condition: People and Policy in the Metropolis*, ed. Leonard J. Duhl (New York: Simon & Schuster,

1963), 151–171; Goksenin Inalhan and Edward Finch, "Place Attachment and Sense of Belonging," *Facilities* 22, no. 5–6 (2004): 120–128; Douglas Porteous and Sandra Smith, *Domicide: The Global Destruction of Home* (Montreal: McGill-Queen's University Press, 2001).

22. Fried, "Grieving for a Lost Home."

23. Alawadi, "Place Attachment as a Motivation."

24. In her work on young street gangs in Russia, Svetlana Stephenson (2011) argues that gangs "responded to the increased insecurity and uncertainty" in their communities' lives by building strong neighborhood organizations. However, she explains that when "the economic and political situation in Russia stabilised, the state re-asserted its sovereignty. With the strengthening of the Russian state, the need for informal social regulation became weaker." In pre-oil Kuwait, it was the *freej* inhabitants who were responsible for the provision of public services rather than the government. For instance, orphans who did not have extended families were often adopted into the family of the unofficial "head" of the quarter, and street cleaning, garbage collection, and road repairs were the responsibilities of the *freej* residents (Al-Nakib, *Kuwait Transformed*, 59-60). Al-Nakib argues that "the increased level of bureaucratic intervention in the internal affairs of the townspeople led to the reduction of neighborhood involvement in the provision of community services" (62). Similarly, having only become independent in 1971, Emirati institutions consolidated over time. People came to rely more on the state and less on the community.

25. John Clammer, "Framing the Other: Criminality, Social Exclusion and Social Engineering in Developing Singapore," *Social Policy and Administration* 31, no. 5 (1997): 138.

26. Clammer, "Framing the Other," 140.

27. Elle Metz, "Why Singapore Banned Chewing Gum," *BBC*, March 28, 2015, https://www.bbc.co.uk/news/magazine-32090420.

28. Clammer, "Framing the Other," 143.

29. Nili Steinfeld, "Track Me, Track Me Not: Support and Consent to State and Private Sector Surveillance," *Telematics and Informatics* 34, no. 8 (2017): 1663–1672; Martin Gill, Jane Bryan, and Jenna Allen, "Public Perceptions of CCTV in Residential Areas: 'It Is Not as Good as We Thought It Would Be,'" *International Criminal Justice Review* 17, no. 4 (2007): 304–324; Hee Jhee Jiow and Sofia Morales, "Lateral Surveillance in Singapore," *Surveillance and Society* 13, no. 3–4 (2015): 327–337.

30. Steinfeld, "Track Me, Track Me Not"; Jiow and Morales, "Lateral Surveillance in Singapore"; Laura Huey, "False Security or Greater Social Inclusion? Exploring Perceptions of CCTV Use in Public and Private Spaces Accessed by the Homeless," *British Journal of Sociology* 61, no. 1 (2010): 63–82; Terry Honess and Elizabeth Charman, "Closed Circuit Television in Public Places:

Its Acceptability and Perceived Effectiveness," *London: Home Office Police Department* 35 (1992); Martin Gill, Jane Bryan, and Jenna Allen. 2007. "Public Perceptions of CCTV in Residential Areas: 'It Is Not as Good as We Thought It Would Be'."

31. Jiow and Morales, "Lateral Surveillance in Singapore"; Nur Amali Ibrahim, "Everyday Authoritarianism: A Political Anthropology of Singapore," *Critical Asian Studies* 50, no. 2 (2018): 219–231.

32. Steinfeld, "Track Me, Track Me Not."

33. Huey, "False Security or Greater Social Inclusion?"

34. Ibrahim, "Everyday Authoritarianism."

35. Neha Vora, *Impossible Citizens: Dubai's Indian Diaspora* (Durham, NC: Duke University Press, 2013).

36. From the *Gulf News* archive.

37. Ibrahim, "Everyday Authoritarianism."

38. Jane Jacobs, *The Death and Life of Great American Cities* (New York: Vintage Books, 1961).

39. Sophie Cranston and Jenny Llyod, "Bursting the Bubble: Spatialising Safety for Privileged Migrant Women in Singapore," *Antipode* 51, no. 2 (2019): 478–496.

40. Angela Davis, *Policing the Black Man: Arrest, Prosecution, and Imprisonment* (New York: Vintage Books, 2018); Ruth Wilson Gilmore, *Golden Gulag: Prisons, Surplus, Crisis, and Opposition in Globalizing California* (Berkeley: University of California Press, 2007); Prison Research Education Action, *Instead of Prisons: A Handbook for Abolitionists* (Syracuse, NY: Critical Resistance, 2005).

41. Lavaanya Kathiravelu, *Migrant Dubai: Low Wage Workers and the Construction of a Global City* (London: Palgrave Macmillan, 2016).

42. Neha Vora, Ahmed Kanna, and Amélie Le Renard, "Space, Mobility, and Shifting Identities in the Constitution of the 'Field,'" in *Beyond Exception: New Interpretations of the Arabian Peninsula*, ed. Ahmed Kanna, Amélie Le Renard, and Neha Vora (Ithaca, NY: Cornell University Press, 2020), 38.

43. Vora, Kanna, and Le Renard, "Space, Mobility, and Shifting Identities," 41.

44. Vora, Kanna, and Le Renard, 39.

45. Vora, Kanna, and Le Renard, 41.

46. Hassan Fattah, "Dubai Swats Pests Ogling Beach Beauties," *New York Times*, November 12, 2006, https://www.nytimes.com/2006/11/12/world/middleeast/12dubai.html.

47. Ahmed Kanna and Najib B. Hourani, "'A Group of Like-Minded Lads in Heaven': Everydayness and the Production of Dubai Space," *Journal of Urban Affairs* 36, no. 2 (2014): 605–620.

48. Shaundel Nicole Sanchez, "Migrating to the Middle East in Search of Safety," *Anthropology News*, August 14, 2019, https://www.anthropology-news .org/articles/migrating-to-the-middle-east-in-search-of-safety/.

49. Sanchez, "Migrating to the Middle East in Search of Safety."

CONCLUSION

1. Nandini Kochar, "Into the UAE: Grappling with the Male Gaze as a Female Photographer in Abu Dhabi," *The Gazelle*, October 3, 2020, https://www .thegazelle.org/issue/184/features/into-the-uae-the-male-gaze-from-a-female-lense.

Bibliography

Abu-Lughod, Lila. "The Romance of Resistance: Tracing Transformations of Power through Bedouin Women." *American Ethnologist* 17, no. 1 (1990): 41–55.

Acuto, Michele. "High-Rise Dubai Urban Entrepreneurialism and the Technology of Symbolic Power." *Cities* 27 (2010): 272–284.

Akinci, Idil. "Culture in the 'Politics of Identity': Conceptions of National Identity and Citizenship among Second-Generation Non-Gulf Arab Migrants in Dubai." *Journal of Ethnic and Migration Studies* 46, no. 11 (2019): 2309–2325.

———. "Dressing the Nation? Symbolizing Emirati National Identity and Boundaries through National Dress." *Ethnic and Racial Studies* 43, no. 10 (2020): 1776–1794.

Al Awadhi, Jassim, and Geoffrey Martin. "Where the Bus At? Public Transportation Challenges in Kuwait." *LSE Middle East Centre* (blog). January 21, 2020. https://blogs.lse.ac.uk/mec/2020/01/21/where-the-bus-at-public-transportation-challenges-in-kuwait.

Alawadi, Khaled. "Urban Redevelopment Trauma: The Story of a Dubai Neighbourhood." *Built Environment* 40, no. 3 (2014): 357–375.

———. "Place Attachment as a Motivation for Community Preservation: The Demise of an Old, Bustling, Dubai Community." *Urban Studies* 54, no. 13 (2017): 2973–2997.

———. "Lifescapes beyond Bigness: The UAE's Exhibition at the Venice Architecture Biennale 2018." Public lecture given at NYUAD, Abu Dhabi, April 11, 2018.

———. "Whatever Happened to Dubai's Public Spaces?" *International Journal of Middle Eastern Studies* 50 (2018): 562–567

Ali, Sayed. *Dubai: Gilded Cage.* New Haven, CT: Yale University Press, 2010.

Al-Kamali, Reem. "Bin Souqat Mall." *Al-Bayan,* September 18, 2019. https://www.albayan.ae/opinions/white-ink/2019-09-18-1.3651603.

AlMutawa, Rana. "Monolithic Representations and Orientalist Credence in the UAE." *Identity & Culture in the 21st Century Gulf* (Autumn 2016): 23–25. https://www.academia.edu/30056784/Monolithic_Representations_and_Orientalist_Credence_in_the_UAE.

———. "National Dress in the UAE: Constructions of Authenticity." *New Middle Eastern Studies* 6 (2016): 1–13.

———. "'Glitzy' Malls and Coffee Shops: Everyday Places of Belonging and Social Contestation in Dubai." *Arab Studies Journal* 28, no. 2 (2020): 44–75.

Al-Nakib, Farah. *Kuwait Transformed: A History of Oil and Urban Life.* Stanford, CA: Stanford University Press, 2016.

———. "'This Is Not What I Thought': The Pitfalls and Potentials of Kuwait's Segregated Nocturnal Landscape." Presented at After Dark: Nocturnal Landscapes and Public Spaces in the Arabian Peninsula, Harvard University, Cambridge, MA, 2017.

Al-Naqeeb, Khaldoun. *Society and State in the Gulf and Arab Peninsula: A Different Perspective.* London: Routledge, 1990.

Alraouf, Ali. "Dubaization vs. Glocalization: Arab Cities Transformed." Presentation at Gulf First Urban Planning and Development Conference, Kuwait. Cited from T. Botz-Bornstein, "A Tale of Two Cities: Hong Kong and Dubai, Celebration of Disappearance and the Pretension of Becoming," *Transcience* 3, no. 2 (2012): 1–16.

AlRayes, Hamad Ahmed. "An Introduction Regarding Systemic Issues and Solutions in the GCC States" [*Muqadima hawl awjuh alkhalal almuzmina wasubul islahiha fee agtar majlis alta3awen lildewal alkhaleej alaraby*]. Gulf Centre for Development Policies, Working Paper 1, 2012.

Al Serkal, Mariam. "Dubai Clamps Down on Dirty Cars with Dh500 Fine." *Gulf News,* September 30, 2018. https://gulfnews.com/uae/transport/dubai-clamps-down-on-dirty-cars-with-dh500-fine-1.2284212.

AlShehabi, Omar. "AlMuharraq and the Changing City of the Arab Gulf" [*Almuharraq wal madina almutahawilla*]. Gulf Centre for Development Policies, 2019. https://gulfpolicies.org/2019-05-18-07-30-16/2019-05-18-10-21-49/1601-2019-07-02-12-02-59.

————. "Removing Roots" [*Iqtilaa' aljuthoor*]. Gulf Centre for Development Policies, 2019. https://gulfpolicies.org/2019-05-18-07-30-16/2019-05-18-10-21-49/1595-2019-07-02-12-00-35.

————. "Right to the City" [*Alhaq fee almadina*]. Gulf Centre for Development Policies, 2019. https://gulfpolicies.org/2019-05-18-07-30-16/2019-05-18-10-21-49/1592-2019-07-02-11-59-19.

Amster, Randall. "Patterns of Exclusion: Sanitizing Space, Criminalizing Homelessness." *Social Justice* 30, no. 1(91) (2003): 195–221.

Antonsich, Marco. "Searching for Belonging—An Analytical Framework." *Geography Compass* 2, no. 6 (2010): 644–659.

Armbrust, Walter. "Bourgeois Leisure and Egyptian Media Fantasies." In *New Media in the Muslim World: The Emerging Public Sphere*, edited by Dale F. Eickelman and Jon W. Anderson, 106–32. Bloomington: Indiana University Press, 1999.

Assaf, Laure. "Le Shopping Mall Comme Moment Urbain" [The Shopping Mall as an Urban Moment]. *Ateliers d'Anthropologie* 44 (2017).

————. "'Abu Dhabi Is My Sweet Home': Arab Youths, Interstitial Spaces, and the Building of a Cosmopolitan Locality." *City* 24, no. 5–6 (2020): 830–841.

Attwood, Karen, and Mark Leftly. "Dubai Babylon: The Glitz, the Glamor—And Now the Gloom." *The Independent*, November 28, 2009. https://www.independent.co.uk/news/world/middle-east/dubai-babylon-the-glitz-the-glamour-ndash-and-now-the-gloom-1830672.html.

Augé, Marc. *Non-places: Introduction to an Anthropology of Supermodernity*. London: Verso, 1995.

Bagheri, Nazgol. "The Emancipated Flâneuse in Tehran's Shopping Malls." In *Walking in Cities: Quotidian Mobility as Urban Theory, Method and Practice*, edited by Timothy Shortell and Evrick Brown, 83–100. Philadelphia, PA: Temple University Press, 2015.

Bayat, Asef. *Life as Politics: How Ordinary People Change the Middle East*. Stanford, CA: Stanford University Press, 2013.

Beblawi, Hazem, and Giacomo Luciani. *The Rentier State*. Berkeley: University of California Press, 1990.

Benjamin, Walter. *The Arcades Project*. Translated by Howard Eliland and Kevin McLaughlin. Cambridge, MA: Harvard University Press, 1999.

Benz, Terressa. "Urban Mascots and Poverty Fetishism: Authenticity in the Postindustrial City." *Sociological Perspectives* 59, no. 2 (2016): 460–478.

Bergamaschi, Maurizio, Marco Castrignanò, and Pia De Rubertis. "The Homeless and Public Space: Urban Policy and Exclusion in Bologna." *Papers in Political Economy* 51 (2014). https://journals.openedition.org/interventionseconomiques/2441.

Binnie, Jon, Julian Holloway, Steve Millington, and Craig Young, eds. *Cosmopolitan Urbanism*. London: Routledge, 2006.

Bourdieu, Pierre. *Distinction*. Translated by Richard Nice. Cambridge, MA: Harvard University Press, 1984.

Brammer, John Paul. "I'm from a Mexican Family. Stop Expecting Me to Eat 'Authentic' Food." *Washington Post,* May 15, 2019.

Brickell, Katherine, Melissa Fernández Arrigoitia, and Alexander Vasudevan. *Geographies of Forced Eviction: Dispossession, Violence, Resistance.* London: Palgrave Macmillan, 2017.

Bristol-Rhys, Jane. *Emirati Women: Generations of Change*. Oxford: Hurst, 2010.

Broudehoux, Anne-Marie. "Delirious Beijing: Euphoria and Despair in the Olympic Metropolis." In *Evil Paradises: Dreamworlds of Neoliberalism,* edited by Mike Davis and Daniel Bertrand Monk, 87–101. New York: New Press, 2007.

———. "Spectacular Beijing: The Conspicuous Construction of an Olympic Metropolis." *Journal of Urban Affairs* 29, no. 4 (2007): 383–399.

———. "Images of Power: Architectures of the Integrated Spectacle at the Beijing Olympics." *Journal of Architectural Education* 63, no. 2 (2010): 52–62.

Brown, Barbara, and Douglas Perkins. "Disruptions in Place Attachment." In *Place Attachment*, edited by Irwin Altman and Setha M. Low, 279–304. New York: Plenum Press, 1992.

Brown, Gavin. "Cosmopolitan Camouflage: (Post-)Gay Space in Spitalfields, East London." In *Cosmopolitan Urbanism*, edited by Jon Binnie, Julian Holloway, Steve Millington, and Craig Young, 130–145. London: Routledge, 2006.

Brubaker, Roger. *Ethnicity without Groups*. Cambridge, MA: Harvard University Press, 2004.

Buckley, Michelle. "Locating Neoliberalism in Dubai: Migrant Workers and Class Struggle in the Autocratic City." *Antipode* 45, no. 2 (2012): 256–274.

Buckner, Elizabeth. "The Other Gap: Examining Low-Income Emiratis' Educational Achievement." Working Paper 15. Ras Al-Khaimah, UAE: Al Qasimi Foundation, 2018.

Castro, Fatimah. "Afro-Colombians and the Cosmopolitan City: New Negotiations of Race and Space in Bogotá, Colombia." *Latin American Perspectives* 40, no. 2 (2013): 105–117.

Centner, Ryan. "On Not Being Dubai: Infrastructures of Urban Cultural Policy in Istanbul and Beirut." *International Journal of Cultural Policy* 26, no. 6 (2020): 722–739.

Centner, Ryan, and Manoel Pereira Neto. "Peril, Privilege, and Queer Comforts: The Nocturnal Performative Geographies of Expatriate Gay Men in Dubai." *Geoforum* 127 (2021): 92–103.

Clammer, John. "Framing the Other: Criminality, Social Exclusion and Social Engineering in Developing Singapore." *Social Policy and Administration* 31, no. 5 (1997): 136–153.

Cooke, Miriam. *Tribal Modern: Branding New Nations in the Arab Gulf.*
Oakland: University of California Press, 2014.

Cranston, Sophie, and Jenny Llyod. "Bursting the Bubble: Spatialising Safety
for Privileged Migrant Women in Singapore." *Antipode* 51, no. 2 (2019):
478–496.

Crawford, Margaret. "Contesting the Public Realm: Struggles over Public Space
in Los Angeles." *Journal of Architectural Education*, 49, no. 1 (1995): 4–9.

Crenshaw, Kimberle. "Demarginalizing the Intersection of Race and Sex: A
Black Feminist Critique of Antidiscrimination Doctrine, Feminist Theory
and Antiracist Politics." *University of Chicago Legal Forum* (1989): 139–167.

Crowley, John. "The Politics of Belonging: Some Theoretical Considerations." In
The Politics of Belonging: Migrants and Minorities in Contemporary Europe,
edited by Andrew Geddes and Adrian Favell. Aldershot: Ashgate, 1999.

Davis, Angela. *Policing the Black Man: Arrest, Prosecution, and Imprisonment.*
New York: Vintage Books, 2017.

Davis, Mike. *City of Quartz: Excavating the Future in Los Angeles.* London:
Verso, 1990.

———. "Sand, Fear and Money in Dubai." In *Evil Paradises: Dreamworlds of
Neoliberalism*, edited by Mike Davis and Daniel Bertrand Monk. New York:
New Press, 2007.

Debord, Guy. *Comments on "The Society of the Spectacle."* Translated by
Malcom Imrie. London: Verso, 1988.

de Certeau, Michel. *The Practice of Everyday Life.* Translated by Steven
Rendall. Berkeley: University of California Press, 1984.

de Koning, Anouk. *Global Dreams: Class, Gender, and Public Space in Cosmopolitan Cairo.* Cairo: AUC Press, 2009.

Derderian, Elizabeth. "Authenticating an Emirati Art World: Claims of Tabula
Rasa and Cultural Appropriation in the UAE." *Journal of Arabian Studies* 7,
no. 1 (2017): 12–27.

Deulgaonkar, Parag, and Mohamad El Sidafy. "Dh1,500 Fine for Hanging Clothes
in Balcony." *Emirates 24/7*, July 21, 2011. https://www.emirates247.com
/news/dh1-500-fine-for-hanging-clothes-in-balcony-2011-07-21-1.408894.

Douglas, Gordon C. C. "Privilege and Participation: On the Democratic Implica-
tions and Social Contradictions of Bottom-Up Urbanism." In *The Palgrave
Handbook of Bottom-Up Urbanism*, edited by Mahyar Arefi and Conrad
Kickert, 305–321. Cham: Palgrave Macmillan, 2019.

Dresch, Paul. "Debates on Marriage and Nationality in the United Arab
Emirates." In *Monarchies and Nations: Globalisation and Identity in the
Arab States of the Gulf*, edited Paul Dresch and James P. Piscatori. London:
I. B. Tauris, 2013.

"Dubai Police Combat Menace of Begging, Arrest 416 since the Beginning of
Ramadan." *Gulf Today*, May 22, 2020. https://www.gulftoday.ae/news

/2020/05/22/dubai-police-arrest-416-beggars-since-the-beginning-of-ramadan.

Duncan, Gillian. "Coronavirus: Seven-Year-Old Reunited with Mother after Writing to RAK Ruler." *The National*, May 13, 2020. https://www.thenationalnews.com/uae/health/coronavirus-seven-year-old-reunited-with-mother-after-writing-to-rak-ruler-1.1018912.

Elsheshtawy, Yasser. *Planning Middle Eastern Cities: An Urban Kaleidoscope*. London: Routledge, 2004.

———. "Navigating the Spectacle: Landscapes of Consumption in Dubai." *Architectural Theory Review* 13, no. 2 (2008): 164–187.

———. *Dubai: Behind an Urban Spectacle*. New York: Routledge, 2009.

———. "Mapping Nightscapes: Scenes from Dubai and Abu Dhabi." Presented at After Dark: Nocturnal Landscapes and Public Spaces in the Arabian Peninsula, Harvard University, Cambridge, MA, 2017.

———. "We Need to Talk about the Modernism Fetish in the Gulf." *Dubaization*, December 26, 2017. http://dubaization.com/post/168964409563/we-need-to-talk-about-the-modernism-fetish-in-the-Gulf.

———. "The Dubai of . . . Urban Loss in the Shadow of Gulf Urbanity." *Middle East Research and Information Project* 287 (2018).

———. *Temporary Cities: Resisting Transience in Arabia*. London: Routledge, 2019.

———. "Urban Enclaves and Transient Cosmopolitanism." *City* 24, no. 5–6 (2020): 805–817.

Fattah, Hassan. "Young Iranians Follow Dreams to Dubai." *New York Times*, December 4, 2005. https://www.nytimes.com/2005/12/04/world/middleeast/young-iranians-follow-dreams-to-dubai.html.

———. "Dubai Swats Pests Ogling Beach Beauties." *New York Times*, November 12, 2006.

Florida, Richard. *The Rise of the Creative Class . . . and How It's Transforming Work, Leisure, Community and Everyday Life*. New York: Basic Books, 2002.

Frazer, Nancy. "Rethinking the Public Sphere: A Contribution to the Critique of Actually Existing Democracy." *Social Text*, no. 25–26 (1990): 56–80.

Fried, Marc. "Grieving for a Lost Home." In *The Urban Condition: People and Policy in the Metropolis*, edited by Leonard J. Duhl, 151–171. New York: Simon & Schuster, 1963.

Gardner, Andrew. *City of Strangers: Gulf Migration and the Indian Community in Bahrain*. Ithaca, NY: Cornell University Press, 2010.

Garmany, Jeff, and Matthew A. Richmond. "Hygienisation, Gentrification, and Urban Displacement in Brazil." *Antipode* 52, no. 1 (2019): 124–144.

Gaudio, Rudolph. "Coffeetalk: Starbucks™ and the Commercialization of Casual Conversation." *Language in Society* 32, no. 5 (2003): 659–691.

Ghannam, Farha. *Remaking the Modern Space, Relocation, and the Politics of Identity in a Global Cairo.* Berkeley: University of California Press, 2002.

Gill, Martin, Jane Bryan, and Jenna Allen. "Public Perceptions of CCTV in Residential Areas: 'It Is Not as Good as We Thought It Would Be.'" *International Criminal Justice Review* 17, no. 4 (2007): 304–324.

Gilmore, Ruth Wilson. *Golden Gulag: Prisons, Surplus, Crisis, and Opposition in Globalizing California.* Berkeley: University of California Press, 2007.

Gooptu, Nandini. "Neoliberal Subjectivity, Enterprise Culture and New Workplaces: Organised Retail and Shopping Malls in India." *Economic and Political Weekly* 44, no. 22 (2009): 45–54.

Gray, Matthew. "A Theory of 'Late Rentierism' in the Arab States of the Gulf." Occasional Paper no. 7. Center for International and Regional Studies, Georgetown University School of Foreign Service in Qatar, 2011.

Grazian, David. *Blue Chicago: The Search for Authenticity in Urban Blues Clubs.* Chicago: University of Chicago Press, 2003.

Halnon, Karen Bettez. *The Consumption of Inequality: Weapons of Mass Distraction.* New York: Palgrave Macmillan, 2013.

Hannerz, Ulf. *Transnational Connections: Culture, People, Places.* London: Routledge, 2006.

Harvey, David. "From Managerialism to Entrepreneurialism: The Transformation in Urban Governance in Late Capitalism." *Geografiska Annaler* 71, no. 1 (1989): 3–17.

———. *A Brief History of Neoliberalism.* Oxford: Oxford University Press, 2007.

———. "The Right to the City." *New Left Review* 53 (September/October 2008).

Hatem, Mervat. "In the Shadow of the State: Changing Definitions of Arab Women's 'Developmental' Citizenship Rights." *Journal of Middle East Women's Studies* 1, no. 3 (2005): 20–45.

Hedetoft, Ulf, and Mette Hjort. *The Post-National Self: Belonging and Identity.* Minneapolis: University of Minnesota Press, 2002.

Herb, Michael. *The Wages of Oil: Parliaments and Economic Development in Kuwait and the UAE.* Ithaca, NY: Cornell University Press, 2014.

Hilgers, Mathieu. "The Three Anthropological Approaches to Neoliberalism." *International Social Science Journal* 61, no. 202 (2010): 351–364.

Hiller, Harry H. 2000. "Mega-Events, Urban Boosterism and Growth Strategies: An Analysis of the Objectives and Legitimations of the Cape Town 2004 Olympic Bid." *International Journal of Urban and Regional Research* 24, no. 2 (2000): 439–458.

Holes, Clive. "Language and Identity in the Arabian Gulf." *Journal of Arabian Studies* 1 (2011): 129–145.

Honess, Terry, and Elizabeth Charman. "Closed Circuit Television in Public Places: Its Acceptability and Perceived Effectiveness." Police Research Group

Crime Prevention Unit Series, Paper no. 35. Home Office Police Department, London, 1992.

Huey, Laura. "False Security or Greater Social Inclusion? Exploring Perceptions of CCTV Use in Public and Private Spaces Accessed by the Homeless." *British Journal of Sociology* 61, no. 1 (2010): 63–82.

Ibrahim, Nur Amali. "Everyday Authoritarianism: A Political Anthropology of Singapore." *Critical Asian Studies* 50, no. 2 (2018): 219–231.

Inalhan, Goksenin, and Edward Finch. "Place Attachment and Sense of Belonging." *Facilities* 22, no. 5–6 (2004): 120–128.

Isakjee, Arshad. "Dissonant Belongings: The Evolving Spatial Identities of Young Muslim Men in the UK." *Environment and Planning A: Society and Space* 48, no. 7 (2016): 1337–1353.

Issa, Wafa. "Gang Violence Rises in Some Dubai Neighbourhoods." *The National*, May 13, 2012. https://www.thenationalnews.com/uae/gang-violence-rises-in-some-dubai-neighbourhoods-1.394773.

Jackson, Peter. "Domesticating the Street: The Contested Spaces of the High Street and the Mall." In *Images of the Street*, edited by Nicholas Fyfe, 176–191. London: Routledge, 1998.

Jacobs, Jane. *The Death and Life of Great American Cities*. New York: Vintage Books, 1961.

Jenkins, Simon. "As They Did Ozymandias, the Dunes Will Reclaim the Soaring Folly of Dubai." *The Guardian*, March 20, 2009. https://www.theguardian.com/commentisfree/2009/mar/20/dubai-decline-middle-east.

Jiow, Hee Jhee, and Sofia Morales. "Lateral Surveillance in Singapore." *Surveillance and Society* 13, no. 3–4 (2015): 327–337.

Jones, Calvert. *Bedouins into Bourgeois: Remaking Citizens for Globalization*. Cambridge: Cambridge University Press, 2017.

Kanna, Ahmed. *Dubai: The City as Corporation*. Minneapolis: University of Minnesota Press, 2010.

———. "Class Struggle and De-exceptionalizing the Gulf." In *Beyond Exception: New Interpretations of the Arabian Peninsula*, edited by Ahmed Kanna, Amélie Le Renard, and Neha Vora, 100–122. Ithaca, NY: Cornell University Press, 2020.

Kanna, Ahmed, Amélie Le Renard, and Neha Vora. *Beyond Exception: New Interpretations of the Arabian Peninsula*. Ithaca, NY: Cornell University Press, 2020.

Kanna, Ahmed, and Najib B. Hourani. "'A Group of Like-Minded Lads in Heaven': Everydayness and the Production of Dubai Space." *Journal of Urban Affairs* 36, no. 2 (2014): 605–620.

Karp, David A. "Hiding in Pornographic Bookstores: A Reconsideration of the Nature of Urban Anonymity." *Urban Life and Culture* 1, no. 4 (1973): 427–451.

Kathiravelu, Lavaanya. *Migrant Dubai: Low Wage Workers and the Construction of a Global City.* London: Palgrave Macmillan, 2016.

Keshavarzian, Arang. "From Port Cities to Cities with Ports: Towards a Multiscalar History of Persian Gulf Urbanism in the Twentieth Century." In *Gateways to the World: Port Cities in the Persian Gulf,* edited by Mehran Kamrava, 19–41. Oxford: Oxford University Press, 2016.

Khalaf, Sulayman. "National Dress and the Construction of Emirati Cultural Identity." *Journal of Human Sciences* 11 (2005): 230–267.

———. "The Evolution of the Gulf City Type, Oil, and Globalization." In *Globalization and the Gulf,* edited by John W. Fox, Nada Mourtada-Sabbah, and Mohammed Al Mutawa, 244–265. London: Routledge, 2006.

Koch, Natalie. "Urban 'Utopias': The Disney Stigma and Discourses of 'False Modernity.'" *Environment and Planning A: Society and Space* 44 (2012): 2445–2462.

———. "Is Nationalism Just for Nationals? Civic Nationalism for Noncitizens and Celebrating National Day in Qatar and the UAE." *Political Geography* 54 (2015): 43–53.

———. "We Entrepreneurial Academics: Governing Globalized Higher Education in 'Illiberal' States." *Territory, Politics, Governance* 4, no. 4 (2016): 438–452.

———. "Orientalizing Authoritarianism: Narrating US Exceptionalism in Popular Reactions to the Trump Election and Presidency." *Political Geography* 58 (2017): 145–147.

———. *The Geopolitics of Spectacle: Space, Synecdoche, and the New Capitals of Asia.* Ithaca, NY: Cornell University Press, 2018.

———. "Post-Triumphalist Geopolitics: Liberal Selves, Authoritarian Others." *ACME* 18, no. 4 (2019): 909–924.

Koch, Natalie, and Neha Vora. "Laboratories of Liberalism: American Higher Education in the Arabian Peninsula and the Discursive Production of Authoritarianism." *Minerva* 57 (2019): 549–564.

Kochar, Nandini. "Into the UAE: Grappling with the Male Gaze as a Female Photographer in Abu Dhabi." *The Gazelle,* October 3, 2020. https://www.thegazelle.org/issue/184/features/into-the-uae-the-male-gaze-from-a-female-lense.

Krane, Jim. *Dubai: City of Gold.* New York: St. Martin's Press, 2009.

Krishnan, Sneha. "Clubbing in the Afternoon: Worlding the City as a College-Girl in Chennai." *City, Culture and Society* 19 (2018).

———. "Style-ish Girls and Local Boys: Young Women and Fashion in Chennai." In *Styling South Asian Youth Cultures: Fashion, Media and Society,* edited by Lipi Begum, Rohit K. Dasgupta, and Reina Lewis, 49–64. London: I. B. Tauris, 2018.

Kubo, Michael. "Building Identities: Transnational Exchange and the Authorship of Modern Gulf Heritage." Presented at Re-engaging with the Gulf Modernist City, Gulf Research Meeting, Cambridge, UK, 2019.

Kumar, Anjana. "All You Need to Know: How to Sponsor Your Family in the UAE." *Gulf News*, November 5, 2019. https://gulfnews.com/uae/all-you-need-to-know-how-to-sponsor-your-family-in-the-uae-1.1572935794448.

"Kuwait: Population by Nationality Group 2018." Gulf Labour Markets, Migration and Population. https://gulfmigration.org/kuwait-population-by-nationality-group-2018/.

"Kuwaiti Hospital 'Will Refuse to Treat Migrant Labourers.'" *The Independent*, February 22, 2017. https://www.independent.co.uk/news/world/middle-east/kuw3ait-city-migrant-workers-discrimination-new-hospital-a7593406.html.

"Kuwait's Prime Minister Resigns after Protests." *BBC*, November 28, 2011. https://www.bbc.co.uk/news/world-middle-east-15931526.

Lawati, Abbas. "Gulf Cities Have a Long Way to Go before Leading the Arab World." *Al-Monitor*, October 13, 2014. https://www.al-monitor.com/pulse/ar/originals/2013/10/gulf-dubai-abu-dhabi-doha-arab.html.

Lees, Loretta. "Urban Renaissance and the Street: Spaces of Control and Contestation." In *Images of the Street*, edited by Nicholas Fyfe, 236–253. London: Routledge, 1998.

Lefebvre, Henri. *Writings on Cities*. Translated by Eleonore Kofman and Elizabeth Lebas. Oxford: Blackwell, 1996.

Le Renard, Amélie. "Shopping Mall Practices by Young Saudi Women: Sociability and Consumerism in Riyadh" [Pratiques du shopping mall par les jeunes Saoudiennes: Sociabilité et consumérisme à Riyad]. In *Mondes et places du marché en Méditerranée: Formes sociales et spatiales de l'échange*, edited by Franck Mermier and Michel Peraldi, 188–190. Paris: Editions Karthala, 2011.

———. "How Western Residents in Riyadh and Dubai Produce and Challenge Exceptionalism." In *Beyond Exception: New Interpretations of the Arabian Peninsula*, edited by Ahmed Kanna, Amélie Le Renard, and Neha Vora, 55–79. Ithaca, NY: Cornell University Press, 2020.

———. *Western Privilege: Work, Intimacy, and Postcolonial Hierarchies in Dubai*. Translated by Jane Kuntz. Stanford, CA: Stanford University Press, 2021.

Ley, David. *The New Middle Class and the Remaking of the Central City*. Oxford: Oxford University Press, 1996.

Longva, Anh Nga. *Walls Built on Sand: Migration, Exclusion, and Society in Kuwait*. Boulder, CO: Westview Press, 1997.

———. "Neither Autocracy nor Democracy but Ethnocracy: Citizens, Expatriates and the Socio-political System in Kuwait." In *Monarchies and Nations:*

Globalisation and Identity in the Arab States of the Gulf, edited by Paul Dresch and James Piscatori. London: I. B. Tauris, 2013.

Lori, Noora. "National Security and the Management of Migrant Labor: A Case Study of the United Arab Emirates." *Asian and Pacific Migration Journal* 20, no. 3–4 (2011): 315–337.

———. *Offshore Citizens: Permanent Temporary Status in the Gulf.* Cambridge: Cambridge University Press, 2019.

Maceda, Cleofe. "15.8 Million People Visited Dubai in 2017." *Gulf News,* February 7, 2018. https://gulfnews.com/business/tourism/158-million-people-visited-dubai-in-2017-1.2169807.

Mahdavi, Pardis. *Gridlock: Labor, Migration, and Human Trafficking in Dubai.* Stanford, CA: Stanford University Press, 2011.

Mahmood, Saba. *Politics of Piety: The Islamic Revival and the Feminist Subject.* Princeton, NJ: Princeton University Press, 2004.

Mangieri, Tina. "Refashioning South-South Spaces: Cloth, Clothing and Kenyan Cultures of Economies." PhD diss., University of North Carolina at Chapel Hill Graduate School, 2007.

Marrus, Michael. *The Holocaust in History.* Toronto: Key Porter, 2000.

Matthews, Hugh, Mark Taylor, Barry Percy-Smith, and Melanie Limb. "The Unacceptable Flaneur: The Shopping Mall as a Teenage Hangout." *Childhood* 7, no. 3 (2000): 279–294.

Metz, Elle. "Why Singapore Banned Chewing Gum." *BBC,* March 28, 2015. https://www.bbc.co.uk/news/magazine-32090420.

Mitchell, Timothy. *Colonising Egypt.* Berkeley: University of California Press, 1988.

Moghadam, Amin. "From Imagined Iran to New Homes of Iran: Transnational Practices and Spaces of Iranians in Dubai" [De l'Iran imaginé aux nouveaux foyers de l'Iran: Pratiques et espaces transnationaux des Iraniens à Dubaï]. *Arabian Humanities* 2 (2013).

———. "The Staging of Cultural Diversity in Dubai: The Case of Dubai Art Fair." *Identities: Global Studies in Culture and Power* 28, no. 6 (2021): 717–733.

Munyal, Panna. "I Speak More Hindi on the Streets of Dubai than I Did in Mumbai—Why I Might Live in the UAE Forever." *The National,* October 31, 2019. https://www.thenationalnews.com/lifestyle/comment/i-speak-more-hindi-on-the-streets-of-dubai-than-i-did-in-mumbai-why-i-might-live-in-the-uae-forever-1.931256.

Nash, Jennifer C. "Re-thinking Intersectionality." *Feminist Review* 89 (2008): 1–15.

Nasir, Kamaludeen Mohamed, and Bryan S. Turner. *The Future of Singapore Population, Society and the Nature of the State.* London: Routledge, 2013.

Nasir, Sarwat. "Heart-Warming Moment German Mum Is Reunited with Daughter in Abu Dhabi after a Month." *The National,* April 7, 2020. https://

www.thenationalnews.com/uae/transport/heart-warming-moment-german-mum-is-reunited-with-daughter-in-abu-dhabi-after-a-month-1.1003000

Nassar, Ahmed, G. Alan Blackburn, and J. Duncan Whyatt. "Developing the Desert: The Pace and Process of Urban Growth in Dubai." *Computers, Environment and Urban Systems* 45 (2014): 50–62.

Nissen, Sylke. "Urban Transformation: From Public and Private Space to Spaces of Hybrid Character." *Czech Sociological Review* 44, no. 6 (2008): 1129–1449.

"Number of Population." Dubai Statistics Centre, 2020. https://www.dsc.gov.ae/Report/DSC_SYB_2020_01_03.pdf.

Onley, James. "Transnational Merchant Families in the Nineteenth- and Twentieth-Century Gulf." In *The Gulf Family: Kinship and Politics*, edited by Alanoud Alsharekh, 37–56. London: Al Saqi Books and London Middle East Institute SOAS, 2007.

Osella, Caroline, and Filipo Osella. "Nuancing the Migrant Experience: Perspectives from Kerala, South India." In *Transnational South Asians: The Making of a Neo-diaspora*, edited by Susan Koshy and R. Radhakrishnan, 146–178. Oxford: Oxford University Press, 2008.

Pacione M. "City Profile Dubai." *Cities*, 22, no. 3 (2005): 255–265.

Peck, Jamie, Nik Theodore, and Neil Brenner. "Neoliberalism Resurgent? Market Rule after the Great Recession." *South Atlantic Quarterly* 111, no. 2 (2009): 265–288.

Pécoud, Antoine. "Entrepreneurship and Identity: Cosmopolitanism and Cultural Competences among German–Turkish Businesspeople in Berlin." *Journal of Ethnic and Migration Studies* 30, no. 1 (2004): 3–20.

Peterson, J. E. "Rulers, Merchants and Shaikhs in Gulf Politics." In *The Gulf Family: Kinship Policies and Modernity*, edited by AlAnoud AlSharekh, 1–37. London: Al Saqi Books and London Middle East Institute SOAS, 2012.

Peterson, Mark Allen. *Connected in Cairo: Growing Up Cosmopolitan in the Modern Middle East*. Bloomington: Indiana University Press, 2011.

Phillips, Deborah. "Parallel Lives? Challenging Discourses of British Muslim Self-Segregation." *Environment and Planning D: Society and Space* 24 (2006): 25–40.

Platz Robinson, Teresa. *Café Culture in Pune: Being Young and Middle Class in Urban India*. New Delhi: Oxford University Press, 2014.

"Population by Gender." Dubai Statistics Centre, 2018. https://www.dsc.gov.ae/Report/DSC_SYB_2018_01%20_%2001.pdf.

Porteous, Douglas, and Sandra Smith. *Domicide: The Global Destruction of Home*. Montreal: McGill-Queen's University Press, 2001.

Prison Research Education Action. *Instead of Prisons: A Handbook for Abolitionists*. Syracuse, NY: Critical Resistance, 2005.

Purcell, Mark. "Excavating Lefebvre: The Right to the City and Its Urban Politics of the Inhabitant." *GeoJournal* 58, no. 2–3 (2002): 99–108.

Raco, Mike. "Remaking Place and Securitising Space: Urban Regeneration and the Strategies, Tactics and Policies of Policing in the UK." *Urban Studies* 40 (2003): 1869–1887.

Reichenbach, Anke. "A Ladies' Paradise? Reflection on the Shopping Mall as a Place for Female Flânerie." Presented at Varieties of Emirati Womanhood, NYUAD, Abu Dhabi, 2018.

Reichenbach, Anke, and Najla Ibrahim. "Pulling at Our Heartstrings: Emirati-Themed Leisure Venues as Places of Belonging." *Urban Anthropology* 48, no. 1–2 (2019): 129–181.

Reisz, Todd. "Future Flyovers: Dubai in 1971." *Architectural Design* 85, no. 1 (2015): 100–105.

———. *Showpiece City: How Architecture Made Dubai.* Stanford, CA: Stanford University Press, 2020.

"Revealed: The Nationalities Investing the Most in Dubai's Real Estate." *Arabian Business*, November 15, 2020. https://www.arabianbusiness.com /real-estate/454595-revealed-the-nationalities-investing-the-most-in-dubais-real-estate.

Robinow, Paul. *French Modern: Norms and Forms of the Social Environment.* Cambridge, MA: MIT Press, 1988.

Roseberry, William. "The Rise of Yuppie Coffees and the Reimagination of Class in the United States." *American Anthropologist* 98, no. 4 (1996): 762–775.

Rothe, Dawn L., and Victoria E. Collins. "The Integrated Spectacle: Neoliberalism and the Socially Dead." *Social Justice* 43, no. 2 (2016): 1–20.

Salamandra, Christa. A *New Old Damascus: Authenticity and Distinction in Urban Syria.* Bloomington: Indiana University Press, 2005.

Salazar Parrenas, Rhacel. *Unfree: Migrant Domestic Work in Arab States.* Stanford, CA: Stanford University Press, 2021.

Sanchez, Shaundel Nicole. "Migrating to the Middle East in Search of Safety." *Anthropology News*, August 14, 2019. https://www.anthropology-news.org /articles/migrating-to-the-middle-east-in-search-of-safety/.

———. "Alhamdulilah, We Live in a Muslim Country: Searching for Safety and Constructing Belonging." PhD diss., Syracuse University, 2020.

Sanderson, Daniel. "Pregnant American Teacher Flown Home to UAE after Government Help." *The National*, March 30, 2020. https://www.the nationalnews.com/uae/health/pregnant-american-teacher-flown-home-to-uae-after-government-help-1.999425.

Sardar, Ziauddin. "After the Sheikhs: The Coming Collapse of the Gulf Monarchies, by Christopher Davidson." *The Independent*, January 18, 2013. http:// www.independent.co.uk/arts-entertainment/books/reviews/after-the-sheikhs-the-coming-collapse-of-the-gulf-monarchies-by-christopher-m-davidson-8456206.html.

Seidman, Steven. "The Politics of Cosmopolitan Beirut: From the Stranger to the Other." *Theory, Culture and Society* 29, no. 2 (2012): 3–36.

"Sheikh Mohammed Orders Stunt Drivers to Clean Dubai Streets." *Khaleej Times*, February 24, 2017. https://www.khaleejtimes.com/news/crime /stunt-drivers-to-clean-dubai-streets-for-reckless-driving-at-city-walk.

Shin, Hyun Bang. "Unequal Cities of Spectacle and Mega-Events in China." *City* 16, no. 6 (2012): 728–744.

Signé, Landry. "What the United Arab Emirates Can Teach Resource-Rich Countries in Africa. *Brookings*, December 19, 2019. https://www.brookings .edu/blog/order-from-chaos/2019/12/19/what-the-united-arab-emirates-can-teach-resource-rich-countries-in-africa/.

Smith, Benjamin. "The Sheikh of Araby Rides a Cadillac: Popular Geoeconomic Imaginations, Positional Anxiety and Nouveau Riche Territories." *Environment and Planning D: Society and Space* 34, no. 3 (2016): 564–580.

Sorkin, Michael. *Variations on a Theme Park: The New American City and the End of Public Space*. New York: Hill & Wang, 1992.

Soudy, Nada. "Home and Belonging: A Comparative Study of 1.5 and Second-Generation Egyptian 'Expatriates' in Qatar and 'Immigrants' in the U.S." *Journal of Ethnic and Migration Studies* 43, no. 9 (2017): 1544–1561.

Stansell, Christine. *City of Women: Sex and Class in New York, 1789–1860*. Urbana: University of Illinois Press, 1986.

Steinfeld, Nili. "Track Me, Track Me Not: Support and Consent to State and Private Sector Surveillance." *Telematics and Informatics* 34, no. 8 (2017): 1663–1672.

Stephan-Emmrich, Manja. "Playing Cosmopolitan: Muslim Self-fashioning, Migration, and (Be-)Longing in the Tajik Dubai Business Sector." *Central Asian Affairs* 4, no. 3 (2017): 270–290.

Stephenson, Svetlana. "The Kazan Leviathan: Russian Street Gangs as Agents of Social Order." *Sociological Review* 59, no. 2 (2011): 324–347.

Stevens, Quentin, and Kim Dovey, "Pop-Ups and Public Interests: Agile Public Space in the Neoliberal City." In *The Palgrave Handbook of Bottom-Up Urbanism*, edited by Mahyar Arefi and Conrad Kickert, 323–337. Cham: Palgrave Macmillan, 2019.

Stratton, Jon. *Race Daze: Australia in Identity Crisis*. London: Pluto Press, 1998.

Thiollet, Hélène, and Laure Assaf. "Cosmopolitanism in Exclusionary Contexts." *Population, Space and Place* 27, no. 1 (2020).

Tonkiss, Fran. *Space, the City and Social Theory: Social Relations and Urban Forms*. Cambridge: Polity Press, 2005.

Volkov, Vadim. *Violent Entrepreneurs: The Use of Force in the Making of Russian Capitalism.* Ithaca, NY: Cornell University Press, 2002.

Vora, Neha. *Impossible Citizens: Dubai's Indian Diaspora.* Durham, NC: Duke University Press, 2013.

———. "The Political Life of Illiberal Death." *Jadaliyya*, March 7, 2016. https://www.jadaliyya.com/Details/33054/The-Political-Life-of-Illiberal-Death.

———. *Teach for Arabia: American Universities, Liberalism, and Transnational Qatar.* Stanford, CA: Stanford University Press, 2018.

———. "Anthropology and the Educational Encounter." In *Beyond Exception: New Interpretations of the Arabian Peninsula*, edited by Ahmed Kanna, Amélie Le Renard, and Neha Vora, 80–99. Ithaca, NY: Cornell University Press, 2020.

Vora, Neha, Ahmed Kanna, and Amélie Le Renard. "Space, Mobility, and Shifting Identities in the Constitution of the 'Field.'" In *Beyond Exception: New Interpretations of the Arabian Peninsula*, edited by Ahmed Kanna, Amélie Le Renard, and Neha Vora, 26–54. Ithaca, NY: Cornell University Press, 2020.

Walsh, Katie. "'It Got Very Debauched, Very Dubai!' Heterosexual Intimacy amongst Single British Expatriates." *Social and Cultural Geography* 8, no. 4 (2007): 507–533.

Wieczorek, Marta. "Introduction: Anthropological Debates on Place-Making." *Urban Anthropology* 48, no. 1–2 (2019): 1–12.

Werbner, Pnina. "Global Pathways: Working Class Cosmopolitans and the Creation of Transnational Ethnic Worlds." *Social Anthropology* 7, no. 1 (1999): 17–35.

Wilson, Elizabeth. *The Sphinx in the City.* Berkeley: University of California Press, 1992.

Wright, Andrea. *Between Dreams and Ghosts Indian Migration and Middle Eastern Oil.* Stanford, CA: Stanford University Press, 2021.

Wynn, L. L. *Pyramids and Nightclubs: A Travel Ethnography of Arab and Western Imaginations of Egypt, from King Tut and a Colony of Atlantis to Rumors of Sex Orgies, Urban Legends about a Marauding Prince, and Blonde Belly Dancers.* Austin: University of Texas Press, 2007.

Yurchak, Alexei. "The Cynical Reason of Late Socialism: Power, Pretense, and the Anekdot." *Public Culture* 9, no. 2 (1997): 161–188.

———. "Soviet Hegemony of Form: Everything Was Forever, Until It Was No More." *Comparative Studies in Society and History* 45, no. 3 (2003): 480–510.

———. *Everything Was Forever, Until It Was No More: The Last Soviet Generation.* Princeton, NJ: Princeton University Press, 2005.

Yuval-Davis, Nira. "Belonging and the Politics of Belonging." *Patterns of Prejudice* 40, no. 3 (2006): 197–214.

———. "Intersectionality, Citizenship and Contemporary Politics of Belonging." *Critical Review of International Social and Political Philosophy* 10, no. 4 (2007): 561–574.

Zukin, Sharon. *Naked City: The Death and Life of Authentic Urban Places.* Oxford: Oxford University Press, 2009.

Index

'abayas: colored, publicly wearing, 92, 199, 241n30; discomfort without, Dubai Mall, 129–30; as Emirati dress, 84, 233n75; jogging without, 143; men wearing to harass women, 212; not wearing in Europe, 170; as outdoor dress of respectability, 197; at posh lounges and hotels, 112, 128; at public beaches, 121, 123–24; Saudi tourists in Dubai, 153; woman smoking sheesha in, 96, 242n41

Abdulla, Abdulkhaleq, 62

Abu-Lughod, Lila, 12

Acuto, Michele, 28

adaptive agents: and ambivalence toward development trajectory, 35, 119–20; and ambivalent forms of belonging, 14, 35, 126–27, 224–25; changing social norms, 94–96, 97*fig.*, 98, 123, 139–40, 209; and cosmopolitan subjectivities, 118, 137–38, 141–42; and creative class, connections to, 42; decentering resistance of, 13; and foreign spectacles, 107*fig.*; as former *shaabiya* residents, 202; inhabiting the spectacle, 7, 11, 33, 73–79, 101, 127, 224; limits of adaptivity, 39; negotiating nostalgia, 48–49; as normal subjects, 13–14, 173; and reliance on state

order and regulation, 158, 163, 168, 207, 213, 218; relocation without cultural dislocation, 146, 148, 181; shaping politics of belonging, 12, 19, 92. *See also* developments, spectacular; Dubai, cosmopolitanism of; Dubai, modernity of; illiberalism; malls, shopping

Al Awadhi, Jassim and Geoffrey Martin, 160

Alawadi, Khaled, 25, 74, 196, 202

alcohol, 120, 127–28, 154, 175, 176, 202, 207

Al Diyafa Street, 49

Al-Ghurair Center, 24, 98–99, 200

alienation: author's sense of, 31; and citizenship, 47; and cultural homogeneity, 105–7, 112–15, 124–25; and discourses of authenticity, 1, 7, 13, 39, 42; and forced relocation, 44–47; in UAE countries, 66, 134. *See also* citizenship; loss, sense of; marginalization

Al-Kamali, Reem, 72, 84

Al Maktoum Hospital, 5–6

AlNeaimi, Abdulla, 101

Al-Quoz, 186, 199

Al-Rashoud, Tala, 31

Al Seef, 52

AlShehabi, Omar, 12, 58, 61–62, 108

neoliberalism: critiques of, 222; and Dubai's image, 51, 159–60; and flexible citizens, 119; neoliberal subjectivities, 182; neo-liberal subjectivity, 3, 10–11, 166, 181. *See also* liberalism/illiberalism binaries

neoorthodox tendencies, 119, 121

new Dubai: creation of, 7; diversity of, 102, 109, 244n15; as feeling international, 130; gendered comfort in, 172, 214; as glitzy, 109; as mirage, 38; as policymaker focus, 51–53, 105; research in, 20. *See also* adaptive agents; authenticity; dis-course of; Brand Dubai; developments, spectacular; Dubai, cosmopolitanism of; old Dubai; segregation; Westerners, cater-ing to

New York University, Abu Dhabi (NYUAD), 58, 62

noncitizen/citizen binaries, 18, 46–48, 109, 123, 150, 246n10. *See also* citizenship

nonplaces, 9, 38, 60, 81, 100–101, 227n3

"normal" lives, leading: in Dubai, 34, 143, 150, 182, 224; as *khaleejis* in Dubai, 152, 173; and normal subjects, 13–14, 173, 228n8; parallels examples to Dubai, 165–66; and spaces of alterity, 169–70, 176; and Western faculty, 17

norms, social and cultural: beaches and changes to, 122–24; as different in Dubai from other GCC states, 143, 170; and Emirati spaces of display, 128; malls and changes to, 94–96, 97*fig.*, 139–40; repli-cating *meela's* in coffee shops, 84; and spectacular spaces, 73, 92–98; Western inhabitant's disrespect for, 137–41; West-ern inhabitant's disrespect for, 117, 137; and Western women's dress changing, 209; women in low- vs. middle-class, 197

nostalgia: adaptability, coexisting with, 35, 48–49; and development trajectory, opposition to, 66; low-income teenage experience, 42–43, 55–56; for malls, 98–102; and older Emiratis, 40–41, 45–46; and positive views of order and control, 208, 218; for *shaabiyas*, 194; vs. standard of living, 197; teenagers at malls, 85, 87, 99

observation, social: of Arab women in Arab-dominated spaces, 132–33; coffee shops as sites of, 84; and cultural homogeneity, 115; Emiratis at Dubai Mall, 129–30; freedom from, 174; malls and social con-testation, 87–88, 92–98; in old Dubai, 104

oil, Dubai discovery of, 5

old Dubai: diversity of, 108; erasure from image and experience of Dubai, 53; ex-residents' experiences of, 104–5; as Indian Ocean cosmopolitanism, 109; as less sanitized, 7, 243n1; sense of commu-nity in, 188; sense of marginalization of, 51. *See also* communities, social; develop-ment trajectory, Dubai; new Dubai; nos-talgia; sanitization

Orientalism: and Al Seef megaproject, 46; and discourse of authenticity, 35–36; Gulf vs. Western modernity, 9; and lib-eral/illiberal binaries, 61; and low-income spaces, 54; and narratives about Dubai, 3, 8, 39; and othering authoritari-anism, 65; and position of Gulf academ-ics, 31; and practices of social distinction, 64, 66–67

Osella, Caroline and Filipo Osella, 179–80, 245n1

overexceptionalism, 11, 27, 37, 109, 112

Palm Islands (the Palm), 7, 93, 119

pay equity, 51

police-owned *shaabiya*, 195–98

policing, community, 204–7

policing, Dubai: discriminatory, 204; feeling heard by, 212; increase of, 206–7; as normalized modernity, 218; as pleasant, 161; positive views of, 208, 211

policymakers, Dubai: and balance of East and West advertising, 135, 148; and elite noncitizens, 164; and exclusionary cul-tural events, 69; focus on Dubai's image, 50, 57, 146; and foreign privileged over local, 57–58; selective diversity, promoting, 107–8. *See also* Brand Dubai; Dubai, public service structures of; sanitization; segregation; Westerners, catering to

Port Rashid, 6

poverty, 69–70, 110, 183

power-centered frameworks, 74–75, 79

privacy, 121, 129–33, 171, 191, 197, 218

public spheres, malls as, 93–94

public universities, UAE, 62–63

Pune, India, 98

Quran, 214

Founded in 1893,
UNIVERSITY OF CALIFORNIA PRESS
publishes bold, progressive books and journals
on topics in the arts, humanities, social sciences,
and natural sciences—with a focus on social
justice issues—that inspire thought and action
among readers worldwide.

The UC PRESS FOUNDATION
raises funds to uphold the press's vital role
as an independent, nonprofit publisher, and
receives philanthropic support from a wide
range of individuals and institutions—and from
committed readers like you. To learn more, visit
ucpress.edu/supportus.